PENGUIN PLAYS

PL30

# RIGHT YOU ARE! (IF YOU THINK SO)
## ALL FOR THE BEST
### HENRY IV

LUIGI PIRANDELLO

# LUIGI PIRANDELLO

*Right You Are! (If You Think So)*
*All for the Best*
*Henry IV*

INTRODUCED AND EDITED BY

E. MARTIN BROWNE

PENGUIN BOOKS

Penguin Books Ltd, Harmondsworth, Middlesex
AUSTRALIA: Penguin Books Pty Ltd, 762 Whitehorse Road,
Mitcham, Victoria

—

*Così è (se vi pare)* first published 1918
This translation first published 1962 in Penguin Books
Copyright © the heirs of Luigi Pirandello and
Frederick May, 1962

*Tutto per bene* first published 1920
This translation first published 1962 in Penguin Books
Copyright © the heirs of Luigi Pirandello and
Henry Reed, 1962

*Enrico Quarto* first published 1922
This translation first published 1962 in Penguin Books
Copyright © the heirs of Luigi Pirandello and
Frederick May, 1962

—

Made and printed in Great Britain
by R. & R. Clark Ltd
Edinburgh
Set in Monotype Bembo

# CONTENTS

# INTRODUCTION

TWENTY years after his death, the English theatre is still almost totally neglecting Luigi Pirandello. Yet he is one of the greatest masters of the contemporary drama: and the word 'contemporary' still applies to him as it does to few of those who lived in his time. I hope that the publication in this series of two volumes of his plays may widen the interest in him and perhaps lead to more of his plays being produced in English.

Pirandello was born in 1867, and grew up with the sentimentality of later nineteenth-century literature as his staple food. He was the foremost among those in Italy who reacted violently against it, the Futurists as they called themselves. While he was developing his talent by writing novels and short stories, several lesser dramatists were preparing the way for him in the Italian theatre. The 'Teatro del Grottesco' sought to break away from the well-made play by bringing on to the stage situations of a bizarre or fantastic kind, and treating them with an exaggerated humour. The most famous and successful of these plays was Luigi Chiarelli's *The Mask and the Face*, a brilliantly funny caricature of the romantic drama which allows a serious idea to be developed within itself. Pirandello uses the same approach for purposes more profound; for to him the drama must be the expression of the intellect: 'One of the novelties that I have given to drama', he says, 'consists in converting the intellect into passion.' This makes his plays intensely exciting to those who are willing to use their brains in the theatre; but let it not be supposed that Pirandello relies on the intellectual content of his plays to replace the craftsmanship of the playwright. On the contrary, most of them are extremely well constructed and hold our interest quite apart from what they have to say.

Pirandello was a Sicilian, born in Agrigento where the Greek temples stand ruined amidst some of the island's most picturesque scenery. His father was a rich proprietor of sulphur mines, a strong, overbearing man. When Luigi was a young man floods destroyed the mines, and the family was reduced from prosperity to poverty. For Luigi this was the cause of a far worse disaster. He had been married by his father to a woman who was driven by their financial troubles into an hysterical form of insanity. Unreasonably jealous, she made his life a hell; but he endured it until, in 1919, she entered a nursing home. This is the background against which his imagination worked, and accounts for the intensification of his pessimism.

7

The problem of the nature of personality, which has dominated philosophical thinking in this century, is acute for Pirandello, and perhaps more so because he must have lived for so many years a double life, as himself and as the twisted version of himself in his wife's mind. He may have wondered which was the real self; certainly his characters wrestle with such doubts. His plays stimulate reflection upon the mystery of life, which is in perpetual flux, the nature of which we no sooner think we have grasped than it slips away from us, the truth of which we really prefer to hide from ourselves by illusions since we know we can never pin it down.

This antithesis between reality and illusion is the theme of *Right You Are! (If You Think So) (Cosí è (se vi pare)*, 1918). Pirandello was always concerned with this question. Here he created two characters each of whom says that the other is mad. When the curious neighbours wish to produce documents to settle which is right, Laudisi, who acts as a sort of Chorus to the play, speaks to them thus:

'They have created, she for him and he for her, a world of fantasy that has all the substance of reality itself, a world in which they now live in perfect peace and harmony. And it cannot be destroyed, this reality of theirs, by any of your documents, because they live and breathe in it!'

The dramatist intrigues us into chasing as excitedly as the neighbours after the solution of the mystery; and he leaves us, as he leaves them, with the mystery returned to our own minds:

'I am just whoever you think I am.'

Reality, in Pirandello's view, is what we have in ourselves; for each of us it is different, and the only proof of it is the effect it produces.

*All for the Best (Tutto per bene*, 1920) shows this problem of reality from another angle, and perhaps in the most movingly human fashion of any Pirandello play. The chief character, Martino Lori, cherishes the memory of his wife who died sixteen years before the play opens. In the first act he learns the distasteful truth about her. He tries to break away from the part he has been playing, without knowing (though everyone else knew) that he was doing so, in regard to her. At last he realizes that he must go on playing it, but now without illusions. This he is strengthened to do by the affection of another person who had formerly held aloof from him. His plight is pitiful, but redeemed by his dignity as a man and by the gain of a fellow-creature with whom to share it.

*Henry IV* (*Enrico Quarto*, 1922) is usually reckoned to be Pirandello's masterpiece. It is on a larger scale than any of his other plays; and the study of reality is extended to cover madness as well as sanity, so that the chief character acquires a breadth which is rare in modern drama. We do not know till late in the play whether Henry is mad or not, nor whether he has ever been mad: in this respect the play recalls *Hamlet*. But in any case *Henry IV* is true tragedy, the tragedy of a man whom time has passed by, for whom there is no place in life today, since he was put out of life years ago. This reveals another aspect of Pirandello's concern with reality: is time, as much as matter, what the human mind makes it for each one of us? Pirandello is always apt to give long monologues to his principal characters; in this play, the practice is developed to a point which recalls the Shakespearean soliloquy; and this again enlarges the character of the hero and deepens the size of the tragedy.

E. MARTIN BROWNE

# RIGHT YOU ARE! (IF YOU THINK SO)

*Cosí è (se vi pare)*

TRANSLATED BY FREDERICK MAY

This play, translated by Arthur Livingston and under the title *And That's the Truth*, was first presented in English at the Lyric Theatre, Hammersmith, on 17 September 1925, with the following cast:

| | |
|---|---|
| LAMBERTO LAUDISI | *Nigel Playfair* |
| SIGNORA FROLA | *Nancy Price* |
| SIGNOR PONZA | *Claude Rains* |
| SIGNORA PONZA | *Dorothy Green* |
| COMMENDATORE AGAZZI | *Guy Lefeuvre* |
| AMALIA | *Margaret Scudamore* |
| DINA | *Paula Cinquevalli* |
| SIGNOR SIRELLI | *J. Leslie Frith* |
| SIGNORA SIRELLI | *Dorothy Cheston* |
| THE PREFECT | *Frank Allenby* |
| AN INSPECTOR | *Scott Russell* |
| SIGNORA CINI | *Minnie Blagden* |
| SIGNORA NENNI | *Mary Fenner* |
| A MANSERVANT | *Alfred Harris* |
| 1ST GENTLEMAN | *Arnold Pilbeam* |
| 2ND GENTLEMAN | *Julian Browne* |

Produced by Nigel Playfair

Frederick May's version was first presented by Queen Mary College Dramatic Society at Toynbee Hall Theatre, London, on 3 December 1947, with the following cast:

| | |
|---|---|
| LAMBERTO LAUDISI | *Peter Caldwell* |
| MRS FROLA | *Jean Revett* |
| PONZA | *Frank Lovis* |
| MRS PONZA | *June Rickards* |
| AGAZZI | *Bill Wright* |
| AMALIA | *Grace Sorrell* |
| DINA | *Kay Edwards* |
| SIRELLI | *Allan Wilkinson* |
| MRS SIRELLI | *Betty Haigh* |
| THE PREFECT | *Gordon Harris* |
| CENTURI | *Stanley Goodwin* |
| MRS CINI | *Isabel Kinnish* |
| MRS NENNI | *Rosemary Tyler* |
| BUTLER | *William Sinton* |
| 1ST GENTLEMAN | *Frederick May* |
| 2ND GENTLEMAN | *Frederick May* |
| A LADY | *Joan Gaster* |

Produced by Jean W. Bloor

# CHARACTERS

LAMBERTO LAUDISI

MRS FROLA

MR PONZA, her son-in-law

MRS PONZA, his wife

MR AGAZZI, provincial councillor

AMALIA, his wife, sister of Lamberto Laudisi

DINA, their daughter

MRS SIRELLI

MR SIRELLI, her husband

THE PREFECT

MR CENTURI, commissioner of police

MRS CINI

MRS NENNI

THE BUTLER in the Agazzi household

A NUMBER OF LADIES AND GENTLEMEN

SCENE: A provincial capital *
TIME: The present (1917)

* An approximate English equivalent would be a county-town

# ACT ONE

---

*The drawing-room in the home of Councillor Agazzi. The principal
entrance is at the back. There is another door left and one right.*

> [*When the curtain rises* LAMBERTO LAUDISI *is irritatedly
> walking up and down the room. He is about forty, quick of
> movement and elegant without affectation. He is wearing a
> violet-coloured smoking-jacket with black lapels and black-
> braided edges and frogging.*]

LAUDISI: H'm! So he's gone off to take the matter up with the
Prefect?

AMALIA [*is about forty-five and grey-haired. Her manner reveals a
considerable sense of her own importance, which is derived from
the position her husband occupies in society. She gives you to
understand, nevertheless, that if it rested with her, she could play
the part all by herself and would behave quite differently on many
an occasion*]: But, good heavens, Lamberto, the man's a subordinate of his!

LAUDISI: A subordinate at the office – not at home!

DINA [*is nineteen years old and has an air of knowing everything a
little better than her mother – and than her father, too. But this air
of superiority is softened by her vivacious, youthful charm*]: But
he's deliberately set his mother-in-law up in a flat in this very
building, and on the same floor as us!

LAUDISI: And why not? He's his own master, isn't he? There
was a suitably small flat to let and he's taken it for his mother-
in-law. Or perhaps you think that one's mother-in-law is in
duty bound to call upon, and pay her respects to, the wife
and daughter of her son-in-law's superior? [*He says this with
some emphasis, deliberately prolonging the sentence.*]

AMALIA: But who's talking about *duty*? I seem to remember
that it was we who made the first move, Dina and I. We
called on the lady in question, *and she wouldn't receive us.*

LAUDISI: In that case what has your husband gone running to the Prefect for? Is he going to ask him to use his authority to *wring* this act of courtesy out of the man?

AMALIA: It would only be what was right and proper, anyway! It's just not *done* to leave two ladies standing like that outside the front door, looking like a couple of dummies!

LAUDISI: You're being very high-handed, aren't you? Outrageously high-handed! Are people no longer to be allowed to keep themselves to themselves, even in their own homes?

AMALIA: Oh well, if you don't *want* to realize that we were only trying to be polite! She's new to the town and we wanted, purely out of courtesy, to call on her first.

DINA: Now, now, Uncle dear, don't get so worked up about it! If you must have the truth . . . Well, we'll be quite honest with you, and admit that our great politeness really arose out of our curiosity. But tell me, doesn't it seem natural to you that we *should* be curious?

LAUDISI: Oh yes, quite, quite natural! Because you've nothing better to do with your time.

DINA: Now, look, Uncle dear. . . . Suppose you're standing there, just where you are now, not taking the slightest notice of what anyone around you is doing. Good! I come along, and then, bang in the middle of this little table that's just in front of you, quite im-per-turb-ably. . . . Or rather, wearing an expression like that gallowsbird we're talking about . . . I put . . . oh, heaven knows what! . . . well, let's say a pair of Cook's shoes, for instance!

LAUDISI [*with a start*]: And what have Cook's shoes got to do with what we're talking about?

DINA [*immediately*]: There, you see! You see? I've startled you! It seems queer to you! So you immediately start trying to find out the why and wherefore.

LAUDISI [*very still, very silent for a moment, a cold smile playing on his lips; but he quickly regains countenance*]: Dina, you're a darling. And you're very clever. But you're dealing with me now, you know. You come and put Cook's shoes on this little table in front of me here, solely in order to arouse my curiosity. Well then, since you did it on purpose, you obviously can't blame me if I ask, 'But why, my dear, have you put Cook's shoes on here?' And now you must prove to me that this Mr Ponza – this rascally boor, as your father calls him – came here and settled his mother-in-law in the flat next door with the same degree of malice aforethought.

DINA: All right, then! Let's suppose he didn't do it on purpose. But you certainly can't deny that that man conducts his life in an extremely odd manner! It was bound to set the whole town buzzing with curiosity. It's only natural! Look here! He arrives. He rents a small flat on the top floor of that large, gloomy house out there, right on the outskirts, by the orchards. . . . Have you ever seen it? I mean from the inside?

LAUDISI: I suppose *you've* been to have a look at it?

DINA: Yes, Uncle dear. I went with Mummy. And we're not the only ones who've been out there either, you know! Everyone's been to have a look at it. There's a courtyard – it's ever so dark, just like a well – with an iron balustrade way up above – running along the top floor balcony. It's ever so high up! And there are several baskets hanging from it on ropes.

LAUDISI: And what is the point of all this?

DINA [*in wonder and indignation*]: Why, that's where he's dumped his wife! Up there!

AMALIA: And he's found a flat for his mother-in-law here, next door to us!

LAUDISI: He settles his mother-in-law in a nice comfortable little flat right in the middle of town! Lucky little old lady!

AMALIA: Oh, yes! Very kind of him! And he forces her to live on her own . . . tears her away from her daughter!

LAUDISI: Who told you so? Isn't it possible that his wife's mother prefers this arrangement? So that she shall be more free to come and go as she wishes.

DINA: Oh no, no, Uncle dear, how *could* she? Everybody knows it's his fault.

AMALIA: Listen to me a moment! Everybody realizes that when a young woman marries, she'll leave her mother's home and go off to live with her husband, and that she may even go off to live in another town, perhaps. That's all perfectly understandable. But when a poor mother, unable any longer to put up with having to live so far away from her daughter, follows her, and then, though they're both strangers here, is forced to live in another part of the town. . . . Well, I ask you . . . that's not so understandable . . . now, *is* it? Go on, own up!

LAUDISI: Of course it isn't! But how stupid you are, floundering and flailing about after the truth in this idiotic fashion! Does it really take such a very great effort of imagination to realize that, either through his fault or through hers, or perhaps through the fault of neither, to realize that they just don't get on together? So that even in the circumstances you . . .

DINA [*interrupting him in astonishment*]: What, Uncle . . .? Not get on together . . .? Mother and daughter?

LAUDISI: Why do you say mother and daughter?

AMALIA: Why, because it couldn't possibly be him and his mother-in-law! They're as thick as thieves, those two!

DINA: Mother-in-law and son-in-law! That's what amazes everybody so!

AMALIA: He comes here every evening to keep his mother-in-law company.

DINA: He comes during the day too. At least once every day. Sometimes twice.

LAUDISI: I take it that you suspect them of making love together, mother-in-law and son-in-law?

DINA: Oh, no! How can you suggest such a thing? Why, she's ever so old! A frail, little old lady!

AMALIA: But he never brings her daughter with him! He never, never brings his wife to see her mother! Never!

LAUDISI: The poor girl's probably ill . . . probably can't leave the house . . .

DINA: What nonsense! Her mother goes out there to that . . .

AMALIA: Yes, she goes all the way out there! To look at her from a distance! We know for an absolute certainty that that poor mother is forbidden to go up to her daughter's flat!

DINA: She can only talk to her from the courtyard!

AMALIA: From the courtyard! You do realize, don't you . . .?

DINA: To her daughter, mind you! Her daughter comes out on to the balcony and peers down, just as if she were looking down from Heaven. The poor woman goes into the court-yard, pulls the rope on the basket and rings the bell. Her daughter comes out on to the balcony . . . and her mother has to talk to her from down there . . . from inside that well . . . twisting her neck like this in order to see her. Just imagine it! And she doesn't even manage to see her daughter, she's so dazzled by the light pouring down from up there!

[*A knock is heard at the door and the* BUTLER *appears.*]

BUTLER: Excuse me, madam, there are some people to see you.

AMALIA: Who is it?

BUTLER: Mr and Mrs Sirelli and another lady.

AMALIA: Oh, show them in. [*The* BUTLER *bows and goes out. Enter* MR *and* MRS SIRELLI *and* MRS CINI.]

AMALIA: My dear! How nice to see you.

MRS SIRELLI [*is a plump, healthy-looking, energetic sort of woman. Still young and pleasing to look at. She is dressed – over-dressed, rather – with what passes for elegance in the provinces. She is consumed by a restless curiosity. Her manner towards her husband is harsh*]: I hope you won't mind, but I've brought a very good friend of mine with me – Mrs Cini. She so very much wanted to meet you.

AMALIA: How do you do, Mrs Cini? Please sit down, every-body. [*She introduces the others.*] This is my daughter, Dina . . . My brother, Lamberto Laudisi.

SIRELLI [*a bald-headed man of about forty. What remains of his hair is slicked down with brilliantine. He is fat and with some pretensions to elegance. As he walks his well-polished shoes squeak*]: How do you do? How do you do? [*He bows to each*

19

*of the ladies in turn as he greets her. He then shakes hands with*
LAUDISI.]

MRS SIRELLI: My dear, we've come to you as to the fount of
all knowledge! We're two poor women positively *thirsting*
for news!

AMALIA: But news about what, ladies?

MRS SIRELLI: Why, news about this blessed new secretary at
the Prefecture, of course! The whole town's talking of nothing else.

MRS CINI [*is a stupid old woman, greedy and malicious. She masks
her faults, however, with an air of ingenuousness*]: We're all so
intrigued by the whole affair.... We're simply agog with
curiosity! There's never been anything like it!

AMALIA: But we know no more than anyone else, Mrs Cini,
believe me.

SIRELLI [*to his wife, as if celebrating a victory*]: What did I tell
you? They know just about as much as I do! Perhaps even
less than I do! [*Then, turning to the others*] For example ...
The *real* reason why this poor woman can't go and visit her
daughter ... do you know what it is?

AMALIA: I was just discussing that very question with my
brother.

LAUDISI: You all seem to me to have gone out of your minds,
the whole pack of you.

DINA [*immediately, before anyone can pay attention to what her
uncle has said*]: They say it's because her son-in-law forbids
her to!

MRS CINI [*in wailing tones*]: That's not a good enough reason,
Miss Agazzi.

MRS SIRELLI [*pressing the point*]: It most certainly is *not* good
enough! There's more to it than that.

SIRELLI [*with a gesture, to gain their attention*]: I've got a fresh
item of news for you ... something that's only just been
confirmed. [*Then, deliberately, stressing the syllables*] He keeps
her under lock and key.

AMALIA: His mother-in-law?

SIRELLI: No, Mrs Agazzi, his wife!

MRS SIRELLI: His wife! His wife!

MRS CINI [*in her wailing voice*]: Under lock and key!

DINA: There, Uncle? Do you realize what . . .? And there were you trying to find excuses . . .!

SIRELLI [*astonished*]: What? Trying to find excuses for that monster?

LAUDISI: But I'm not trying to find excuses for him! Nothing of the sort! All I'm trying to say is that your curiosity – with all due deference to the ladies – is insufferable. If for no other reason than that it's quite pointless.

SIRELLI: Pointless?

LAUDISI: Pointless! Yes, pointless, dear ladies.

MRS CINI: Pointless? Our trying to find out?

LAUDISI: Forgive my asking . . . find out *what*? What can we really know about other people? Who they are? What sort of people they are? What they do? Why they do it?

MRS SIRELLI: Well, by trying to get information, by asking for news, we can . . .

LAUDISI: But if there's anyone, according to that reckoning, who should be thoroughly *au fait* with what's going on, it's you, Mrs Sirelli . . . with a husband like yours, a man who is always so well-informed about everything.

SIRELLI [*trying to interrupt him*]: Excuse me, but . . .

MRS SIRELLI: No, dear, listen! It's only too true! [*She turns to* AMALIA.] The truth of the matter is, my dear, that for all my husband's always saying he knows *everything*, I never succeed in getting to know *anything*.

SIRELLI: And no wonder! She's never content with what I *do* tell her! She always has her *doubts* as to whether a thing can really be as I've said it is. Furthermore, she'll maintain that what I've told her just cannot be true. Why, she even goes so far as deliberately to suppose that the real truth is the exact opposite of what I've told her!

MRS SIRELLI: Now, just a minute. . . . Some of the things you tell me. . .!

LAUDISI [*laughing loudly*]: Ha! Ha! Ha! May I, Mrs Sirelli? I'll answer your husband for you. My dear man, how do you expect your wife to be content with what you tell her if . . . as is quite natural . . . you present things to her as they appear to you?

MRS SIRELLI: And as they just simply cannot be!

LAUDISI: Oh no, Mrs Sirelli! Forgive me, but I must tell you that there you're wrong. You may be quite sure that for your husband things are exactly as he describes them to you.

SIRELLI: And, what's more, *as they are in reality! As they are in reality!*

MRS SIRELLI: Nonsense! Nothing of the kind! You're constantly making mistakes about things!

SIRELLI: Believe me, *you're* the one that's constantly making mistakes, *not me*!

LAUDISI: No! No! My dear good people, the fact is that neither of you really makes mistakes. May I explain? I'll prove it to you. [*He rises and stands in the middle of the room.*] Now both of you can see me standing here. You *can* see me, can't you?

SIRELLI: Why, of course!

LAUDISI: No, no! Don't be in such a hurry to say yes, my dear fellow! Come over here! Come on over!

SIRELLI [*looking at him, an uncertain smile on his lips. He is perplexed and a little disconcerted, rather as if he were reluctant to take part in a joke he doesn't understand*]: Why?

MRS SIRELLI [*irritatedly*]: Go on. [*She gives him a push.*]

LAUDISI [*to* SIRELLI, *as hesitantly he advances towards him*]: Can you see me? Take a better look at me. Touch me.

MRS SIRELLI [*to her husband who, not at all sure whether he wants to take part in this incomprehensible joke, is still hesitating as to whether to touch* LAUDISI]: Go on, touch him! [SIRELLI *lifts a hand and touches* LAUDISI *gingerly on the shoulder.*]

LAUDISI: Good man, that's right! You're quite sure that you're touching *me* . . . the *me* that you can see . . . aren't you?

SIRELLI: I should say so.

LAUDISI: Of course you're sure! You haven't the slightest doubt whatsoever about it! Now go and sit down again.

MRS SIRELLI [*to her husband, as he stands there stupidly in front of* LAUDISI]: It's no use your standing there, blinking your eyes! Come and sit down again!

LAUDISI [*to* MRS SIRELLI, *when her somewhat shattered husband has returned to his seat*]: Now, will *you* please come here, Mrs Sirelli? [*Immediately, forestalling her objection*] No, no! Of course! I'll come to you! [*He comes and stands in front of her and then goes down on one knee.*] You *can* see me, can't you? Lift up your tiny hand and touch me. [*And as* MRS SIRELLI *puts her hand out towards his shoulder, he bends his head to kiss it.*] What a charming little hand!

SIRELLI: I say! Hold on!

LAUDISI: Take no notice of him! Are you sure that you too are touching *me*, the *me* that you can see? You *are* sure . . . You have no doubt whatsoever that it's me you're touching. But please, I beg you, don't tell your husband, or my sister, or my niece, or Mrs Thingummy here . . .

MRS CINI [*prompting him*]: Mrs Cini.

LAUDISI: . . . Or Mrs *Cini*, how I appear to you, because all four of them will immediately tell you that you're quite mistaken. Whereas in reality you're not mistaken at all, because actually I *am* as you see me. But, Mrs Sirelli, that in no way alters the fact that I am really what I seem to be to your husband, or to my sister, or to my niece or to Mrs – er –

MRS CINI [*prompting him*]: Cini.

LAUDISI: – to Mrs Cini here. And they, too, are in no way mistaken.

MRS SIRELLI: But how on . . .? You mean you're a different person for each one of us then?

LAUDISI: Why, of course, I am, dear lady! And you . . .? I suppose you *aren't*? You're *not* a different person?

MRS SIRELLI [*very quickly*]: Oh, no, no, no, no! I assure you that, as far as I'm concerned, I'm never anybody different!

LAUDISI: And as far as *I'm* concerned *I'm* never anybody different either! And I could quite well maintain that unless you see me as I see myself then you're all mistaken. All of which doesn't alter the fact that, for me to say *that* would be an inexcusable act of presumption on my part, as inexcusable as the one you're making is on yours, dear lady.

SIRELLI: You'll forgive my asking, but what do you hope to achieve with all this rigmarole?

LAUDISI: So you think there's no conclusion to be drawn from it? Good Lord! I find you all anxiously trying to search out who other people are, and what things are really like . . . Just as if people and things were like this or like that, simply because they are what they are.

MRS SIRELLI: According to you, then, we can *never* know the truth?

MRS CINI: Things have come to a pretty pass if we're no longer to believe in what we can see and touch!

LAUDISI: Oh yes, dear lady, you must believe . . .! However, let me urge you to respect what others see and touch, even if it is the exact opposite of what you yourself see and touch.

MRS SIRELLI: Oh, listen to him! I'm going to turn my back on you! And I shan't say another word to you! I don't want to go mad!

LAUDISI: No! No! I've finished! Go on talking about Mrs Frola and her son-in-law, Mr Ponza. I shan't interrupt you again.

AMALIA: Oh, thank goodness for that! Lamberto dear, it would be best if you were to go into the other room!

DINA: Yes, Uncle dear, it would! In you go! Go on, into the other room with you!

LAUDISI: No, why should I? I'm enjoying myself, listening to you people talk. Don't you worry, I'll be a good boy and keep quiet. At the very worst, I may occasionally laugh up my sleeve . . . and if you should happen to hear me once or twice . . . well, you'll just have to forgive me.

MRS SIRELLI: And to think that we came here to find out . . .!

But, really, Amalia, isn't this Mr Ponza a subordinate of your husband's?

AMALIA: That's all very well when he's at the office. But when he's in his own home, my dear . . .

MRS SIRELLI: Of course, I quite understand! But haven't you even *tried* to see his mother-in-law next door?

DINA: I should just say we have! Twice, Mrs Sirelli!

MRS CINI [*starting; then, greedily and intently*]: Ah! So you've . . . So you've actually spoken to her?

AMALIA: She was not at home to us, Mrs Cini.

SIRELLI, MRS SIRELLI, and MRS CINI: What? Oh! Oh! How was that?

DINA: And this morning, moreover . . .

AMALIA: The first time we called we stood for more than a quarter of an hour outside the door. No one came and opened it, so we couldn't even leave a card. We tried again today . . .

DINA [*with a gesture expressing horror*]: And *he* came to answer the door!

MRS SIRELLI: How horrid! That face of his! Yes, there's something really evil about it! He's upset the whole town with that face of his! And then, the way he always dresses in black. They all three dress in black, don't they? His wife as well? The daughter, I mean.

SIRELLI [*annoyance and disgust in his voice*]: Now how can you possibly know *that*, if no one has ever seen the daughter? If I've told you once, I've told you a thousand times . . . it's quite *probable* that she dresses in black. . . . They come from a small town, in Marsica, you know.

AMALIA: Yes, it was completely destroyed, so it seems.

SIRELLI: By the last earthquake. Just razed to the ground. There's not one stone left standing on another.

DINA: It's said that they lost all their relatives.

MRS CINI [*anxiously trying to bring the conversation back to where it was before the digression*]: Yes, yes! So . . . So *he* opened the door?

AMALIA: The moment I saw him standing there in front of me, with that face of his, what I was going to say just stuck in my throat! I managed to stammer out that we'd come to call on his mother-in-law and . . . he didn't say a word! Not even 'Thank you'!

DINA: Oh no, be fair, Mummy! He did bow!

AMALIA: Yes . . . But only just! It was more of a nod than a bow. Like this!

DINA: But his eyes said all sorts of things, didn't they? Those eyes of his . . .! They're a wild beast's eyes, not a man's!

MRS CINI [*still trying to keep to the main issue*]: And then? What did he say *then*?

DINA: He was all embarrassed . . .

AMALIA: . . . and all untidy. He told us that his mother-in-law was indisposed . . . was very grateful to us for our kindness in calling . . . and then just stood there in the doorway, waiting for us to go.

DINA: It was so terribly humiliating!

SIRELLI: The ill-mannered ruffian! Oh, you can be absolutely sure it's all his fault! For all we know he may be keeping his mother-in-law under lock and key, too!

MRS SIRELLI: The nerve of the man! To treat a lady like that, and the wife of his superior at that!

AMALIA: Oh, as for that . . . this time my husband did take it rather badly. He considered it a very grave lack of respect on his part. So he's gone to make a strong complaint to the Prefect and to demand an apology.

DINA: Talking of angels, here comes Daddy now.

[AGAZZI *joins them.*]

AGAZZI [*is fifty, with rather unkempt red hair and beard. He is wearing gold-rimmed spectacles. His manner is scornfully, spitefully authoritarian*]: My dear Sirelli, how are you? [*He comes up to the settee, bows, and then shakes hands with* MRS SIRELLI.] Good afternoon, Mrs Sirelli.

AMALIA [*presenting him to* MRS CINI]: My husband . . . Mrs Cini.

AGAZZI [*he bows and shakes hands*]: Delighted. [*Then turning – almost solemnly – to his wife and daughter*] I have to tell you that Mrs Frola will be arriving any moment now.

MRS SIRELLI [*clapping her hands exultantly*]: She's coming? She's actually coming here?

AGAZZI: Well, I had to do something about it! I couldn't possibly tolerate such an insult to my family honour, such flagrant rudeness to my own wife and daughter, now could I?

SIRELLI: Of course not! That's just what we were saying!

MRS SIRELLI: And it might have been a good idea to take this opportunity to . . .

AGAZZI [*breaking in*]: . . . To give the Prefect an account of all the gossip that's going round town about this gentleman? Don't you worry! I've seen to that all right!

SIRELLI: Oh, good! Good man!

MRS CINI: Such inexplicable things, too! Absolutely inconceivable!

AMALIA: Positively *beastly*! But did you know that he keeps them under lock and key? *Both* of them!

DINA: No, Mummy, that's not true! We still don't know about the old lady!

MRS SIRELLI: But it's certainly true about his wife.

SIRELLI: And what did the Prefect say?

AGAZZI: Oh, yes! Well . . . he was very . . . yes, what I told him made a very deep impression on him. . . .

SIRELLI: Well, that's good news!

AGAZZI: A stray rumour or two had reached him already, and . . . well, he too sees that here's a good opportunity to clear up the mystery . . . once and for all . . . and really to get at the truth.

LAUDISI [*laughing loudly*]: Ha! Ha! Ha!

AMALIA: Your laughter, my dear Lamberto, is singularly inappropriate just now!

AGAZZI: Why is he laughing?

MRS SIRELLI: Why, because, according to him, it's quite impossible to discover the truth about anything.

[*The* BUTLER *comes in.*]

BUTLER [*appearing in the doorway*]: Mrs Frola is here. Shall I show her in?

SIRELLI: Ah! Here she is.

AGAZZI: Now, my dear Lamberto, we shall soon see whether it's impossible or not.

MRS SIRELLI: Good! Oh, I'm so glad she's come.

AMALIA [*getting up*]: Shall I ask him to show her in?

AGAZZI: No, my dear, *you* sit down. Wait till she's shown in. We must remain just as we are! It's most important that when she comes in we should all be sitting down and behaving quite naturally. [*To the* BUTLER] Show her in.

[*The* BUTLER *goes out. He returns almost immediately with* MRS FROLA. *All rise.* MRS FROLA *is a neat little old lady, retiring, yet very friendly and courteous. There is a profound sadness in her eyes, but it is softened by the sweet smile which is always on her lips.* AMALIA *goes up to her and holds out her hand.*]

AMALIA: Oh, please do come in, Mrs Frola. [*Taking her by the hand she introduces her to the others.*] Mrs Sirelli, a dear friend of mine ... Mrs Cini ... my husband ... Mr Sirelli ... my daughter Dina ... my brother, Lamberto Laudisi. And now, please do sit down, Mrs Frola.

MRS FROLA: I must apologize for having neglected my duty for so long. I'm very sorry. It was most gracious of you, Mrs Agazzi, to honour me with a visit ... when really it was my place to have called on you first.

AMALIA: Among neighbours, Mrs Frola, one doesn't worry about who should call first. Especially as I thought that you, being a stranger here and all on your own, might quite well be in need of ...

MRS FROLA: Oh, thank you, thank you. ... You're too kind. ...

MRS SIRELLI: You're all by yourself in our dear little town, then?

MRS FROLA: No, I have a married daughter here. She hasn't been here very long either.

SIRELLI: Mrs Frola's son-in-law is the new secretary at the Prefecture . . . Mr Ponza, isn't it?

MRS FROLA: Yes, that's right. And I hope that Mr Agazzi will be very kind and forgive me. And forgive my son-in-law too.

AGAZZI: To tell the truth, Mrs Frola, I did take it a little amiss. . . .

MRS FROLA [*interrupting him*]: And you were quite right to. . . . Quite, quite right! But you must forgive him! Believe me . . . we're still utterly overwhelmed by . . . the dreadful thing that happened to us.

AMALIA: Yes, of course, of course! You were involved in that awful disaster!

MRS SIRELLI: Did you lose any relatives in the . . .?

MRS FROLA: All of them. . . . Every one, Mrs Sirelli. There's hardly a trace of our village left now. Just a heap of ruins out there among the fields . . . completely deserted.

SIRELLI: Yes, we heard about it.

MRS FROLA: I only lost my sister and her unmarried daughter. Yes, she had a daughter too. My poor son-in-law, however, suffered much more grievously. He lost his mother, two brothers and their wives, a sister and her husband . . . And there were the children as well . . . his little nephew and niece . . .

SIRELLI: An absolute massacre!

MRS FROLA: A tragedy like that haunts you all your life! You're left . . . Well, it's just as if you'd been stunned!

AMALIA: It must be!

MRS SIRELLI: And to happen just like that . . . in a flash! Why it's enough to send you out of your mind!

MRS FROLA: Your mind stops working. So you sometimes fail in your social duties, without really meaning to do anything of the sort, Mr Agazzi.

AGAZZI: Of course! I quite understand. Let's say no more about it, Mrs Frola.

AMALIA: It was really . . . Well, partly on account of this . . . er . . . misfortune of yours that my daughter and I came to call on you . . . first.

MRS SIRELLI [*writhing with curiosity*]: Of course! Knowing that you were so very much alone, Mrs Frola. . . . Yet you must forgive my rudeness if I presume to ask how it is that, having your daughter here in the town . . . and after such a terrible misfortune as that . . . that. . . . [*Growing abashed after having made such a magnificent start*] Well, it seems to me that . . . it ought to make the survivors feel the need to keep together. . . . So how is it that . . .?

MRS FROLA [*completing her remark, so as to rescue her from her predicament*]: . . . That I should always be so very much alone? Is that it?

SIRELLI: Yes, to be quite frank with you, it *does* seem strange.

MRS FROLA [*sadly*]: Yes, I understand. [*Then, as if trying to find a way out*] But, you know, it's my belief that when your son or your daughter gets married, they should be left very much to themselves, so that they can live their life in their own way. That's what I . . .

LAUDISI: And you're quite right! Quite, quite right! Because of sheer necessity it must be an altogether different sort of life, founded as it is on a new relationship, the relationship between husband and wife.

MRS SIRELLI: But it's not so different, if you'll forgive my saying so, Laudisi, that it means shutting one's mother completely out of one's life.

LAUDISI: Who said anything about shutting her out? If I understand things correctly, at this particular moment we're talking about a mother who realizes that her daughter can and should no longer be tied to her apron-strings . . . as she has been hitherto . . . because she now has a life of her own to lead . . . a very *different* kind of life.

MRS FROLA [*very grateful to him for this*]: Yes, that's quite right! That's exactly how things are! Thank you, Mr Laudisi! That's precisely what I wanted to say.

MRS CINI: But your daughter probably comes here . . . I imagine . . . comes here pretty often and keeps you company. . . .

MRS FROLA [*on tenterhooks*]: Yes, of course . . . we do see each other. . . . We certainly do see . . .

SIRELLI [*immediately*]: But your daughter never leaves the house! At least, no one has ever seen her do so!

MRS CINI: Perhaps she has her children to look after!

MRS FROLA [*instantly*]: No, there are no children yet. And perhaps there won't be any at all . . . *now*. She's been married . . . oh, it's over seven years now. She has a great deal to do about the house, of course. But that's not the reason. [*She smiles sadly, and then goes on – trying to find a new way out.*] We women who come from small towns, you know . . . we're used to staying at home all the time.

AGAZZI: Even when we have our mother to go and see? Our mother . . . who's no longer with us all day long. . . .

AMALIA: But Mrs Frola probably goes and sees her daughter!

MRS FROLA [*immediately*]: Of course! Why shouldn't I? I go at least once a day . . . sometimes twice!

SIRELLI: And once or twice a day you climb all the way up those stairs? Right up to the top floor of that huge building?

MRS FROLA [*growing pale, but still trying to smile through the torment that she is suffering at this questioning*]: Why no, to tell the truth, I don't climb all the way up. You're quite right, Mr Sirelli, the stairs would be too much for me. No, I don't go upstairs. My daughter comes out and looks down on the courtyard side and . . . well, we can see each other and have a chat.

MRS SIRELLI: Is that the only way you see one another? Oh! Don't you ever see her close to?

DINA [*putting her arm round her mother's neck*]: Speaking as a daughter, I certainly shouldn't expect my mother to climb up hundreds of stairs every day on my account. But I most definitely shouldn't be content only to see her and speak to her from a distance, without being able to give her a hug . . . or have the comfort of feeling her near me.

MRS FROLA [*thoroughly perturbed and embarrassed*]: You're quite right! Yes, I see that I'll have to explain exactly how . . . I wouldn't want you to think anything that wasn't true about my daughter . . . that she's in any way lacking in affection or consideration for me . . . or about me, her mother, either. . . . All those hundreds of stairs would be no barrier to a mother, old and tired though she might be, when at the end she would have the reward of being able to press her daughter to her heart.

MRS SIRELLI [*triumphantly*]: There you are! That's just what we were saying, Mrs Frola. We said there must be a reason.

AMALIA [*pointedly*]: There, do you see, Lamberto? There *is* a reason!

SIRELLI [*promptly*]: Your son-in-law, eh?

MRS FROLA: Oh no, please don't think ill of him! He's such a good boy! You can't imagine just how good he is . . . how tender and how delicate is his affection for me! How attentive he is – and how concerned for my comfort! To say nothing of the love he has for my daughter and the care that he lavishes on her. Oh, believe me, I couldn't have wished for a better husband for her.

MRS SIRELLI: But . . . In that case . . .?

MRS CINI: In that case he probably *isn't* the reason!

AGAZZI: Of course not! It doesn't seem even remotely possible to me that he should forbid his wife to go and visit her mother, or forbid his mother-in-law to go up to her daughter's flat and spend a little while with her!

MRS FROLA: Oh, no! There's no question of *forbidding*! I didn't say that it was he who forbade it. It's *our* decision . . . Believe me . . . Mine and my daughter's. We refrain from visiting each other of our own accord, out of our regard for him.

AGAZZI: But, forgive my asking, what could he possibly take offence at? I'm afraid I don't understand!

MRS FROLA: It's not that he'd take offence, Mr Agazzi. It's a feeling . . . A feeling that is perhaps not altogether easy to understand. [*This is to the ladies*] When you do understand, however, you won't find it at all difficult to sympathize, believe me ... Though it does undoubtedly mean no light sacrifice on my part ... And on my daughter's too.

AGAZZI: Mrs Frola, you must admit that all this that you've been telling us is very strange ... To say the least.

SIRELLI: Yes, and absolutely guaranteed to arouse a good deal of curiosity ... And justifiable curiosity, too.

AGAZZI: And, one might even add, a certain amount of suspicion.

MRS FROLA: Of him? Oh, for pity's sake, please don't say that! What sort of suspicion, Mr Agazzi?

AGAZZI: None at all. Now ... Please don't get worried. I only said that one *might* be inclined to suspect something.

MRS FROLA: No! No! Suspect what? Why, there's perfect agreement between us! We're happy, very very happy ... I'm perfectly happy and so is my daughter.

MRS SIRELLI: Perhaps the root of the trouble is jealousy.

MRS FROLA: Jealousy ... of his wife's mother? I don't think you could call it that ... although ... I don't really know. This is how things are ... He wants to keep his wife's heart completely to himself ... and so intense is his desire that he even wants the love that my daughter should have for her mother ... and he admits it! Of course he does! Why shouldn't he? ... He wants her love to reach me through him. ... By way of him! There ... that's how things are!

AGAZZI: Oh! ... Forgive me for saying so, but that seems outrageously cruel to me!

MRS FROLA: Oh, no! Not cruel! Please don't call it cruel, Mr Agazzi! It's something quite quite different, believe me! Oh, how can I make you understand what I mean? His nature ... yes, that's it! But ... no! Oh, dear! It's a kind of disease, maybe. ... Yes, let's call it that, if you wish! It's like a fullness of love ... all locked up ... yes ... so as to keep out everybody and everything. In that fullness of love his wife must live without ever coming out ... and no one else must ever be allowed to enter into it.

DINA: Not even her mother?

SIRELLI: Downright selfishness, I call it!

MRS FROLA: Perhaps . . . but a selfishness that gives itself utterly and completely, like a world of tenderness and devotion, to the woman he loves. After all, it would be I who would be selfish if I tried to force my way into this closed world of love, when I know that my daughter lives happily in it, and that he adores her so. That ought to be enough for a mother, oughtn't it? [*This is to the ladies.*] Besides, so long as I can see my daughter and talk to her . . . [*With a graceful, confiding gesture*] There's a little basket that we send up and down . . . in the courtyard . . . it always carries a note from me and a word or two from her . . . just giving the day's news. I'm quite content with that. And now . . . well, I'm quite used to it now. Resigned, if you like. I don't suffer any more.

AMALIA: Well, after all, if *you're* happy, you and your daughter . . . !

MRS FROLA [*rising*]: Oh yes, we *are* . . . as I told you. Because he's so very good. Believe me, I couldn't wish for a better son-in-law. We all have our weaknesses and we must learn to bear with one another. [*She takes her leave of* AMALIA.] Goodbye, Mrs Agazzi. [*She next takes her leave of* MRS SIRELLI *and* MRS CINI: *then of* DINA. *Then, turning to* AGAZZI] I hope you really *will* forgive me for . . .

AGAZZI: There's nothing to forgive, Mrs Frola. We're most grateful to you for calling on us.

MRS FROLA [*a slight inclination of the head to* SIRELLI *and* LAUDISI. *Then, turning to* AMALIA]: No, Mrs Agazzi, please don't bother . . . please don't bother to come to the door . . . don't disturb yourself . . . please . . .

AMALIA: Why, of course I must! It's my duty, Mrs Frola! [MRS FROLA *goes out, accompanied by* AMALIA, *who comes back shortly.*]

SIRELLI: Well! Well! What utter nonsense! Were you satisfied by her explanation?

AGAZZI: What explanation? God only knows what terrible mystery there is hidden away in that story of hers . . .

MRS SIRELLI: And Heaven knows how she must be suffering as a mother! Deep down in her heart!

DINA: And her daughter, too! Oh, dear! Oh, dear! [*A pause.*]

MRS CINI [*from the corner of the room where she has hidden herself to conceal her crying, her words coming like a shrill explosion*]: The tears were trembling in her voice!

AMALIA: Yes ... when she said she would think nothing of climbing up hundreds and hundreds of stairs, just to be able to press her daughter to her heart.

LAUDISI: For my part I noticed above all a studied carefulness in her manner. ... No, it was more than that ... there was a marked determination to ward off any suspicion that might conceivably fall on her son-in-law.

MRS SIRELLI: Oh, nonsense! Good heavens, you could see she just didn't know how to excuse his behaviour!

SIRELLI: Excuse it! Huh! Is there any excuse possible for such violent behaviour? Such downright barbarity?

[*The* BUTLER *comes in.*]

BUTLER [*appearing in the doorway*]: Mr Agazzi, Mr Ponza is here. He would like to see you for a few minutes.

MRS SIRELLI: Oh! *Him!*

[*There is general surprise and a movement of anxious curiosity, almost of dismay, rather.*]

AGAZZI: He wants to speak to me?

BUTLER: Yes, sir, that was what he said.

MRS SIRELLI: Please speak to him in here, Mr Agazzi. I'm almost afraid ... but I'm ever so curious to see him at close quarters! The Monster!

AMALIA: But what can he possibly want?

AGAZZI: Well, we shall soon find out. Please sit down, everybody! Please sit down! We must try and look as unconcerned as possible. [*To the* BUTLER] Show him in.

[*The* BUTLER *bows and goes out.* MR PONZA *enters shortly after. He is dark, short, thick-set, and of an almost ferocious appearance. He is dressed entirely in black. He has thick black hair, a low forehead, and a great black moustache. He talks with*]

*an effort, his speech giving you a sense of violence restrained
with difficulty: he is continually clenching and unclenching his
fists. Every now and again he mops the sweat off his face with a
black-bordered handkerchief. As he speaks, his eyes remain
fixed in a hard and gloomy stare.*]

AGAZZI: Please come in, Mr Ponza, please come in. [*Introducing him*] Mr Ponza, the new secretary . . . My wife . . . Mrs
Sirelli . . . Mrs Cini . . . my daughter . . . Mr Sirelli . . . my
brother-in-law, Laudisi. Please sit down.

PONZA: Thank you. I shan't take up more than a moment of
your time, and then I'll relieve you of the burden of my
company.

AGAZZI: Would you prefer to speak with me in private?

PONZA: No, I can . . . I can speak in front of everybody. As a
matter of fact, it's something everybody really ought to
know. I feel it's my duty to . . .

AGAZZI: You mean about your mother-in-law's not coming
to call on us? You don't need to bother any more about that,
because . . .

PONZA: No, it's not that, sir. It's rather that I want you to
know that Mrs Frola, my mother-in-law, would undoubtedly have called on your wife before she and your
daughter were so kind as to visit her, if I had not done all I
could to prevent her from doing so . . . because I simply
could not allow her either to visit anyone or to be herself
visited by anyone.

AGAZZI [*with proud resentment*]: And why not, may I ask?

PONZA [*getting more and more excited, despite his efforts to restrain
himself*]: Has my mother-in-law been talking to you about
her daughter? Did she tell you that I forbid her to see her
daughter . . .? That I forbid her to enter my house?

AMALIA: Why, no! There was nothing but kindness and affection for you in everything she said.

DINA: She had nothing but good to say of you.

AGAZZI: She said, moreover, that it was she who refrained
from visiting her daughter . . . out of consideration for some

36

peculiar feeling of yours. . . . All of which, I tell you quite frankly, we find completely incomprehensible.

MRS SIRELLI: And, what is more, if we had to say just exactly what we think of the whole affair. . . .

AGAZZI: Yes! It seemed very cruel to us. Yes, absolutely cruel!

PONZA: It's precisely in order to throw some light on that matter that I am here, sir. That woman is in a most pitiable condition. But I myself am no less to be pitied . . . Not least because I am obliged to justify my actions . . . and to have to tell you all about a misfortune which only . . . only such violence as this could have forced me to reveal to you. [*He stops a moment to look at everybody*. Then he says slowly and with emphasis] Mrs Frola is mad.

ALL [*with a start*]: Mad?

PONZA: She has been mad for the last four years.

MRS SIRELLI [*with a cry*]: Oh, dear! And it doesn't show in the slightest.

AGAZZI [*utterly astounded*]: What do you mean, mad?

PONZA: She doesn't *appear* to be mad, but she *is* mad. And her madness consists in this very thing, in her believing that I don't want to let her see her daughter. [*With an access of strong, almost ferocious emotion*] Which daughter, in God's name? Her daughter has been dead for the last four years!

ALL [*flabbergasted*]: Dead? Oh! What do you mean? Dead?

PONZA: She died four years ago. That is what drove her mother mad.

SIRELLI: But, if this is true, who is the lady who's . . . living with you now?

PONZA: She is my second wife. I married her two years ago.

AMALIA: And Mrs Frola thinks it's still her daughter who's your wife?

PONZA: That has been her good fortune . . . if you can call it such. She was in a nursing home . . . under close supervision. One day, as she was looking out of her window, she happened to see me walking along the street with my second

37

wife. Immediately she became fixed in the fantastic belief that in her she saw her own daughter . . . alive. She started to laugh, and to tremble all over. Suddenly she was free from the brooding despair into which she had fallen, only to find herself in this other world of madness. At first she was in a highly excited, ecstatic condition. Then, little by little, she became calmer. But her heart is still full of anguish. And yet she's somehow managed to submit to it with resignation. She's quite happy, however, as you've been able to see for yourselves. She persists in believing that it's not true that her daughter is dead, but that I want to keep her entirely to myself, without ever letting her mother see her again. She appears to be completely cured. And in fact, to hear her talk, you'd think she was no longer mad at all.

AMALIA: That's very true! You wouldn't have the slightest suspicion!

MRS SIRELLI: Yes, she *did* say she was happy as things were.

PONZA: She says that to everyone. But she really is very grateful, and most affectionate towards me. Because I try to back her up as much as I possibly can, even at the cost of grave personal sacrifice. I have to keep up two homes. I have to ask my wife, who fortunately is very charitable and so agrees, to preserve the illusion for her continually . . . The illusion that she is her daughter. She comes to the window, she speaks to her, she writes to her. But there is a limit to charity, ladies and gentlemen, a limit to duty! I cannot compel my wife to live with her. And in the meantime that poor unfortunate woman is virtually a prisoner in her own home, under lock and key, for fear that *she* might one day walk in. Yet, she's quiet enough, a very gentle woman . . . but, as you'll readily appreciate, it would strike horror into my wife to have to accept the caresses that *she* would lavish upon her! It would make her shudder from head to foot!

AMALIA [*bursting out, horror and pity mingling in her voice*]: Oh yes! The poor woman! Just imagine how dreadful it would be!

MRS SIRELLI [*to her husband and to* MRS CINI]: There, do you hear? She actually *wants* to be kept locked up!

PONZA [*to cut things short*]: You will realize, sir, that I couldn't possibly let her make this visit unless I was absolutely forced to do so.

AGAZZI: I do indeed. I fully appreciate your difficulty. Yes . . . yes . . . I see very clearly now why . . .

PONZA: Anyone who suffers a misfortune as terrible as this must be kept from contact with the outside world. When I was compelled to let my mother-in-law call on you, it became my imperative duty to come here and tell you what I have just told you. It was my duty, if I had a due regard for the position I occupy. So that this terrible accusation against a public official . . . that I could be so cruel, either from jealousy or from some other motive, as to prevent a mother from seeing her own daughter . . . shall not be believed by the people of this town. [*He rises.*] I beg your pardon, ladies, for having upset you. It was quite unintentional. . . . [*He bows.*] Good afternoon, sir. [*He bows again, then nods to* LAUDISI *and* SIRELLI.] Good afternoon. [*And he goes out through the door centre-back.*]

AMALIA: So she's mad! Oh!

MRS SIRELLI: Poor lady! Mad!

DINA: And that's why there's all this . . . She thinks she's Mrs Ponza's mother . . . but she's *not* her daughter! [*She buries her head in her hands in horror.*] Oh, God!

MRS CINI: But who would ever have supposed it?

AGAZZI: And yet, you know . . . the way she talked . . .

LAUDISI: You mean . . . you'd already guessed?

AGAZZI: No . . . but, at the same time, she was obviously none too sure about how to put what she wanted to say.

MRS SIRELLI: No wonder, poor creature! She doesn't see things rationally.

SIRELLI: All the same . . . forgive me for pressing the point. . . . She's behaving very strangely if she really *is* mad. It's very true that she didn't talk about things rationally. But the way she was constantly trying to explain to herself why her son-in-law didn't want her to see her daughter . . . the way she was forever trying to find excuses for him, and then adapting herself to the excuses she had herself invented. . . .

AGAZZI: Good grief, man! Why, that's the very thing that proves she's mad! That frantic hunting for excuses for her son-in-law, without ever succeeding in finding a single one that would pass muster!

AMALIA: Yes, she'd say something and then take it back again.

AGAZZI [to Sirelli]: Do you honestly believe that if she weren't mad she could possibly accept her present way of life? Only to see her daughter up there at the window. . . . And the only reason why she mayn't see more of her to be the one she gave us, the morbid love of a husband who wants to keep his wife for himself alone?

SIRELLI: All right! But do you honestly believe that it's because she's mad that she accepts her present way of life? That it's because she's mad that she's resigned to it? It seems very fishy to me! Very fishy indeed! [To LAUDISI] What do you say?

LAUDISI: Me? Why, nothing!

BUTLER [knocking on the door, and then appearing in the doorway. He looks somewhat perturbed]: I beg your pardon, sir, but Mrs Frola is here again.

AMALIA [dismay in her voice]: Oh dear, what does she want now? Suppose we can't get rid of her again!

MRS SIRELLI: I understand just how you feel . . . now that we know she's mad.

MRS CINI: Oh, dear! Oh, dear! Heaven only knows what she's come to tell us this time! I'm dying to hear what she has to say, though!

SIRELLI: I'm rather curious too. I'm not in the least convinced that she is mad.

DINA: Yes, Mummy, do ask her in. There's nothing to be afraid of! You saw how quiet she is!

AGAZZI: We certainly must ask her in. Let's hear what it is she wants. If there's any trouble we'll be able to cope with it. But do sit down, everybody! Please sit down! We must remain seated! [*To the* BUTLER] Show her in. [*The* BUTLER *goes out.*]

AMALIA: Oh, please help me, everybody, for goodness' sake! I haven't the slightest idea what to say to her now that we . . .

[MRS FROLA *enters.* AMALIA *rises and, somewhat afraid, goes to greet her. The others are looking at* MRS FROLA *in some dismay.*]

MRS FROLA: May I come in?

AMALIA: Please do, Mrs Frola, please do. . . . My friends are still here, as you see . . . .

MRS FROLA [*she is smiling, but there is a pronounced sadness in the gentle courtesy of her smile*]: And they're all looking at me just as if I were some poor mad woman. Yes, you too, dear Mrs Agazzi. . . . [*Then, to them all*] You are, aren't you?

AMALIA: No, no, Mrs Frola! How can you suggest such a thing?

MRS FROLA [*profound regret in her voice*]: It would have been better to have left things as they were, when I was rude enough to keep you standing outside the door, the first time you called! I could never have supposed that you would return and oblige me to make this visit, the consequences of which, alas! I foresaw only too clearly.

AMALIA: No! No! Believe me, we're very pleased to see you again.

SIRELLI: Something is distressing Mrs Frola. . . . We don't know what. . . . Suppose she tells us what it is.

MRS FROLA: Didn't my son-in-law leave here a moment or so ago?

AGAZZI: Oh, yes . . . yes! But he came to. . . er . . . er . . . talk to me about some . . . er . . . er . . . official matters, Mrs Frola. Yes, *official* matters!

MRS FROLA [*hurt and dismayed*]: Oh, what pitiful lies you're telling me . . . just so that I shan't worry . . .

AGAZZI: No! No! Mrs Frola. You may rest assured that it's the truth I'm telling you.

MRS FROLA [*the hurt and dismay still marked*]: He was quite calm, I hope. . . . *Was* he? Did he speak calmly?

AGAZZI: Oh, yes . . . quite calm. . . . He was very calm indeed, wasn't he?

[*All nod assent – confirming his words.*]

MRS FROLA: Oh dear, you all think you're reassuring me . . . And all the time *I* want to reassure *you* about *him.*

MRS SIRELLI: But what need is there for you to do so, Mrs Frola, if we tell you again that . . .?

AGAZZI: . . . It was official matters he came to talk to me about.

MRS FROLA: But I can see how you're looking at me. Please be patient with me. It's not for my own sake that I'm telling you all this! From the way in which you're looking at me, I can see quite plainly that he's been here and given you proof of . . . something that I would never have revealed, not for all the wealth in creation! You can all bear witness that when I was here just a short time ago I didn't know how to answer your questions. They were very cruel questions, believe me. And I gave you an explanation of our way of life which, I admit, could satisfy no one! But could I possibly tell you the real reason? Or could I tell you, as he goes about saying, that my daughter died four years ago, and that I am a poor mad woman who believes her to be still alive, and that he doesn't want to let me see her?

AGAZZI [*quite stunned by the profound accent of sincerity with which* MRS FROLA *has spoken*]: Oh! Do you mean to say . . .? Your daughter?

MRS FROLA [*immediately, anxiously*]: You see, it's true! Why are you trying to hide the truth from me? That *is* what he told you . . .!

SIRELLI [*hesitant, studying her*]: Yes . . . as a matter of fact . . . he *did* say . . .

MRS FROLA: I know he did. And unfortunately I know too the

42

pain it causes him, finding himself obliged to say such things about me! Ours is a misfortune, Mr Agazzi, which has inflicted terrible suffering upon us. By unceasing effort we have been able to come to terms with it. But only at the cost of living as we now live. I can very well appreciate how odd it must look to other people . . . what suspicion it must arouse . . . the scandal it provokes. But, on the other hand, he's an excellent worker, most conscientious and completely scrupulous. But you'll have found that out already, no doubt.

AGAZZI: Well, to tell you the truth, I haven't . . . I've had no chance to, as yet.

MRS FROLA: Please don't judge him by appearances! He really is an excellent boy. Everybody he's ever worked for has said that! So why must you torture him with this investigation into his private life? Into this misfortune of his? A misfortune, I repeat, that he has got over, but one which . . . if people got to know about it . . . might injure his career.

AGAZZI: Mrs Frola, please don't distress yourself so! Nobody wants to torture him.

MRS FROLA: Oh dear, how can you expect me not to be distressed, when I see him obliged to give to all and sundry an explanation that is absurd, *horrible*? Can you really seriously believe that my daughter is dead? That I am mad? And that this woman who's living with him now is his second wife? But, believe me, it is necessary, absolutely necessary for him to say all this! By this means alone has he been able to regain his tranquillity and his belief in life. He himself is well aware of the enormity of what he says, and when he is forced to say it, he gets excited and overwrought. You'll have noticed that for yourselves!

AGAZZI: Yes, as a matter of fact, he was a little . . . a little . . . excited.

MRS SIRELLI: Oh dear, do you mean to say . . . ? Then *he's* the one that's mad now, is he?

SIRELLI: Why, of course he is! It must be him! [*Triumphantly*] I told you so!

43

AGAZZI: Good Lord! Is it really possible? [*A lively agitation among the others.*]

MRS FROLA [*immediately, clasping her hands*]: Oh, please, everyone, what are you thinking now? *No!* It's only on this one subject that he's so sensitive. But would I leave my daughter alone with him if he really were mad? Would I? No! And there's the evidence of his work at the office. . . . You can see for yourself, Mr Agazzi. He carries out all his duties perfectly. No one could possibly do better.

AGAZZI: H'm! But you'll still have to explain to us exactly how things stand, Mrs Frola. And very clearly too! Do you really mean to say that your son-in-law came here and made up all that story purely for our benefit?

MRS FROLA: Yes. . . . I'll explain everything to you. But you must forgive him, Mr Agazzi, you *must!*

AGAZZI: But do you really mean to say . . . ? Isn't it true that your daughter's dead?

MRS FROLA [*in horror*]: Oh, no! God forbid!

AGAZZI [*thoroughly annoyed, shouts*]: Then he's the one that's mad!

MRS FROLA [*entreating*]: No! No! Look. . . .!

SIRELLI [*triumphantly*]: Yes, yes, of course, he must be mad!

MRS FROLA: No! Look! Look! He's not mad! He's not mad! Please let me speak! You've seen him. He's a tremendously powerful, virile, rather violent sort of man. When he got married he was carried away by an absolute frenzy of love. My daughter's a very delicate girl and he came very near to destroying her with the violence of his passion. On the advice of the doctors, the members of the two families decided that . . . his relatives agreed as well . . . they're dead now, poor things! . . . that she should be taken away in secret and put in a nursing home. He was naturally already a little unbalanced as a consequence of his . . . excessive love . . . so that when he could no longer find her in the house he . . . he fell into a kind of furious despair! [*This to the ladies*] He really believed that his wife was dead. He wouldn't hear

44

anything to the contrary. He insisted on wearing black. He did all sorts of mad things. And there was no way in which you could get him to budge from his obsession. So much so that when, just about a year later, my daughter, now completely well and blooming again, was brought back to him, he said no, it couldn't be his wife. No, no . . . he looked at her . . . no, no, it wasn't his wife at all. How terrible it was! [*This to the ladies*] She went up to him, and it seemed for a moment that he recognized her, and then, again, no, no . . . and finally, so as to bring him to accept my daughter again, we had to have a make-believe second wedding with the connivance of some friends.

MRS SIRELLI: Ah! So that's why he says . . .

MRS FROLA: Yes, but not even he really believes it any longer. And he hasn't for some time now. But he needs to keep up the pretence before others. He can't help it. He does it so that he can banish his sense of insecurity. Do you understand? Because, perhaps, every now and again there flashes into his mind the fear that his darling wife might once more be taken away from him. [*In a lower tone, smiling confidingly*] That's why he keeps her under lock and key . . . to keep her all to himself. But he adores her! Of that I'm quite sure. And my daughter is happy. [*She rises.*] I must go. I shouldn't like him to call on me suddenly now, all overwrought, as you say he is, and not find me at home. [*She sighs softly, gesturing with her clasped hands.*] We must be patient. That poor girl must pretend to be, not herself, but someone else, and I . . . yes, I have to pretend to be mad. [*This to the ladies*] But what of it? So long as *he's* at peace . . .! Please don't trouble, I know the way. Goodbye, goodbye. [*Bowing and smiling her farewells, she retires hurriedly through the door, centre-back. They all remain on their feet, staring at one another, utterly bewildered, utterly astounded. Silence.*]

LAUDISI [*stepping into the centre of the group*]: So . . . you're all staring at one another? Well, well! And the *truth*? [*He bursts into noisy laughter.*] Ha! Ha! Ha! Ha!

# ACT TWO

---

AGAZZI's *study. Antique furniture: old paintings on the walls: a door back, with a hanging curtain. There is a door left leading into the drawing-room. This too has a hanging curtain. To the right is a fireplace of ample proportions, and resting on the mantelshelf is a large mirror. On the desk is a telephone. For the rest there are a couch, armchairs, chairs, etc.*

[AGAZZI *is standing near the writing-desk with the telephone receiver to his ear.* LAUDISI *and* SIRELLI, *who are seated, are looking expectantly at him.*]

AGAZZI: Hello! Yes. Is that you, Centuri? Well? Oh, yes. . . . Good man! [*He listens for some time.*] What's that? Really? Do you mean to say that . . .? [*He listens again for some time.*] Yes, I do understand! But suppose we get down to it a little more energetically. . . . M'm? . . . [*A long pause.*] It's really most strange, that we shouldn't be able to . . . [*A pause.*] Oh yes, I quite appreciate . . . I do realize. [*A pause.*] Ah well, that'll have to do for the moment. . . . We'll wait a bit, and see . . . . Goodbye! [*He puts down the receiver and comes forward.*]

SIRELLI [*anxiously*]: Well?

AGAZZI: Absolutely nothing.

SIRELLI: Can't they find anything at all?

AGAZZI: Everything's been destroyed or got lost in the confusion. The Town Hall, the Records Office, the Registrar's . . .

SIRELLI: But couldn't they at least have got some sort of information from the survivors?

AGAZZI: There's no record of there being any survivors. And even if there were any, it would be exceedingly difficult to trace them after all this time.

SIRELLI: So there's no option but to believe one or other of them? Just on what they say, without a scrap of proof either way?

AGAZZI: Unfortunately!

LAUDISI [*getting up*]: Would you care to take my advice? Believe them both.

AGAZZI: That's all very well, but . . .

SIRELLI: Suppose she says one thing and he says the direct opposite?

LAUDISI: In that case, don't believe either of them!

SIRELLI: Oh, you're just trying to be funny. It's quite true that the proof we need is missing. . . . The exact facts of the case, that is. . . . But, good heavens, the truth must lie with one or other of them!

LAUDISI: Precisely, the facts of the case! And what would you deduce from *them*?

AGAZZI: Oh, really! The death certificate of the daughter, for example. . . . If Mrs Frola is the one who's mad, there must have been such a certificate at some time or other. Unfortunately it's no longer to be found, for the simple reason that we can no longer find *anything*. But it might be found tomorrow. And once it was found, it would be perfectly obvious that *he* was right . . . the son-in-law, I mean.

SIRELLI: Would you be able to deny such evidence of his being right, if tomorrow we were to present you with this certificate?

LAUDISI: Me? I'm not denying anything! I'm most careful not to do anything of the sort. It's you, not I, who have need of the precise facts of the case, of documents to deny this or to affirm that! I don't care a brass farthing for them, because as far as I'm concerned they don't constitute reality. Reality for me lies in the minds of those two, and I can only hope to penetrate to that reality through what they tell me about themselves.

SIRELLI: Very well! And don't they themselves quite definitely say that one or other of them is mad? Either *she's* mad, or else *he* is. That fact there's no escaping! Now which of them is it?

AGAZZI: That is the question!

LAUDISI: First of all it's not true that both of them do say that. Mr Ponza says it about his mother-in-law. Mrs Frola denies that it's true, not only about herself, but about him, too. At most, she says, he was a little overwrought mentally owing to his excessive passion for his wife. But now he's all right again, quite all right.

SIRELLI: Ah, so you're inclined to believe what the mother-in-law says . . . like me?

AGAZZI: Well, it's certainly true that if you accept what she says everything's accounted for very neatly.

LAUDISI: But you can explain everything equally well if you accept what the son-in-law says!

SIRELLI: So, neither of them is mad? But, good heavens above, one of them must be!

LAUDISI: And which of them is it? You can't tell, any more than anyone else can. And not only because those documents that you're so busily hunting for have been totally obliterated . . . destroyed or dispersed by this disaster . . . whatever it was . . . a fire or something . . . this *earthquake*! No, but because they have obliterated everything in themselves, in their own minds, if you understand what I mean. They have created, she for him and he for her, a world of fantasy that has all the substance of reality itself, a world in which they now live in perfect peace and harmony. And it cannot be destroyed, this reality of theirs, by any of your documents, because they live and breathe in it! They can see it, feel it, touch it! At most a document might comfort *you* a little, might satisfy your stupid curiosity. But such a document is just not to be found, and so you're condemned to the wonderful torment of having before your very eyes, suddenly very close to you, on the one hand, this world of fantasy and on the other, *reality* . . . and of not being able to distinguish one from the other!

48

AGAZZI: Philosophy, my dear Lamberto, sheer philosophy! We shall see, we shall soon see if it's possible to distinguish one from the other or not!

SIRELLI: Look! We've heard his story and we've heard hers. Now, if we put them side by side, do you really mean to say that we shan't discover which is the world of fantasy and which reality?

LAUDISI: All I ask is your permission to go on laughing at your efforts, right to the bitter end.

AGAZZI: All right! All right! But we'll see who has the last laugh! Now, don't let's waste any more time! [*He goes to the door left and calls*] Amalia . . . Mrs Sirelli . . . please be so kind as to join us, will you?

[AMALIA, MRS SIRELLI, *and* DINA *join them.*]

MRS SIRELLI [*to* LAUDISI, *shaking her finger threateningly at him*]: What, are *you* here again?

SIRELLI: He's incorrigible!

MRS SIRELLI: But how is it that you manage to keep so cool, calm, and collected when all the rest of us are simply *itching* to get to the bottom of this mystery? Why, it's pretty nearly driven us all mad, we're so worked up! Do you know, I didn't sleep a wink all last night!

AMALIA: Oh, please don't bother with him, Mrs Sirelli!

LAUDISI: Indeed you mustn't. Give all your attention to my brother-in-law, who is about to ensure that you get a good night's sleep tonight.

AGAZZI: Well, then. Let's get things organized. This is what you have to do. . . . You three will go and call on Mrs Frola . . .

AMALIA: And will she be at home to us?

AGAZZI: She most decidedly will be!

DINA: It's our duty to return her visit.

AMALIA: But what about his not wanting her to pay or receive calls?

SIRELLI: Oh, that was before. Because nobody knew anything then. But now that Mrs Frola has been obliged to call, and has spoken to us and explained in her own way the reason for her being so reserved. . . .

MRS SIRELLI [*pursuing his line of reasoning*]: . . . She might, in fact, be only too pleased to talk to us about her daughter.

DINA: She's perfectly delightful, isn't she? Oh, as far as I'm concerned, I have absolutely no doubt whatsoever as to who's telling the truth. He's the one that's mad!

AGAZZI: Steady on! Don't let's rush to hasty conclusions. Now, listen to me. [*He looks at his watch.*] You will only stay a short while. A quarter of an hour. No longer.

SIRELLI [*to his wife*]: Now for goodness' sake remember that!

MRS SIRELLI [*her anger rising*]: And why say that to me?

SIRELLI: *Why?* Because once you start talking . . .

DINA [*forestalling a quarrel between the two of them*]: A quarter of an hour, a quarter of an hour! I'll see that we stay no longer.

AGAZZI: I'm going as far as the Prefecture, and I'll be back at eleven. In about twenty minutes' time.

SIRELLI [*fretfully*]: And what do I do?

AGAZZI: Wait. [*To the women*] Just before I'm due home again you'll find some excuse for bringing Mrs Frola back here with you.

AMALIA: What sort of an excuse?

AGAZZI: Any excuse will do! Something is bound to come up in the course of conversation. You're not likely to lack an excuse. You're not women for nothing. And you've got Dina and Mrs Sirelli to help you. . . . When you come back, you will go into the drawing-room, of course. [*He goes to the door left and opens it wide, drawing the curtain to one side.*] This door must remain like this, open quite wide, so that we can hear what's being said in there when *we're* in here. On my desk I shall leave these papers . . . which I really ought to take with me. It's an official brief especially prepared for Mr Ponza. I shall pretend that I've forgotten it, and on that pretext I shall return here, bringing Mr Ponza with me. Then . . .

SIRELLI [*still fretting away*]: Forgive my interrupting, but what about *me*? When shall I come?

AGAZZI: At a few minutes past eleven. When the ladies are already in the drawing-room and I'm in here with Ponza. You'll have come to collect your wife. You get them to show you in here. And then I'll ask the ladies to be good enough to join us. . . .

LAUDISI [*immediately*]: And the truth will be revealed!

DINA: But, Uncle dear, once they're face to face . . .

AGAZZI: Oh, for goodness' sake, don't pay any attention to him! Now, off you go! Off you go! There's no time to be lost!

MRS SIRELLI: Yes, let's go! Let's be on our way! I won't even say goodbye to you!

LAUDISI: In that case, I shall say goodbye to myself on your behalf, Mrs Sirelli. [*He shakes one hand with the other.*] Good luck!

[*Exeunt* AMALIA, DINA, *and* MRS SIRELLI.]

AGAZZI [*to* SIRELLI]: I think we'd better be going too, don't you? Without wasting any more time!

SIRELLI: Yes, let's push off! Goodbye, Lamberto!

LAUDISI: Goodbye! Goodbye!

[AGAZZI *and* SIRELLI *go out.*]

LAUDISI [*wanders round the study for a little while, grinning to himself and shaking his head. Then he stops in front of the large mirror which rests on the mantelpiece, looks at his own reflection and starts talking to it*]: Ah, there you are! [*He gives his reflection a mock salute with a couple of fingers, winks one eye cunningly, and grins at it.*] Well, my dear fellow! Now which of us two is mad? [*He raises his hand, pointing the forefinger at his reflection, which, in turn, points its forefinger at him. He grins again, then*] Ah yes, I know! I say *you* and you point at *me*! Dear me! Dear me! Between you and me and the gatepost we know one another pretty well, you and I! But what an awful fix you're in, old chap! Other people don't see you the way *I* see you! So what do you become? I can say that, as far as I'm concerned, standing in front of you as I am now, I'm able to see myself and touch myself. But as for you, when it's a question of how other people see you, what happens to you? You become a phantom, my dear fellow, a creature of fantasy! And yet, do you see what these lunatics are up to? Without taking the slightest notice of their own phantom, the phantom that is implicit within *them*, they go haring about, frantic with curiosity, chasing after other people's phantoms! And they believe they're doing something quite quite different.

[*The* BUTLER *enters and is rather taken aback as he hears* LAUDISI'S *last words to the mirror. Then he says*]:

BUTLER: Mr Laudisi!

LAUDISI: M'm?

BUTLER: Two ladies have called, sir. Mrs Cini and another lady.

LAUDISI: Do they want me?

BUTLER: They asked for Mrs Agazzi. I said that she had gone to call on Mrs Frola next door and then . . .

LAUDISI: Then . . .?

BUTLER: They looked at one another and clapped their hands. 'Oh, yes?' they said. 'Oh, yes?' Then they asked me, sir, with some anxiety, if that meant that nobody was, in fact, at home.

LAUDISI: And you replied that there was nobody at home.

BUTLER: I replied that *you* were at home, sir.

LAUDISI: Me? No, not at all. Only the Laudisi they know! That is, if there's *anybody*.

BUTLER [*more taken aback than ever*]: What do you mean, sir?

LAUDISI: Forgive my asking, but do you think that I and that Laudisi are the same person?

BUTLER [*is still utterly astounded: his mouth is open and he tries miserably to smile*]: I'm afraid I don't understand, sir.

LAUDISI: Who are you talking to?

BUTLER [*flabbergasted*]: Eh? . . . who . . . who am I talking to . . .? Why . . . to *you*, sir. . . .

LAUDISI: And you're absolutely certain that I am the same person as the one the ladies are asking for?

BUTLER: Well, I couldn't really say. . . . They asked for Mrs Agazzi's brother. . . .

LAUDISI: Good man! Ah, well . . . yes, then it is me! It is me they want. . . . Show them in, show them in . . .

[*The* BUTLER *goes out, turning round several times to look back at him, as if he can no longer believe his own eyes.*]

MRS CINI: May I come in?

LAUDISI: Please do, Mrs Cini! Of course!

MRS CINI: They told me that Mrs Agazzi was not at home. I'd brought my friend, Mrs Nenni, with me. [*She introduces her, an elderly lady, even more stupid and affected than* MRS CINI *herself. She too is filled with avid curiosity, but hers is a cautious, rather abashed curiosity.*] She was most anxious to meet Mrs . . .

LAUDISI [*immediately*]: . . . Frola?

MRS CINI: No, no . . . your sister.

LAUDISI: Oh, she won't be long. She'll be back very soon. And Mrs Frola too. Please sit down, won't you? [*He invites them to sit on the couch and then gracefully insinuates himself between them.*] May I? There's ample room for the three of us on this couch, isn't there? Mrs Sirelli has gone with them.

MRS CINI: Yes, I know, the butler told me.

LAUDISI: It's all been planned in advance, you know. Oh, there'll be a most interesting scene! Tremendous! It won't be long now. At eleven o'clock. Here.

MRS CINI [*stunned by all this*]: All been planned? Excuse me, but *what* has all been planned?

LAUDISI [*he becomes very mysterious. First of all a mystifying gesture . . . he joins the tips of his forefingers . . . then he goes on in mysterious tones*]: Their meeting! [*A gesture of admiration.*] A wonderful idea.

MRS CINI: What, *what* meeting?

LAUDISI: The meeting of *those two*. First of all *he* will come in *here*.

MRS CINI: Mr Ponza?

LAUDISI: Yes. And *she* will be taken in *there*. [*He gestures towards the drawing-room.*]

MRS CINI: Mrs Frola?

LAUDISI: Yes, Mrs Cini. [*He repeats his performance . . . first the hands, then the voice.*] And *then*, both of them in here, face to face with one another. And the rest of us all round to see and hear what happens. A wonderful idea!

MRS CINI: So as to find out . . .?

LAUDISI: . . . the truth! But, of course, we know that already. All that remains is for its mask to be stripped off!

MRS CINI [*with surprise and the most lively anxiety*]: Oh! the truth is known already? And which of them is it? Which of them is it? Which?

LAUDISI: Now, let's see! Guess! Which of them would *you* say it was?

MRS CINI [*exultant, but hesitating to give her opinion*]: Why . . . I . . . well, I should . . . it's . . .

LAUDISI: Him or her? Let's see if . . . Come on . . . guess! Don't be frightened!

MRS CINI: I . . . well, I'd say it was him.

LAUDISI [*looks at her for a short while, then*]: It *is*!

MRS CINI [*exultantly*]: It is? There! What did I say? Of course it is! It had to be him! It *had* to!

MRS NENNI [*exultantly*]: It's him! There, that's what we women have been saying all along!

MRS CINI: And how did they, how did they manage to find out? Some proofs have come to light, I suppose? Documents?

MRS NENNI: I suppose the Police found it out, didn't they? That's what we always said! It just wasn't possible for us not to get at the truth once the Prefect set things moving!

LAUDISI [*motions them to sit nearer to him. Then in a mysterious tone, almost weighing out the syllables, he says quietly and slowly*]: The certificate of the second marriage.

MRS CINI [*as if she had been punched on the nose*]: Of the *second* marriage?

MRS NENNI [*bewildered*]: What do you mean? What do you mean? *The certificate of the second marriage?*

MRS CINI [*recovering, but thoroughly put out*]: But . . . but in that case *he'd* be the one who was right!

LAUDISI: Well, there you are, the documents in the case, ladies. The certificate of the second marriage . . . as far as I can see . . . speaks plainly enough.

MRS NENNI [*almost weeping*]: But in that case *she's* the one who's mad!

LAUDISI: Yes! It certainly looks like it.

MRS CINI: But how d'you . . . ? First of all you said it was him, now you say it's her.

LAUDISI: Yes, because, as Mrs Frola herself has assured us, that certificate, Mrs Cini, that second marriage certificate, may very well be a fake. Do you see what I mean? Faked with the help of friends, so as to back him up in his fixation that his wife was not who she really was, but someone else.

MRS CINI: Ah! And in that case a document . . . which is valueless, therefore?

LAUDISI: No, that is . . . that's to say . . . it has whatever value . . . whatever value anyone cares to set on it, ladies! And, then, aren't there the notes Mrs Frola says she receives every day from her daughter, the notes she sends down into the courtyard in the little basket? There are those notes too, aren't there?

MRS CINI: Yes. Well?

LAUDISI: Well . . . documents, Mrs Cini! Documents, all of them! Even those notes! All dependent on the value that you decide you want to set on them! Along comes Mr Ponza and says they've all been faked in order to back up Mrs Frola in her fixation.

MRS CINI: Oh, dear! Oh, dear! Then we can know nothing for certain?

LAUDISI: Nothing? What do you mean, nothing? Don't let's exaggerate! Tell me. . . . How many days in the week are there?

MRS CINI: Why, seven.

LAUDISI: Monday, Tuesday, Wednesday . . .

MRS CINI [*prompted to go on*]: Thursday, Friday, Saturday . . .

LAUDISI: . . . and Sunday. [*Turning to the other woman*] And how many months in the year?

MRS NENNI: Twelve!

LAUDISI: January, February, March . . .

MRS CINI: Oh, oh, now we see what you're . . .! You're trying to make fun of us!

DINA [*rushing in suddenly through the door back*]: Uncle dear, please . . . [*Catching sight of* MRS CINI *she stops*] Oh, *you're* here, Mrs Cini?

MRS CINI: Yes, I came with Mrs Nenni . . .

LAUDISI: . . . Who is very anxious to meet Mrs Frola.

MRS NENNI: Why, no . . .

MRS CINI: He's still making fun of us. Oh, Dina dear! He's made us all so confused, you know. Argued us silly! It's been just like when you go into a railway station! Clackety-lurch! Clackety-lurch! One set of points after another! We're quite dizzy!

DINA: Oh, he's being very naughty just now with everybody, even with us! Please don't mind what he says. Now, there's nothing more I need to do in here, is there? I'll go and tell Mummy that you're here. Yes, everything seems to be all right. Oh, Uncle, if you could only have heard her! She's a perfectly charming old lady. Such a dear! So good and so kind! And how sweet she is about everything! It's a lovely little flat and everything's so neat and tidy. It's all so tasteful. The lovely little white covers on the furniture. She showed us all the notes from her daughter, too.

MRS CINI: Yes . . . but . . . well, suppose, as Mr Laudisi was just saying. . .

DINA: And what does he know about them? He's never even read them!

MRS NENNI: You don't think it's possible that they're forgeries, do you?

DINA: Forgeries indeed! Don't pay any attention to him! Do

you really think that a mother could possibly be mistaken about the way her own daughter would write to her? The last note ... she only got it yesterday ... [*She breaks off as voices in the adjoining drawing-room make themselves heard through the open door.*] Ah, there they are! That must be them now! [*She goes to the drawing-room door to look.*]

MRS CINI [*running after her*]: Is *she* there, too? Is Mrs Frola with them?

DINA: Yes, but come along please, now. Do come along with me. We've all got to stay in the drawing-room. Is it eleven o'clock yet, Uncle?

AMALIA [*coming in all of a sudden from the drawing-room. She too is agitated*]: I think this whole business is most unnecessary! We've already got all the proof we need!

DINA: Of course we have! That's what I think, too. The whole thing's pointless now.

AMALIA [*greeting MRS CINI hastily, sadness and anxiety in her manner*]: How are you, my dear Mrs Cini?

MRS CINI [*introducing MRS NENNI*]: This is Mrs Nenni, who came with me to ...

AMALIA [*hastily greeting MRS NENNI too*]: I'm very pleased to meet you, Mrs Nenni. [*Then*] There can no longer be the slightest doubt! He's the one that's mad!

MRS CINI: It's him, is it? You're sure it's him?

DINA: Oh, if only we could warn Daddy and prevent him from playing this trick on poor Mrs Frola!

AMALIA: Yes! We've brought her back with us. She's in there! It seems like downright treachery to me!

LAUDISI: Of course it is! And most unworthy of you! Most unworthy! You're quite right! So right that you're now beginning to convince me that she must be the one who's mad! Yes it *must* be Mrs Frola who's mad!

AMALIA: Mrs Frola? What on earth do you mean? What *are* you talking about?

LAUDISI: Mrs Frola! Mrs Frola! Mrs Frola!

AMALIA: Come, Lamberto! Don't be tiresome!

DINA: Why . . .! But . . . we're quite convinced now that it's Ponza who's mad.

MRS CINI and MRS NENNI [*both exultant*]: You *are*, are you? You're convinced he's mad?

LAUDISI: I think what I think precisely because you others are so convinced to the contrary.

DINA: Oh, come on! Let's go into the other room! Let's go into the other room! Can't you see he's doing it on purpose?

AMALIA: Yes, let's go. Come along, Mrs Cini! Mrs Nenni, you too. [*She is now by the door left.*] No, please . . . after you . . .

[MRS CINI, MRS NENNI, *and* AMALIA *go out*. DINA *is about to follow them.*]

LAUDISI [*calling her to him*]: Dina!

DINA: No, no! I refuse to listen to you!

LAUDISI: Shut that door, if the test is now pointless as far as you're concerned!

DINA: And what will Daddy say? It was he who left it open like that, remember. He's due back with Mr Ponza any minute now. If he found it shut . . . Well, you know what Daddy's like!

LAUDISI: But you people will be able to convince him that . . . *you* especially . . . that there was no longer any need for it to be left open. Or aren't you quite so sure about that?

DINA: Absolutely sure!

LAUDISI [*with a challenging smile*]: Well then, shut it!

DINA: You want to have the satisfaction of getting me to admit that I still have my doubts, don't you? I'm not shutting that door. But only because Daddy said . . .

LAUDISI [*as before*]: Would you like *me* to shut it?

DINA: On your own head be it!

LAUDISI: But, unlike you, I'm not convinced that Ponza's the one who's mad.

DINA: Then come into the drawing-room and listen to Mrs Frola, as we've been listening to her. You'll see . . . In next to no time you'll be just as convinced as we are. Are you coming?

LAUDISI: Yes, I'm coming! And I think I can shut the door, you know! And on my own head be it!

DINA: There, you see? Even before you've heard her say a word!

LAUDISI: No, my dear. It's because I'm quite sure that your father is at this moment thinking exactly the same thing as you women ... that this test is absolutely pointless.

DINA: Are you sure?

LAUDISI: Of course I am! At this moment he's talking to Ponza, and I haven't the slightest doubt that he is now thoroughly convinced that it's Mrs Frola who's mad. [*He goes resolutely up to the door.*] I'm going to shut the door.

DINA [*immediately restraining him*]: No! [*Then, correcting herself*] Oh, I'm sorry ... but ... if that's what you think ... let's leave it open. ...

LAUDISI [*laughing – as he is wont to do*]: Ha! Ha! Ha!

DINA: I mean because of Daddy!

LAUDISI: And Daddy will say because of you women! Let's leave it open. [*We hear the piano being played in the drawing-room. The piece is an old tune, full of a sweet, sad gracefulness. It comes from Paisiello's 'Nina, Whom Love Drove Mad'.*]

DINA: Ah, it's her. ... Can you hear? That's her playing now.

LAUDISI: The old lady?

DINA: Yes, she told us about how her daughter always used to play that old tune. Before all *that* happened. Do you hear how sweetly she plays it? Let's join them, shall we? Shall we? [*They both go out through the door left.*]

[*After* LAUDISI *and* DINA *go out the stage remains empty for a short while. We still hear the sound of the piano coming from the next room.* MR PONZA *enters with* MR AGAZZI *through the door back. Hearing the music, he is profoundly disturbed. As the scene progresses his perturbation gradually increases.*]

AGAZZI [*standing by the door back*]: Please come in. Please do come in. [*He shows* MR PONZA *in, and then comes in himself.*

*He goes towards the desk, to pick up the papers which he has pretended he has forgotten to take to the office.*] Yes, I must have left them here. Do sit down, please. [MR PONZA *remains standing, looking agitatedly towards the drawing-room from which the sound of the piano is coming.*] Ah, here they are, in fact! [*He picks up the papers and goes over towards* MR PONZA, *leafing through them as he goes.*] It's a terribly complicated case . . . as I was telling you . . . it's been dragging on for years. [*Irritated by the sound of the piano, he also turns to look towards the drawing-room.*] Oh, music! And now of all times! [*As he turns he shrugs a little contemptuously, as if saying to himself: 'These stupid women!'*] Who's that playing, I wonder? [*He goes and looks through the open door into the drawing-room. He sees that it is* MRS FROLA *at the piano, and makes a gesture of amazement.*] Well! Well! Come and see who it is!

PONZA [*coming up to him, greatly agitated*]: My God, is it *Mrs Frola* who's playing? *Is* it?

AGAZZI: Yes, your mother-in-law. How well she plays!

PONZA: What does this mean? Have you brought her here – *again*? Are you getting her to play for you?

AGAZZI: I don't see what harm there can be in that.

PONZA: But not that tune! For heaven's sake don't let her play *that* tune! It's the piece her daughter used to play!

AGAZZI: Ah, I suppose it hurts you to hear it played?

PONZA: Not me! She's the one it hurts. There's really no knowing how deeply it hurts her! I've already told you, sir, and the ladies too, of the sad condition that that poor, unfortunate woman is in . . .

AGAZZI [*attempting to calm him as his agitation grows*]: Yes, yes . . . but look here . . .

PONZA [*sweeping on*]: . . . And she must be left in peace! She mustn't visit people and they mustn't visit her! I, and only I, know how to deal with her! You're killing her! You're killing her!

AGAZZI: Oh, no! Don't exaggerate! My wife and daughter would notice just as soon as you would if . . . [*He suddenly breaks off as the music in the drawing-room stops. A chorus of praise is now to be heard.*] There, you see, you can hear how . . .

[*From the drawing-room the following snatch of dialogue can be distinctly heard*]:

DINA: But you still play most wonderfully, Mrs Frola!

MRS FROLA: Do I? You should hear my dear Lina! You should hear how my dear Lina plays!

PONZA [*trembling, clenching his fists*]: Her dear Lina! Did you hear? She said *her dear Lina!*

AGAZZI: Why, of course, her daughter.

PONZA: But she said *plays! Plays!*

[*Again from the other room may be heard distinctly*]:

MRS FROLA: No, she hasn't been able to play since . . . since *that* happened! And, you know, I think this has probably been the hardest thing of all for her to bear.

AGAZZI: Why, it all seems quite natural to me. She believes that her daughter's still alive. . . .

PONZA: But you oughtn't to let her say such things! She *mustn't* . . . she *mustn't* say such things! Did you hear what she said? 'Since *that* happened.' She said 'since *that* happened!' Talking about her daughter's piano, of course! Oh! you can't possibly understand! She was talking about her poor dead daughter's piano!

[*At this point* SIRELLI *suddenly comes in, and, on hearing* PONZA'S *words and seeing the extreme exasperation on his face, stands stock-still in amazement.* AGAZZI, *who is no less dismayed, beckons him over.*]

AGAZZI: Please ask the ladies to come and join us!

[SIRELLI, *giving* PONZA *a wide berth, goes to the door left and calls the ladies.*]

PONZA: The ladies? In here? No, no! Better . . .

[*The ladies, to whom an absolutely dismayed* SIRELLI *has indicated the state of affairs, come in. They are somewhat dismayed themselves.* PONZA *is trembling all over, almost like a suffering animal.* MRS FROLA, *seeing her son-in-law in his present state of fury, is terror-stricken, and during the ensuing*

61

*scene, as he assails her with ever more extreme violence, she
throws expressive glances of understanding at the other ladies.
The scene unfolds rapidly and is tense with excitement.*]

PONZA: You're here? Again? What have you come for?

MRS FROLA: I came to . . . Oh, don't be cross with me!

PONZA: You came here to tell them again about . . . What
have you told them? What have you told these ladies?

MRS FROLA: Nothing, I swear! Nothing at all!

PONZA: Nothing? What do you mean nothing? I heard what
you said. [*Pointing to* AGAZZI] *He* heard too! You said
plays! *Who* plays? *Lina* plays? You know perfectly well that
your daughter's been dead for the last four years!

MRS FROLA: Why, of course I do, my dear! Now calm yourself! Of course I know! Yes!

PONZA: 'No, she hasn't been able to play since *that*
happened.' No wonder she hasn't been able to play . . .!
How do you expect her to, if she's dead?

MRS FROLA: Why, of course not! And isn't that just what I
said? [*Appealing to the ladies*] Didn't I say that she hadn't been
able to play since . . .? She's dead!

PONZA: Then why are you still brooding about that piano?

MRS FROLA: Oh, but I'm not! I don't think about it any longer!

PONZA: I smashed it up, and you know it! I smashed it up
when your daughter died, so that my second wife shouldn't
touch it! She can't play anyway! You know perfectly well
that my wife can't play!

MRS FROLA: Why, of course I know that she can't play! Of
course I do!

PONZA: And what was your daughter's name? It was Lina,
wasn't it? Lina! Now tell me, what is my second wife's
name! Tell it to everybody! You know it perfectly well!
What's her name?

MRS FROLA: Giulia! That's her name, Giulia! [*Then, to all the
others*] Yes, it's true! Her name *is* Giulia!

PONZA: Giulia, then! *Not* Lina! And don't try to insinuate
anything by winking as you say that her name's Giulia.

MRS FROLA: Winking? Why, I wasn't winking!

PONZA: I saw you! You were winking! I saw you very clearly!
You want to ruin me! You want all these people to think
that I'm still trying to keep your daughter entirely to myself, just as if she were not dead! [*He breaks into terrifying
sobs.*] Just as if she were not dead!

MRS FROLA [*immediately running to him, infinitely tender and
humble*]: Oh, no! No! Of course I don't, my dear boy!
Please be calm! I've never said anything of the sort, have
I? Have I? [*Appealing to the ladies.*]

AMALIA, MRS SIRELLI, DINA: No, of course not! No! She's
never said anything of the sort! She's always said that her
daughter was dead!

MRS FROLA: Yes, that's right! That she was dead . . . that's
what I told them! Why not? And I told them, too, that you
were so kind to me. [*Appealing to the ladies*] Didn't I? Would
I want to ruin you? Would I want to spoil your career?

PONZA [*now very erect, terribly*]: But meanwhile you go into
other people's houses, looking for a piano on which to play
the pieces of music that your daughter was so fond of playing! And you go about saying that Lina plays like that and
better than that!

MRS FROLA: No, it was . . . I did it, as much . . . as much to
prove . . .

PONZA: You can't! You mustn't! What on earth put it into
your head to play again the music that your daughter used
to play?

MRS FROLA: Yes, you're quite right! Oh, my poor boy! My
poor boy! [*Deeply touched, she begins to cry.*] I'll never do it
again! I'll never do it again!

PONZA [*coming quite close, his manner terrible*]: And now, go!
Go! Go home at once!

MRS FROLA: Yes . . . yes . . . I'm going . . . I'm going . . . Oh,
dear!

[*She looks beseechingly at everybody as she backs out, pleading
with them to have pity on her son-in-law. Weeping, she goes*

*off. Everyone is overcome with pity and terror and is staring at* MR PONZA. *But as soon as his mother-in-law has left the room his manner changes completely. He becomes calm and again assumes his normal bearing. Then he says quite simply*]:

PONZA: I must beg your pardon, ladies and gentlemen, for having had to make this unhappy scene in front of you. I *had* to do it, so that I might remedy the harm which, without knowing it and without in the least wishing it, you were doing that unhappy woman, by showing her so much compassion.

AGAZZI [*as astounded as the rest*]: Do you mean to say . . . ? It was all a pretence on your part?

PONZA: A necessary one! Don't you understand that this is the only way to keep up her illusion for her? For me to shout the truth out in that way, as if *I* were mad, and *that* my particular form of madness! You will forgive me, won't you? And now, if you'll pardon me, I must run along and see how she is.

[*He goes out hurriedly through the door back. Once again the others are left astounded and silently staring at one another.*]

LAUDISI [*stepping into the centre of the group*]: Well, everybody, there you are! You've discovered the truth! [*He bursts out laughing.*] Ha! Ha! Ha! Ha!

# ACT THREE

---

*The scene is the same as in Act Two.*

> [LAUDISI *is stretched out in an armchair, reading. Through the door left, which leads into the drawing-room, can be heard the confused noise of many voices. The* BUTLER, *standing at the door centre, ushers in* CENTURI, *the Commissioner of Police.*]

BUTLER: Will you please wait in here a moment? I'll go and tell Mr Agazzi that you've come.

LAUDISI [*turning and seeing* CENTURI]: Why, it's you, Centuri! [*He gets up hurriedly and calls back the* BUTLER, *who is just about to go out.*] Sst! Wait a moment. [*To* CENTURI] Any news?

CENTURI [*tall, stiff, about forty years old, his face set in a perpetual frown*]: Yes, a little.

LAUDISI: Oh, good! [*To the* BUTLER] You needn't bother. I'll call my brother-in-law myself, after I've had a word with Mr Centuri. [*He nods in the direction of the door left. The* BUTLER *bows, and goes out.*] So you've accomplished the miracle! You're the saviour of the town! Can you hear them? Can you hear all the noise they're making? Well? Anything definite?

CENTURI: Well, we've finally managed to trace one or two people . . .

LAUDISI: . . . From Ponza's home town? People who know all about him?

CENTURI: Yes, sir. We've got one or two facts now. . . . Not much to go on, but what we've got is reliable.

LAUDISI: Oh, good! Good! For example?

CENTURI: Well, this is what's been sent me.

> [*He takes from his inside coat pocket an open yellow envelope with a sheet of paper in it and proffers it to* LAUDISI.]

LAUDISI: Let's see! Let's see! [*He extracts the sheet of paper from the envelope and starts reading it to himself, interspersing his reading from time to time with various grunted comments – now an 'Ah!', now an 'M'm!', and so on. First of all these are comments of satisfaction, then of doubt, then almost of commiseration; finally his voice expresses complete disillusionment.*] Why, there's nothing at all here! There's nothing that you could really call definite in what you've got here, Centuri.

CENTURI: Well, that's all they were able to find out.

LAUDISI: But it leaves everything just as doubtful as it was before! [*He looks at him. Then, on the spur of the moment, he says*] Would you like to do us all a really good turn, Centuri? Would you like to render an outstanding service to the community, a service for which the Good Lord will most certainly reward you?

CENTURI [*looking at him perplexedly*]: What sort of a service? I'm afraid I don't follow . . .

LAUDISI: Well, look . . .! Sit down in that chair! [*He points to the chair at the desk.*] Tear off the bit that's got the report on it, and that doesn't tell us a thing! Then on the bottom half write a report which gives some really precise and concrete information.

CENTURI [*amazed*]: You want me to . . .? What on earth do you mean? What sort of report?

LAUDISI: Oh, write anything you like! Write it in the names of these people you've unearthed, who used to live in the same town as him! It's for everybody's good! It'll restore peace and quiet to our town! They want the truth! It doesn't matter *what* truth it is, provided only that it's good, solid, categorical stuff! And you're the man to give it to them!

CENTURI [*forcefully, getting heated, for he feels almost insulted*]: But how can I give them the truth if I haven't got it myself? Do you want me to commit forgery? I'm amazed that you should suggest such a thing to me! I say amazed. . . . I might put it more strongly! And now, please be so kind as to tell Mr Agazzi that I am here!

LAUDISI [*throwing up his arms in a gesture of defeat*]: I'll call him immediately. [*He goes to the door left and opens it. Immediately the noisy clamour of the crowd of people in the drawing-room can be heard more distinctly. But as* LAUDISI *steps through the doorway the noise stops quite suddenly. Then the voice of* LAUDISI *is heard from the other room announcing*] Ladies and gentlemen, Mr Centuri is here, and he's brought some absolutely decisive information, from people *who really know*!

[*This news is welcomed with a burst of applause and shouts of congratulation.* CENTURI *is rather put out by this, knowing quite well that the report he has brought will by no means be adequate to satisfy all the expectation that's building up.* AGAZZI, SIRELLI, LAUDISI, AMALIA, DINA, MRS SIRELLI, MRS CINI, MRS NENNI, *and many other ladies and gentlemen rush in through the door left,* AGAZZI *at their head. They are all exultant, inflamed with excitement. There is a good deal of clapping and there are cries of 'Good man, Centuri!' 'Good work!' and so on.*]

AGAZZI [*with arms outstretched*]: My dear Centuri! I knew it! I never had the slightest doubt! I knew you'd get to the bottom of the whole affair!

ALL: Good work! Good man, Centuri! Let's have a look at the proofs! Let's see what you've got to show us! Out with it! Which of them is it? Which of them is it?

CENTURI [*dismayed, taken aback, astonished*]: Why, I'm afraid ... there isn't ... that is ... Mr Agazzi, I ...

AGAZZI: Please, everyone! Hush! *Please!*

CENTURI: It's quite true that I've done everything I possibly could. Yes! But if Mr Laudisi came in there and told you ...

AGAZZI: ... That you were bringing us some absolutely decisive information ...

SIRELLI: ... Clear-cut ... documents ...

LAUDISI [*in a loud, decisive tone, forestalling him*]: ... Not much information, it's true! But what there is, is quite decisive! From people they've been able to trace. People from Mr Ponza's home town! People who really *know*!

ALL: At last! Ah, at last! At last!

CENTURI [*shrugging his shoulders and holding out the sheet of paper to* AGAZZI]: Here you are, sir.

AGAZZI [*they all crowd round him as he unfolds the sheet of paper*]: Ah, now let's see! Let's see!

CENTURI [*resentfully, going up to* LAUDISI]: But you, Mr Laudisi . . .

LAUDISI [*immediately, in a loud voice*]: Let him get on with reading it! For heaven's sake! Let him read the thing!

AGAZZI: Please be patient for a moment, everybody! Now, just give me a little elbow room! Ah! That's better! Now I can see what I'm doing!

[*There is a moment's silence. Then, into the silence, there cuts the firm, precise voice of* LAUDISI.]

LAUDISI: I've read it already, of course!

ALL [*deserting* AGAZZI *and crowding noisily around* LAUDISI]: You have? Well? What does it say? What's the answer?

LAUDISI [*speaking very formally*]: There is not the slightest doubt, it is an irrefutable fact that, as a former neighbour of Ponza's testifies, Mrs Frola was at one time a patient in a nursing home!

ALL [*disappointment and regret in their voices*]: Oh!

MRS SIRELLI: Mrs Frola?

DINA: But does it really say Mrs Frola?

AGAZZI [*meanwhile has read through the document. He now bursts out, waving the paper as he speaks*]: No! No! It doesn't say anything of the sort here!

ALL [*leaving* LAUDISI *again, and rushing to crowd round* AGAZZI]: What? What *does* it say? What *does* it say?

LAUDISI [*loudly, to* AGAZZI]: But it does! It says 'the lady'! It specifically says 'the lady'!

AGAZZI [*louder still*]: Nothing of the sort! 'I think', he says. He's not the least bit certain. In any case, he doesn't know whether it was the mother or the daughter.

ALL [*satisfiedly*]: Ah!

LAUDISI [*persisting*]: But it must have been the mother! There can be no possible doubt about that!

SIRELLI: What? No, it was the daughter! Of course, it was the daughter!

MRS SIRELLI: Besides, she told us so herself! Mrs Frola, I mean.

AMALIA: Of course! It all fits in. It was when they took her away secretly, without telling her husband. . . .

DINA: And shut her up in a nursing home! Yes, *a nursing home!*

AGAZZI: And what's more, this fellow doesn't even come from the place! He says he used to go there often . . . that he doesn't remember very well. . . . But he *thinks* he heard something of the sort. . . .

SIRELLI: Huh! A lot of airy-fairy speculation, then!

LAUDISI: I do apologize for butting in, but if you're all so sure that Mrs Frola is right, what on earth are you chasing after now? For goodness' sake, have done, once and for all! He's the one that's mad, so let's have an end to all this nonsense!

SIRELLI: That's what I say! But the trouble is the Prefect doesn't agree with us, and he goes out of his way to demonstrate his complete faith in Mr Ponza!

CENTURI: Yes, that's so! The Prefect believes Mr Ponza. He told *me* that, too!

AGAZZI: But that's only because the Prefect hasn't yet had a word with Mrs Frola next door!

MRS SIRELLI: It's pretty obvious he hasn't! He's only talked to *him*!

SIRELLI: And what's more, there are one or two other people here who share the Prefect's viewpoint.

A GENTLEMAN: Me, for instance! Yes, me! Because I know of a similar case, of a mother who went mad over her daughter's death. And *she* believed that her son-in-law was preventing her from seeing her daughter. It's exactly the same!

SECOND GENTLEMAN: No, no, it's not the same. There's the added factor that the son-in-law has remained a widower and no longer has anyone to share his life. But in this case, Mr Ponza *has* someone . . .

LAUDISI [*struck by a sudden thought*]: Good heavens, everybody! Did you hear? Why, he's hit the nail right on the head! Good Lord! It's the old story of Columbus and the egg! [*He claps the* SECOND GENTLEMAN *on the back.*] Good man! Good for you, old man! Did you hear what he said?

ALL [*perplexed, uncomprehending*]: What? What did he say?

SECOND GENTLEMAN [*in utter bewilderment*]: What *did* I say? I don't know. . . .

LAUDISI: What? What did you say? Why, you've solved the whole affair! Now, everybody, if you'll just have a little patience . . . [*To* AGAZZI] Is the Prefect due to come here?

AGAZZI: Yes, we're expecting him any minute. But why do you ask? Explain yourself.

LAUDISI: It's useless his coming here to talk to Mrs Frola! Up to now he's believed the son-in-law. Once he's talked to Mrs Frola he too won't know which to believe! No! No! The Prefect must do something quite different from that! Something that only he *can* do!

ALL: What? What?

LAUDISI [*radiant*]: What? Didn't you hear what this gentleman said? He said that Mr Ponza *has* someone . . . his wife!

SIRELLI: You mean make his wife speak? Oh, yes! *Yes! Yes!*

DINA: But the poor woman's kept locked up, just as if she were in prison, isn't she?

SIRELLI: The Prefect must use his authority and make her speak!

AMALIA: And there's no doubt about it . . . she's the only one who can tell us where the truth lies.

MRS SIRELLI: Nonsense! She'll say just whatever her husband wants her to say!

LAUDISI: That's true! That's exactly what'll happen if she has to speak in front of him! Very true!

SIRELLI: She must speak in private with the Prefect!

AGAZZI: And by virtue of his authority the Prefect can compel Mrs Ponza to tell him in private just what the real state of affairs is! Why, of course! Of course! What do you think, Centuri?

CENTURI: I think you're quite right . . . if the Prefect's willing!

AGAZZI: It's certainly the only solution! We must warn him, and spare him the trouble for the moment of coming to see me. I wonder if you'd go and tell him, Centuri? Would you mind, my dear fellow?

CENTURI: Not at all, sir! Goodbye, sir! Goodbye! [*He bows all round and exit.*]

MRS SIRELLI [*clapping her hands*]: Oh, yes! Laudisi, you *are* a clever boy!

DINA: Yes, Uncle dear! Clever, clever Uncle Lamberto! What a wonderful idea!

ALL: Good man, Laudisi! Good man! Yes, it's the only solution! The one and only!

AGAZZI: Of course it is! And how on earth did we come to overlook it?

SIRELLI: It's not really so surprising that we shouldn't have thought of it before! No one's ever seen her! It's just as if the poor girl didn't exist.

LAUDISI [*as if struck by a new idea*]: Oh, dear! Are you really sure that she does?

AMALIA: What? Oh, good God, Lamberto!

SIRELLI [*with a forced laugh*]: Are you trying to put her very existence in doubt?

LAUDISI: Well, we must proceed with a certain degree of caution. You say yourselves that no one's ever seen her!

DINA: Oh, rubbish! Mrs Frola sees her and speaks to her every day!

MRS SIRELLI: And Mr Ponza states quite definitely that she exists too.

LAUDISI: Fair enough! But just reflect for a moment. By all the laws of logic, there can only be a phantom living in that house.

ALL: A phantom?

AGAZZI: Oh, Lamberto! Now stop this nonsense, once and for all!

LAUDISI: May I just finish what I was saying? It'll be the phantom of the second wife, if *she's* right, if Mrs Frola is

right. Or, if *he's* right, if Mr Ponza is right, the phantom o:
her daughter. What remains to be seen now, ladies and
gentlemen, is whether either his or her phantom is a rea.
person existing in her own right. And having got to tha
point, I think there's a case to be made out for having one':
doubts on that score too!

AMALIA: Rubbish! You're just trying to make us all as mad a:
yourself!

MRS NENNI: Oh, dear, you're making my flesh creep!

MRS CINI: I don't know what satisfaction you get out o:
frightening us like this!

ALL: Nonsense! Nonsense! He's joking. He's only joking!

SIRELLI: You can be pretty sure that she's a real live flesh-and-
blood woman. And we'll make her speak! We'll make her
speak, all right.

AGAZZI: Forgive me for reminding you of the fact, but it wa:
you who proposed that she should be made to have a talk
with the Prefect.

LAUDISI: Very true, it was. But I said ... if there really *is* a
woman living in that house, a woman just like any other
woman! But mark my words, everybody, there just canno·
be a woman, *a woman like any other*, living in that house
There isn't! I at least take leave here and now to doubt tha·
there is!

MRS SIRELLI: Oh, good Lord! He really does want to drive
us mad!

LAUDISI: Well, we shall see! We shall see!

ALL [*confused*]: But other people have seen her too! She look:
down into the courtyard! She writes notes to Mrs Frola
He's doing it on purpose, just to make fools of us!

CENTURI [*dashing in, red in the face, amidst all this hubbub*]: The
Prefect! The Prefect's on his way here!

AGAZZI: What? On his way here? What did you do, then?

CENTURI: I met him in the street, with Mr Ponza, coming in
this direction. . . .

SIRELLI: With Ponza, eh?

AGAZZI: Oh, my God, no! If he's with Ponza, he's probably going to see Mrs Frola next door! Centuri, I wonder if you'd do me a favour and wait by the door, and ask him from me if he'd be so kind as to step in here for a moment, as he promised me he would?

CENTURI: Why certainly, sir, I'll go right away. [*He hurries out through the door back.*]

AGAZZI: Now will you all please go back into the drawing-room, ladies and gentlemen?

MRS SIRELLI: But be sure to explain it all clearly to him! It's the only solution! It's the only solution!

AMALIA [*by the door left, to the ladies*]: Please, Mrs Cini . . . Mrs Nenni . . .

AGAZZI: Sirelli, I'd like you to stay. You too, Lamberto. [*Everyone else goes out through the door left. Then* AGAZZI *says to* LAUDISI] But let *me* do the talking, if you don't mind!

LAUDISI: Don't worry! I shan't throw any spanners in the works! In fact, if you'd prefer that I left too . . .

AGAZZI: No, it's better that you should be here. Ah, here he is. [*The* PREFECT *comes in. He is a man of about sixty, tall and stout. There is an air of easy-going good nature about him.*]

PREFECT: My dear Agazzi, how are you? Ah, you're here too, Sirelli! And how are *you*, Laudisi? [*He shakes hands all round.*]

AGAZZI [*indicating a chair*]: I hope you'll forgive my asking you to come in and see me first.

PREFECT: I'd intended to come in anyway. You remember, I promised you I would. I should certainly have dropped in to see you afterwards, in any case.

AGAZZI [*catching sight of* CENTURI, *who is still on his feet*]: Come over here, Centuri! Come on! Do sit down!

PREFECT: They tell me, Sirelli, that you've got quite excited over this business of our new secretary. From all accounts you really seem to be about the most agitated man in town.

SIRELLI: Oh no, sir! Believe me, everybody's just as worked up about it all as I am.

AGAZZI: That's true. Everybody's running round in small circles.

PREFECT: And I can't for the life of me see why!

AGAZZI: That's because it hasn't fallen to your lot to be present at one or two little incidents. Well, we've had that good fortune! His mother-in-law lives next door, you know!

SIRELLI: Forgive my asking, sir, but you haven't had a chance to talk to the old lady yet, have you?

PREFECT: As a matter of fact, I was just on my way to see her. [*Then, to* AGAZZI] You'll remember that, when you approached me on this matter, I promised you I'd come along here and listen to what she had to say . . . But then her son-in-law came and begged me, simply implored me, to come and see her in her own home. To stop all this gossip, he said. Well, do you really think he'd have done that, if he hadn't been more than certain that my visit would confirm the truth of what he said?

AGAZZI: Why, of course he would! Because in front of him, the poor woman . . .

SIRELLI [*immediately getting his oar in*]: . . . Would have said just whatever he wanted her to say! And that proves she's not the one who's mad!

AGAZZI: Why, we had a sample of how he goes on only yesterday, *here*, in front of us all!

PREFECT: Why, of course, my dear fellow. . . . That was because he deliberately makes her believe that he's the one who's mad! He warned me about that. As a matter of fact, how otherwise could he keep up the illusion for the poor unfortunate creature? Believe me, it's martyrdom, sheer martyrdom for the man!

SIRELLI: Very well! Suppose, instead, that *she's* the one who keeps up the illusion for *him*, the illusion that her daughter's dead, so that he can remain quite secure in his belief that his wife won't be taken away from him again! In that case, as you'll readily see, it is Mrs Frola who is the martyr, and not Ponza at all!

AGAZZI: Exactly! And it's this that makes us all hesitate about believing him. And I would suggest that some such doubt would appear to have crossed *your* mind. . . .

SIRELLI: Just like the rest of us!

PREFECT: Doubt? Why no! On the contrary, it seems to me that, as far as you're concerned, you have no doubts at all on the subject. And neither have I. Only I happen to believe the exact opposite of what you believe. What about you, Laudisi?

LAUDISI: I must ask you to excuse me, sir. I promised my brother-in-law I wouldn't open my mouth.

AGAZZI [*protesting angrily*]: Good God, man! What on earth will you say next? If you're asked a question, by all means reply! As a matter of fact, I did ask him not to say anything. And do you know why? Because for the last couple of days he's been taking a perverse delight in spreading doubt and uncertainty, just for the sheer pleasure of making confusion worse confounded!

LAUDISI: Don't you believe a word he says, sir! Quite the contrary. I've done everything I could to clear matters up.

SIRELLI: Yes, and do you know how? By maintaining that it's impossible to discover the truth! And his last bright idea was to start having doubts as to whether there really was a woman up at Mr Ponza's house, or merely a phantom!

PREFECT [*enjoying himself*]: Well! Well! That's an interesting suggestion!

AGAZZI: Please don't encourage him! You see how it is . . . there's no point at all in listening to *him*!

LAUDISI: And yet, sir, you've been invited to come here on my account.

PREFECT: Because you also think that it would be a good idea if I had a talk with the lady next door?

LAUDISI: Oh, no! Nothing of the kind! I think it would be an excellent idea for you to continue to believe what Mr Ponza tells you.

PREFECT: Oh, good! So you too believe that Mr Ponza . . .?

LAUDISI [*immediately*]: No! I want you to believe what Mr

Ponza tells you, just as I should like everyone to believe what Mrs Frola says. Then the whole affair would be over and done with.

AGAZZI: There, do you see! Does that seem rational to you?

PREFECT: Just a moment. [*To* LAUDISI] According to you, then, we can also believe implicitly what Mrs Frola says?

LAUDISI: Why, of course! Everything she says, and no matter what she's talking about! Just as you can believe quite implicitly everything *he* says.

PREFECT: Forgive me. . . . I'm not quite clear about this. . . . Where do we go from . . .?

SIRELLI: But suppose they contradict each other?

AGAZZI [*irritated, decisively*]: May I say a word? I'm not prejudiced either way . . . either in his favour or in hers. I have no desire to be prejudiced! *He* may be right or *she* may be right. But the matter must be settled once and for all, and there's only one way of doing it!

SIRELLI: And he's the very person that suggested it! [*Pointing to* LAUDISI.]

PREFECT: H'm! Did he now? Well then, let's hear what this suggestion is.

AGAZZI: Since all other positive evidence is lacking, the only thing left to do is this. . . . You must use your authority to get a statement from his wife.

PREFECT: From Mrs Ponza?

SIRELLI: But without her husband's being there, of course!

AGAZZI: So that she can be absolutely free to tell the truth!

SIRELLI: If she's Mrs Frola's daughter, as it seems to us we must believe she is . . .

AGAZZI: Or his second wife, who is consenting to impersonate Mrs Frola's daughter, as Mr Ponza would have us believe. . . .

PREFECT: . . . And as I personally most certainly do believe! But you're quite right. It does appear to be the only way. Believe me, that poor fellow wants nothing better than to convince everyone that he's right. He showed himself most willing to comply with anything I suggested! Yes, he'll be happier than anyone to have the whole affair cleared up! And it has the added advantage, my friends, that it will set *your* minds at rest immediately! Centuri, I wonder [CENTURI *gets up.*] if you'd be so kind as to go next door, and ask Mr Ponza from me if he'd be good enough to come in and see me for a moment or two!

CENTURI: I'll go at once! [*He bows and goes out by the door back.*]

AGAZZI: Now if only he agrees to . . .

PREFECT. You'll see, he'll agree immediately. The whole thing will be settled in next to no time. And here, in this room too, in front of you all.

AGAZZI: What? Here? In my flat?

SIRELLI: Do you really think he'll be willing to bring his wife here?

PREFECT: You leave it to me! Yes, we'll settle it all here. Otherwise, I know quite well, you'd always have a suspicion that I . . .

AGAZZI: Oh, no, no! How could you possibly think such a thing?

SIRELLI: Why, we'd never dream of doing so!

PREFECT: Now, don't try and pretend! Why . . . knowing how sure I am that he's right . . . you might think . . . especially as he's a public official . . . that in order to hush the whole thing up. . . . No! No, I want you all to hear what she has to say. [*Then, to* AGAZZI] Is your wife at home?

AGAZZI: She's in there with some of her friends. . . .

PREFECT: Good heavens! It's a regular den of conspirators you've got here!

[CENTURI *and* MR PONZA *join them.*]

CENTURI: May I come in? Mr Ponza is here.

PREFECT: Thank you, Centuri. [MR PONZA *appears in the doorway.*] Come in, come in, my dear Ponza. [MR PONZA *bows.*]

AGAZZI: Please sit down. [MR PONZA *turns, bows to him, and sits.*]

PREFECT: You know everybody ... Sirelli ... [MR PONZA *rises, bows to him.*]

AGAZZI: Yes, they've met already. ... My brother-in-law, Laudisi. [MR PONZA *bows.*]

PREFECT: I've asked you to come and see me, my dear Ponza, in order to tell you that these friends of mine and I ... [*From his very first words* MR PONZA *has evinced a lively perturbation. He is terribly agitated. The* PREFECT *breaks off.*] Was there something you wanted to say?

PONZA: Yes! That I intend, sir, to ask for an immediate transfer!

PREFECT: But why? Only a short while ago you were talking to me so reasonably about everything ...

PONZA: But I'm being persecuted here, sir! It's an unheard of outrage!

PREFECT: Come! Come! Don't let's exaggerate, my dear fellow!

AGAZZI [*to* PONZA]: An outrage ... on my part, do you mean?

PONZA: On the part of all of you, and that's why I'm leaving here! I'm leaving, sir, because I cannot tolerate this ferocious and unrelenting inquisition into my private life, an inquisition which will end in the total overthrow of an edifice of love and devotion which has cost me so much agony to create, and for which I've sacrificed so much! Oh, it will spoil everything irrevocably! I've loved and respected that poor woman more than I would have my own mother! Yesterday I found myself, here in this very room, compelled to attack her in a most cruel and violent fashion. And just now I arrived to find her in such a state of despair and agitation ...

AGAZZI [*calmly, interrupting him*]: That's very strange! Because when Mrs Frola has talked to *us* she has always been very calm. All the agitation, on the other hand ... or so we've noticed up to now ... came from you. Even now, at this very moment, that seems to be the case.

PONZA: Because you don't know what you're making me suffer!

PREFECT: Now, now! Calm yourself, my dear Ponza! What's the matter? Don't forget that I'm here! You know quite well how I've always listened sympathetically to your case and believed what you've had to say. Now, haven't I?

PONZA: Forgive me! You most certainly have, and I'm grateful to you for that, sir.

PREFECT: Well then, let's see. You say that you love and respect the unfortunate Mrs Frola as if she were your own mother? Now, you must believe me when I tell you that these friends of mine here are so anxious to find out the truth, precisely because they're just as fond of her as you are.

PONZA: But they're killing her, sir! And I've warned them about it more than once!

PREFECT: Now, have just a little patience! You'll see that they won't trouble you any more, once this matter's cleared up! It'll only take a moment or so. . . . It's all very simple really. You have it in your power to rid these people of all their doubts. You don't have to worry about me, because I haven't any. It's quite easy what you have to do, and I can personally guarantee that it'll be successful!

PONZA: But they won't believe me, whatever I do!

AGAZZI: That's not true! When you came here after your mother-in-law's first visit, and told us that she was mad, we were rather astonished, I'll admit. But we all believed you! [*Then, to the* PREFECT] But immediately afterwards, you know, Mrs Frola returned. . . .

PREFECT: Yes, yes, I know! You told me. [*Turning to* PONZA, *he goes on.*] Mrs Frola returned and put forward the same reasons for your behaviour as you yourself are trying to get her to accept. You mustn't be too impatient, you know, if people who listen to poor Mrs Frola, after they've just‧been listening to you, find certain very troublesome doubts gnawing away in their minds. Confronted with what your mother-in-law says, these gentlemen just cannot believe that they may any longer with complete certainty trust what you say to be the truth, my dear Ponza. Well then, it's perfectly clear what we must do! You and your mother-in-law ... Well, suppose you, as it were, step to one side for a moment! *You're* quite certain that you're telling the truth. And so am I! That being so, you can have no objection to its being confirmed here and now by the only person, apart from you two, who *can* confirm it.

PONZA: And who is that?

PREFECT: Why, your wife!

PONZA: My wife? [*Forcefully and angrily*] Oh no, sir! Never!

PREFECT: And why not, if I may ask?

PONZA: Bring my wife here, merely in order to satisfy the curiosity of these people who have no desire whatsoever to believe what I say?

PREFECT [*promptly*]: And in order to satisfy *my* curiosity too, my dear Ponza! What's the difficulty?

PONZA: But, sir! ... No! Not my wife! No, please let's leave my wife out of it! Why can't you believe what *I* tell you?

PREFECT: Now look here. ... You're causing me seriously to wonder ... I too am beginning to think that you're doing everything in your power to *prevent* people from believing you!

AGAZZI: It's how he's been behaving all along! He tried in every way possible to prevent his mother-in-law from coming to talk to us! He even went so far as to insult both my wife and daughter!

PONZA [*bursting out in sheer exasperation*]: But what in the name of God do you people want of me? Isn't it enough for you that you're tormenting the life out of that unfortunate woman? Must you have my wife, too? I cannot tolerate this outrage, sir! My wife never leaves the house, and I am not going to bring her here to satisfy anybody's curiosity! It's enough that *you* believe me, sir! And now I shall go at once and write out my formal request for a transfer from this place! [*He rises.*]

PREFECT [*striking the desk with his fist*]: Wait! First of all, Mr
Ponza, I cannot tolerate your assuming such a tone before
Mr Agazzi and myself! After all, I have spoken to you with
great courtesy and great respect for your feelings. Secondly,
I repeat that this stubborn refusal of yours to give me the
proof which I, and no one else, ask for . . . and ask for in
your own interest. . . . And what I'm asking you to do cannot possibly cause you any harm, as far as I can see. . . . Well,
it makes *me* wonder rather. It would be quite proper for my
colleague and myself to ask your wife to come and see us . . .
Or, if you prefer it, *we* can call on *her*.

PONZA: Then you insist?

PREFECT: I repeat that I ask it of you for your own good. I
can also demand it as your official superior.

PONZA: Very well! Very well! If that's how it is, I'll bring my
wife here and settle the whole matter once and for all. But
who's going to guarantee that that poor woman won't see
her?

PREFECT: Oh, yes! Of course! She lives next door. . . .

AGAZZI [*immediately*]: We should be quite willing to call on
Mrs Ponza.

PONZA: No! I say *no* for your sakes! I don't want you to spring
any more surprises on me! There might be the most terrible
consequences.

AGAZZI: You can rest quite easy on that score, as far as we're
concerned!

PREFECT: Well, if you think you'd rather not, you can
bring your wife along to the Prefecture in your own good
time.

PONZA: No! No! I'll bring her here as soon as I possibly can!
Then I'll go in there and keep an eye on Mrs Frola myself.
I shall go at once, sir, and then the whole thing will be
settled! Settled for good and all! [*Very angry, he goes out by
the door back.*]

PREFECT: I must confess that I didn't expect this opposition on
his part.

AGAZZI: And you'll see, he'll force his wife to say just whatever he wants her to say!

PREFECT: Oh, no! Don't you worry about that. I'll question Mrs Ponza myself!

SIRELLI: You know, the way he's always so terribly worked-up . . . !

PREFECT: No! It's the first time, the very first time I've seen him like that! Perhaps it was the thought of bringing his wife here . . .

SIRELLI: . . . Of letting her out of her prison!

PREFECT: Oh, as for that . . . his keeping her locked up . . . Well, you can explain that easily enough, without having to suppose that he's mad.

SIRELLI: Forgive me for reminding you, sir, but you haven't yet heard what the lady's got to say, poor creature!

AGAZZI: No! He says he keeps her locked up for fear of what Mrs Frola might do.

PREFECT: Well, even supposing that isn't the explanation . . . Why, he might just be jealous! That would be quite an adequate explanation.

SIRELLI: So jealous as not even to keep a servant? So jealous as to force his wife to do all her own housework?

AGAZZI: And to do all the shopping himself every morning?

CENTURI: Yes, sir, it's true. I've seen him myself. He gets an errand-boy to help him to carry it all back.

SIRELLI: And he always makes him wait outside the door!

PREFECT: Dear me, gentlemen! He told me about that, and said how much he regretted having to do it.

LAUDISI: And as a source of information he's unimpeachable, of course!

PREFECT: He does it to save money, Laudisi! He has two homes to keep up. . . .

SIRELLI: But that wasn't why we raised the matter. Do you really think, sir, that a man's second wife would be so self-sacrificing as to . . .

AGAZZI [*pressing the point*]: . . . To do so many of the most menial jobs about the house . . .

SIRELLI [*following him up*]: . . . For the sake of someone who was her husband's mother-in-law, and who, as far as she is concerned, is a perfect stranger?

AGAZZI: Yes, doesn't it seem rather improbable to you? Doesn't it?

PREFECT: M'm! It does *rather* . . .

LAUDISI [*interrupting him*]: If his second wife is, in fact, a woman just like any other woman.

PREFECT [*immediately*]: Well, let's agree on your point. Yes, it *is* improbable. But this too, you know, can quite well be explained . . . if not by generosity on her part . . . by jealousy again. And that he's jealous . . . whether he's mad or not . . . seems to me beyond question. [*At this juncture a confused din of voices makes itself heard from the drawing-room.*]

AGAZZI: Oh, what's happening in there, I wonder?

AMALIA [*entering hurriedly through the door left, in a state of utter consternation*]: Mrs Frola! Mrs Frola's here!

AGAZZI: No! Good God, who asked her to come?

AMALIA: Nobody asked her! She came of her own accord!

PREFECT: Well, she can't stay here now! No! Not now! Please ask her to go home, Mrs Agazzi.

AGAZZI: She must go home at once! Don't let her come in here! You must prevent her somehow! It's absolutely imperative! If *he* were to find her here it really would look like a trap to him!

[MRS FROLA *comes in, handkerchief in hand, and around her crowd the people from the other room – they are all extremely disturbed. She is trembling and crying. Her manner as she speaks is one of entreaty.*]

MRS FROLA: Oh, please! Please, everyone! You tell them, Mr Agazzi, *please*, not to send me away!

AGAZZI [*stepping forward; he is very angry*]: I must ask you, Mrs Frola, to go home at once! You can't stay here! Not just now!

MRS FROLA [*dismayed*]: Why not? Why not? [*To* AMALIA] I appeal to you, Mrs Agazzi ... you're so very kind. ...

AMALIA: But ... please, Mrs Frola ... don't you see ... the Prefect's here ...

MRS FROLA: Oh, *you* are here! Please help me! I was going to come and see you.

PREFECT: You must please excuse me, Mrs Frola. I can't see you just at present You must go now! Please! You must leave here immediately!

MRS FROLA: Very well, I shall go! And I'm going to leave this town! This very day! [*To the* PREFECT] I'm going right away! I'm going away, and I shall never come back!

AGAZZI: But you mustn't do that, Mrs Frola! If you'll just be so good as to return to your flat for a moment or so! Now please do as I ask, as a favour to me! Afterwards you can have a word or two with the Prefect!

MRS FROLA: But why must I go? What's the matter? What's happened?

AGAZZI [*losing patience*]: Your son-in-law is on his way back here! There! Now do you understand?

MRS FROLA: Oh! He's coming back *here*? In that case ... why, yes! Yes! I will go home. I'll go home at once. I should only like to say this one thing to you. Please stop all this! You think you're helping me, but you're really hurting me very much! I shall have to go away altogether if you go on like this! I shall have to go away this very day, so that he may be left in peace! But what do you want with him now? What do you want? Why have you sent for him this time? What do you want him to do now? [*To the* PREFECT] Oh, please. ..!

PREFECT: Now, don't worry, Mrs Frola! It's nothing special! So please keep calm, and just leave us for the present. Please!

AMALIA: Yes, Mrs Frola! Please be a dear, and go!

MRS FROLA: Oh dear, Mrs Agazzi! You'd all rob me of the one remaining comfort I have! It's my only happiness, being

able to see my daughter, even if it's only from a distance!
[*She begins to cry.*]

PREFECT: But who said anything of the sort? You've no need
to go away altogether! We're only asking you to leave us
for a few minutes. So please don't worry!

MRS FROLA: Oh, but I'm thinking about *him*! About *him*!
[*This to the* PREFECT] It was for his sake that I came to ask
you for your help, everybody! Not on my own account!

PREFECT: Yes! Yes! Now that's all right! And you needn't
worry on his account either! I give you my personal
promise! You'll see, we'll straighten everything out in no
time!

MRS FROLA: How? I can see that everybody's all ready to
pounce on him!

PREFECT: No, Mrs Frola, that's not true! I'm here to stand up
for him! So you need have no worry!

MRS FROLA: Oh, thank you! You mean you understand . . .?

PREFECT: Yes, Mrs Frola, I understand.

MRS FROLA: As I've told these ladies and gentlemen over
and over again, it was a misfortune. But he's got over it now,
and he mustn't be made to go back to that nightmare again.

PREFECT: Yes, you're quite right, Mrs Frola. As I told you, I
understand perfectly!

MRS FROLA: We're quite happy to live as we do. My daughter
is very happy. So . . . Please do see to it that . . . Please see
that everything comes out all right! Because if it doesn't,
then there's nothing left for me but to go away altogether
and never to see her again, not even from a distance, as I do
now. Please leave him in peace, everybody! *Please!*
[*At this juncture there is a movement in the crowd, and everybody starts signalling. Some of them look in the direction of the
door. Subdued voices make themselves heard.*]

VOICES: Oh, Lord! . . . Here she is! Here she is!

MRS FROLA [*noticing their dismay and bewilderment, is perplexed.
She trembles and moans*]: What's the matter? What's the
matter?

[*The company falls back on either hand to allow* MRS PONZA *to pass. She comes forward, holding herself very erect. She is in deep mourning, her face hidden by a thick, impenetrable black veil.*]

MRS FROLA [*uttering a piercing cry, full of frantic joy*]: Ah, Lina! Lina! Lina! [*And she throws herself at the veiled woman, twining her arms around her with all the warmth of a mother who has not held her daughter in her arms for a very long time. But at the same time* MR PONZA'S *cries are to be heard, and he immediately rushes on to the stage.*]

PONZA: Giulia! Giulia! Giulia! [MRS PONZA, *on hearing his cries, draws herself up stiffly within the encircling arms of* MRS FROLA. *As he rushes on,* MR PONZA *immediately catches sight of his mother-in-law thus desperately entwined about his wife, and shrieks out furiously.*] Ah! I said this was what would happen! I trusted you, and you've taken advantage of me in this despicable manner!

MRS PONZA [*turning her veiled head towards him. . . . There is an almost austere solemnity about the gesture*]: Never mind! Don't be afraid! Don't be afraid! Just go away, *both of you!*

PONZA [*quietly and affectionately to Mrs Frola*]: Let us go. Yes, let us go. . . .

MRS FROLA [*has released her hold on* MRS PONZA *and is trembling all over. She echoes his words back to him, her voice humble, full of solicitude for him*]: Yes, yes, let us go, my dear . . . let us go. . . . [*And they go out, with their arms round one another, giving each other reassuring caresses from time to time. Their weeping is a sad duet, and, as they go, they murmur affectionately to one another. There is silence. Then, having watched* MRS FROLA *and* MR PONZA *until they have disappeared completely, the rest of the company turns and looks at the veiled woman. Everyone is deeply moved and utterly dismayed by what has happened.*]

MRS PONZA [*looks at them intently through her veil for a moment, and then says, with sombre solemnity*]: What else can you possibly want of me after this, ladies and gentlemen? Here, before your very eyes, you have a terrible misfortune. One that must remain hidden from the world, because only if it does remain hidden can the remedy that compassion has provided be at all effective.

PREFECT [*moved*]: But we have every desire to respect that compassion, Mrs Ponza. We should like you to tell us, however . . .

MRS PONZA [*speaking slowly and distinctly*]: What? The truth? It is simply this . . . that I am . . . yes, I am Mrs Frola's daughter . . .

ALL [*with a sigh of satisfaction*]: Ah!

MRS PONZA [*still speaking slowly and distinctly, carrying straight on*]: . . . And Mr Ponza's second wife . . .

ALL [*astounded and disappointed, in subdued tones*]: Oh? But how on . . . ?

MRS PONZA [*slowly and distinctly, carrying straight on*]: Yes! And for myself, I am nobody! Nobody at all!

PREFECT: Oh, no, Mrs Ponza, that just cannot be! You must be either one or the other!

MRS PONZA: No! As far as I am concerned, I am just whoever you think I am. [*She looks intently at them all for a moment through her veil, and then goes out. There is silence.*]

LAUDISI: And that, ladies and gentlemen, is the voice of truth! [*He throws a derisive, challenging glance round the company.*] Are you happy now? [*He bursts out laughing.*] Ha! Ha! Ha! Ha!

# ALL FOR THE BEST

*Tutto per bene*

TRANSLATED BY HENRY REED

This translation was first presented on the Third Programme of the B.B.C. on 24 November 1953, with the following cast:

| | |
|---|---|
| MARTINO LORI | *George Hayes* |
| SALVO MANFRONI | *Norman Shelley* |
| PALMA LORI | *Violet Loxley* |
| FLAVIO GUALDI | *Michael Bates* |
| LA BARBETTI | *Vivienne Chatterton* |
| CARLO CLARINO (CARLETTO) | *Peter Claughton* |
| SIGNORINA CEI (GINA) | *Janet Burnell* |
| VENIERO BONGIANI | *Eric Anderson* |
| A PORTER | *Henry Mara* |
| A FOOTMAN | *Brian Hayes.* |
| A MANSERVANT | *John Turnbull* |

Produced by Wilfred Grantham

# CHARACTERS

MARTINO LORI, a secretary of state

SALVO MANFRONI, a senator

PALMA LORI

THE MARCHESE FLAVIO GUALDI

LA BARBETTI, a widow, formerly SIGNORA CLARINO,
    and before that, SIGNORA AGLIANI

CARLO CLARINO, her son

THE CONTE VENIERO BONGIANI

A PORTER

GIOVANNI, a footman in Flavio's house

An old MANSERVANT of Manfroni's

SCENE: Rome
TIME: The present (1920)

# ACT ONE

*A room in* MARTINO LORI'S *flat, furnished in a refined but not expensive way. A door on the left leads to the drawing-room; another, on the right, to* PALMA'S *bedroom. In the back wall, towards the right, is another door, giving onto a corridor. It is* PALMA'S *wedding-day; there are large bouquets and baskets of flowers about the room.*

[*When the curtain rises, the room is empty. After a few moments,* LA BARBETTI *enters from the left, followed by her son* CARLO CLARINO.

[LA BARBETTI *is sixty-three. She is wearing a hat. Her hair is dyed and she is over-dressed, in the manner of a wealthy woman from the provinces. She is domineering and vulgar but, underneath it all, by no means unpleasant. Her son,* CARLETTO, *about thirty, is dressed in the latest fashion, and tries to give the impression of being a weary man of the world, bored by everything. Just now he is being dragged by his rich, nagging mother into a situation that embarrasses him. They come in, as though looking for someone; the mother fairly resolute, the son apprehensive.*]

LA BARBETTI [*in the doorway*]: Can I come in? Isn't there anybody here? Come in, Charlie, come in.

CARLETTO [*in the voice of someone expecting trouble*]: Mother, do be careful!

LA BARBETTI: Will you stop nagging! Leaving us stuck in that room like that . . . !

CARLETTO: But we can't wander about other people's houses like this . . .

LA BARBETTI: I want to know what's going on here. . . . There must be someone . . . [*She looks round.*] Isn't there a bell in the room?

CARLETTO [*with a sigh of resignation*]: Well, if we must make fools of ourselves, we must, I suppose!

LA BARBETTI [*tapping on the door to the right*]: Hello? [*She waits a moment, and taps again.*] Anyone there? [*After a further pause, she pushes the door open and looks in.*] Nobody in there, either. [*Angrily turning on her son*] What do you mean, make fools of ourselves, you great lump! I've brought the girl a nice wedding-present, haven't I? A nice brooch: it cost three thousand seven hundred lire. [*With another glance round the room*] And where's that stupid porter got to, I wonder? [*She crosses to the door at the back, opens it, and calls.*] Porter! Porter!

CARLETTO [*after a pause*]: He'll have gone to the church with the rest of the servants to see the wedding.

LA BARBETTI: What, and leave the house with nobody in it?

CARLETTO [*pleading*]: It may be a stroke of luck, mother. . . . Let's get out of the place, while there's still time!

LA BARBETTI: I've told you, you'll stay here! I'm going to show you what it's like to be among decent respectable people for a change.

CARLETTO: That'll be fun, won't it?

LA BARBETTI: You're not getting any more of my money to pour down the drain, I can tell you!

CARLETTO: Mother, for God's sake . . .!

LA BARBETTI: You'll see, from now on!

CARLETTO: I suppose you think they're going to be pleased to see us?

LA BARBETTI: I don't care whether they're pleased or not. I've not come all the way from Perugia for a joke. I'm willing to start you up properly here, and if your brother-in-law's willing to help you, you can –

CARLETTO [*with a start*]: Mother! Will you please stop calling him my brother-in-law? You make my flesh creep.

LA BARBETTI: Why, of course he's your brother-in-law! Such nonsense!

CARLETTO: Mother: I warn you: if you say that word brother-in-law again, I'm leaving.

LA BARBETTI: What do you want me to say?

CARLETTO: I just don't want to be kicked down the stairs, that's all, if you don't mind.

LA BARBETTI [*with determination, facing him*]: Charlie: are you my son, or aren't you?

CARLETTO: Oh, shut up, mother!

LA BARBETTI: You're not my son?

CARLETTO: I said, shut up, mother! You know you've no business here.

LA BARBETTI [*with sudden ferocity*]: What are you talking about, you great fool, you!

CARLETTO: Please! Do you have to start quarrelling *in here*?

LA BARBETTI: No! I just expect you to treat your mother with respect, that's all!

CARLETTO: But I *am* treating you with respect, mother. It's only because I want everyone else to treat you with respect as well, that I keep on telling you: let's get out of here!

LA BARBETTI: No! I won't! You poor, mean-spirited little worm, you! You silly fool, I never heard such rubbish! Even if me and your father – oh, I'm not afraid to admit it – even if there was a little irregularity just at the start, we got married eventually, didn't we?

CARLETTO: Yes, mother: exactly: *eventually.*

LA BARBETTI: Well, what did it matter? You were just as legitimate as poor dear Silvia, in the end. I know she was only your half-sister, I know she was. That doesn't alter the fact that this Signor Martino Lori here married my poor Silvia. He's my son-in-law, isn't he? Well, then: he'll have to accept you as his brother-in-law. It stands to sense.

CARLETTO: Yes. Splendid. If you can wipe out what happened 'just at the start'.

LA BARBETTI: What do you mean: 'wipe out'?

CARLETTO: What I say! Just you try and wipe out that 'little irregularity', that's all. Just you try.

LA BARBETTI: Rubbish! Who do you think's going to bother about that after all this time? My first husband died twenty years ago.

CARLETTO: Yes, mother. And I wasn't his son, and I'm thirty-two! I should call that a rather *serious* irregularity, from your first husband's point of view. *So* serious, that I'm damned sure if Silvia were still alive, you'd never have dared to show your face here.

LA BARBETTI: Well, is she dead, or isn't she? Hasn't she been dead sixteen years, or has she? Sixteen years: you don't call that last week, I suppose? And now my daughter's daughter's getting married, and I've come to bring her a lovely present for her wedding-day.

CARLETTO: All right. Do, by all means. As her grandmother. *Say* you're her grandmother. You *are* her grandmother, no one's going to deny that. Silvia was your daughter; this is Silvia's daughter. That's all there is to say, and it's not very much: you're her grandmother. But don't get the *men* mixed up in it, mother. God knows, you can never be sure just what relation men are to each other, even father and son, let alone brothers-in-law!

[*At the door at the back, drawn by the sound of their voices,* GINA CEI *appears. Fair-haired, slim, tall, about thirty, she is dressed for the occasion with sober elegance. She is a woman who keeps her own private feelings out of sight, under an appearance of great composure; she is guarded in speech, but highly observant, and at all times shows a natural delicacy and breeding.*]

GINA: Who is it, please?

LA BARBETTI [*turning at the sound of her voice*]: Ah, here we are . . . We did ask if –

GINA: But . . . forgive me . . . May I ask who you are?

LA BARBETTI: I'm the bride's grandmother. And this is her uncle. [*She indicates her son, who makes a gesture of annoyance.*]

GINA [*observing all this in some perplexity*]: Ah, her grandmother?

LA BARBETTI [*deliberately*]: And her uncle. We've come from Perugia.

GINA [*gently*]: But I don't think they were expecting you, so far as I know . . .?

LA BARBETTI: Oh, no: we've come as a surprise.

GINA [*to both of them*]: Please . . . won't you sit down?

LA BARBETTI [*sitting*]: Thank you. I suppose – forgive me for asking – you'd be . . .?

GINA: Oh, I'm . . . what shall I say? I stay here to keep Palma company.

LA BARBETTI: Ah, yes: a lady's companion.

GINA: If you like to call it that . . . But I'm really just a friend of Palma's, that's all.

LA BARBETTI: Ah, yes, of course: Palma. That's her name. [*She repeats the name, as though it were the first time she had heard it*] Palma.

GINA: I'm sorry she didn't let me know that you –

LA BARBETTI: Oh, not at all. Don't you worry. We *want* it to be a surprise.

GINA: Yes, but just at this moment . . .

CARLETTO [*who has been greatly agitated by his mother's previous remark*]: Exactly! That's just what I told my mother.

LA BARBETTI: Just you shut up! [*To* GINA] There's been a bit of a mistake, I'm afraid. You see, we were told the wedding was going to be tomorrow. We wanted to get here the day before.

GINA: Well, as a matter of fact, it was yesterday.

LA BARBETTI: Yesterday? How?

GINA: Yes, the civil marriage took place yesterday. It's the religious ceremony today.

LA BARBETTI: Ah! Civil yesterday, and religious today . . . Fancy!

GINA: I'm expecting them back any minute now.

LA BARBETTI: A big party of them, I suppose? A large wedding-breakfast, and all that?

GINA: Oh, no, nothing like that . . . nothing.

LA BARBETTI: Nothing? Why, that room in there [*pointing off left*] is crammed with flowers. [*She looks round the room.*] And what about all these?

GINA: Yes, but they're not having a party. Yesterday, of

course, we had a reception and a dinner-party: but only jus
the family . . .

CARLETTO: Yes, of course, like everybody does nowadays. Ir
going-away clothes.

GINA: Well, not exactly. There *are* only a few family friend:
coming today; but of course the bride's all in white for the
ceremony, with her veil and orange-blossom. Well, you'l
see her: she looks lovely!

LA BARBETTI: I'm sure she does! A darling! But then, I mean
goodness me – marrying a title and all . . .!

GINA: Yes, but you see, the Marchese's mother –

LA BARBETTI: Didn't want the marriage?

GINA: Oh, no, don't think that! On the contrary! You shoulc
see the presents she's sent! But . . . well . . . she's alway;
rather poorly . . .

CARLETTO [*a man of the world*]: Oh, quite, quite. Quite.

GINA: She will, of course, give a big party for the bride a
her house when they come back from the honeymoon.

LA BARBETTI: So today, you're only having –

GINA: Oh, it's really all over. They'll call in here for a few
moments, I expect, so that Palma can change for the journey
There'll only be the witnesses and a few friends of the
Marchese and the Senator.

LA BARBETTI: My son-in-law? [*To* CARLETTO] Did you hear
that? They've made him a Senator as well!

GINA [*with an imperceptible smile*]: Oh, no: I meant Senato:
Manfroni.

LA BARBETTI: Oh, not my son-in-law? And who is this Manfroni, then?

CARLETTO: Why, Salvo Manfroni, of course, mother! He
was our Member of Parliament, and afterwards he was made
a Minister.

LA BARBETTI: Oh, him! And what's he got to do with it?

CARLETTO: Do with it? Why, it was Manfroni who got you
son-in-law into the Council of State!

LA BARBETTI: Oh, did he?

CARLETTO: When Manfroni was made Minister, he took Martino Lori with him as his chief secretary; don't you remember, I told you in Perugia?

GINA: It's due to Senator Manfroni's kindness that I'm here, too.

CARLETTO: He was one of your first husband's pupils, mother.

LA BARBETTI: Oh, yes, yes, I remember now. . . . A pupil of my first husband.

GINA: Palma's grandfather?

LA BARBETTI: Yes. A professor, you know! My first husband.

GINA [*with barely concealed surprise*]: Ah! Then you must have been the wife of Bernardo Agliani?

LA BARBETTI: Yes, yes, I was!

GINA: What a very great scientist he was!

LA BARBETTI: Has my little granddaughter told you about him?

GINA: Oh, he's in all the school-books, too, of course.

LA BARBETTI: He died from an accident, did you know that? Yes, in his . . . [*To* CARLETTO] what do you call it?

CARLETTO: Laboratory, mother!

LA BARBETTI: His laboratory, yes.

CARLETTO: The physics laboratory.

LA BARBETTI: The physics laboratory, that was it. He blew up! It was in all the papers.

GINA: Oh yes, I know . . .

LA BARBETTI: A shocking business! And oh, I *was* so sorry when it happened! I was so sorry I hadn't had the patience to stay with him till the end. Such a clever man! Always reading and writing! Always publishing! Book after book!

CARLETTO: But, mother, this lady knows all about that. And Salvo Manfroni knows too; I think it was he who brought out Agliani's last, posthumous –

LA BARBETTI: Yes, yes, one of those . . . special books . . . what are they called?

CARLETTO: Posthumous, mother. Posthumous.

LA BARBETTI: No, I mean a book this Manfroni man got hold of, because my husband had left it all in – oh, what is it they call the thing?

CARLETTO: In manuscript.

LA BARBETTI: In what?

CARLETTO: Manuscript, mother.

LA BARBETTI: Yes, that's right. And Manfroni went off with it and made a big name for himself with it: a Senator!

CARLETTO: You mustn't say he went off with it, like that, mother! It sounds as if he'd stolen it. They were just notes, memoranda for a new work.

GINA: Salvo Manfroni took it in hand, and developed and completed it.

LA BARBETTI: Yes, and got a good deal of fuss made over him for it!

GINA: But quite deservedly, I think. He didn't detract in any way from the reputation of his teacher.

LA BARBETTI: Ah, they don't think that up in Perugia! They don't believe that up there! And I wouldn't mind telling him so, either.

CARLETTO: Mother, no, for goodness' sake . . .

GINA: In any case, it all seems to have been very lucky for Palma, from what I've heard her say.

LA BARBETTI: What do you mean, lucky?

GINA: Why, that Senator Manfroni should have found those unpublished papers by his old teacher, in Mr Lori's house.

LA BARBETTI: It was lucky for *him*, all right!

GINA: Yes, possibly. But for Palma too. She was only a little girl at the time. Senator Manfroni was compelled to work here in this house. Apparently Palma's mother wouldn't let her father's papers out of her possession and Senator Manfroni was here so much he grew very fond of the little girl. And when Palma's mother died, he took a great interest in Palma, poor little mite. He's never married, you know, and he's very rich. He brought Palma up almost as if she were his own child: it was he who arranged this wealthy marriage for her.

LA BARBETTI: Yes, I dare say! He's paying her for what he took from her grandpa! He did a lot for my son-in-law as well.

GINA: Oh yes, we've all seen how good he's been to Signor Lori: like a brother.

LA BARBETTI: Tell me, please, if you don't mind: what sort of a man *is* my son-in-law?

GINA: Well, you know him, of course . . .

LA BARBETTI: No, I don't: that's just it. You see: my daughter died a good many years ago. She went in for the teaching. She came down here to Rome after her father died, and met this man Lori, who was working in the Ministry of Education, and got married to him without ever saying a word to me about it at all. Not a word. You see, poor Silvia, she was *also* a bit of a victim, you know, of all this science her poor dear father went in for. She absolutely adored him; you should have seen her create, if anyone said a word against him! Well, of course, you know how it is with science and that: a daughter can *sympathize* with it in a way, I mean . . . but a *wife* can get very tired of it. Very tired. And I don't mind telling you, *I* got tired of it. And so when I . . . separated from her father, I never saw my daughter again. And she'd only been married just seven years, when she died. So you see, I've never actually met my son-in-law.

GINA: Never met him!

LA BARBETTI: Never!

GINA: Nor Palma either, then?

LA BARBETTI: No, never!

GINA: Oh, but in that case –

CARLETTO: We haven't exactly chosen the best moment, have we? It's just what I've been telling my mother.

GINA: It's just that – well, you'll understand . . .

CARLETTO: What with all the confusion, you mean . . .?

GINA: Yes, and –

CARLETTO: It'll be very embarrassing having to explain so much.

LA BARBETTI: Rubbish! Who'll be embarrassed? And what's there to explain? A grandmother's come to bring her little grandchild a wedding-present. I know it would have been nicer if we'd got here the day before. But you don't think she'll bother about things that were over and done with all those years ago, do you? And what's my son-in-law got to worry about? He's been a widower for sixteen years. You don't suppose he'll still be worrying about a father-in-law he never even met? I know Silvia was vexed about what I did . . . but he'll surely have stopped worrying about his wife by now!

GINA: I'm afraid you're quite mistaken there.

LA BARBETTI: You mean he does still worry about her?

GINA: Indeed he does! I don't know . . . but to think so much of a woman makes one almost feel contemptuous – I don't mean towards him, of course. But towards us, because we have such poor opinions of ourselves. To see a man so distracted, and so lost, after so many years, because his wife has died . . .

LA BARBETTI: Really? How do you mean, lost?

GINA: There's an expression in his eyes sometimes. I don't know how to describe it. You should see how he looks at people! And listens! As if everything, every noise he hears, even the voices of the people he knows best in the world, like his daughter and his friends: oh, as if there were something about the way they look and speak that he just can't recognize any more. As if all round him, life had . . . somehow disintergated. Perhaps it's because of the habit he always had of . . .

LA BARBETTI [with an accompanying gesture]: The drink?

GINA [with a shocked smile]: Oh, no, no. What an idea! [Then sadly] No, I mean his habit of going back there every day.

LA BARBETTI: To the cemetery, you mean?

GINA: Every day, whatever the weather's like. And he comes

back home, staring before him as though he saw everything from miles away.

CARLETTO [*rising, after a pause*]: I really think, mother, we'd do much better to postpone our visit to some other day.

LA BARBETTI: You sit down. I want to hear all about this . . . [*Firmly, to* GINA, *in the manner of one who does not intend to be taken in.*] Tell me, please: how old is he?

GINA: Oh, forty-five or forty-six.

LA BARBETTI: Take away sixteen, what's that leave?

GINA: What do you mean?

LA BARBETTI: Forty-six take away sixteen.

GINA: Thirty.

LA BARBETTI: Yes, thirty. And are you trying to make me believe that Signor Lori, who was only thirty when his wife died, still goes and visits his wife's grave every day? My dear young woman! We're all flesh and blood, aren't we?

GINA: What do you imagine he does, then?

LA BARBETTI: Well, it doesn't take much imagining, does it?

GINA: I'm sure you won't think that when you've seen him. Besides, everyone knows –

[*A uniformed* PORTER *comes in through the door at the back and announces hastily*]:

PORTER: Signorina, they're back! They're just coming up! [*He hurries out again.*]

GINA [*rising*]: Here they are, then. Will you excuse me a moment, please? Or would you like to go into the drawing-room, perhaps?

CARLETTO [*rising also*]: No, no, please . . .!

LA BARBETTI: We'll wait in here. . . . That'll be best.

GINA: As you wish.

CARLETTO: Just say it's the young lady's grandmother, please! just the grandmother, that's all. . . .

[GINA *goes out to the left.*]

LA BARBETTI: You're making a fine bright ass of yourself, I must say. A good job *I'm* here.

CARLETTO: But look: what if they're rude to you? What do *I* do?

LA BARBETTI: You won't do anything!

CARLETTO: Am I to let them insult my own mother?

LA BARBETTI: Who d'you think's going to insult me? Why should anyone insult me?

[MARTINO LORI, *agitated and angry, comes in from the left. His hair is almost completely white, though he is not yet fifty. Very careful in dress. Lively, mobile features, especially the eyes; visibly at the mercy of the continuous warnings of a restless, acute sensitiveness, which can however, all at once, vanish, as though he had suddenly become absent-minded, and his spirit were left defenceless, and revealed as melancholy, submissive, and, above all, credulous.*]

LORI: No, no, really, this is inexcusable! I don't know how you have the impudence to appear in my house!

LA BARBETTI: Am I speaking to my son-in-law?

LORI: Certainly not! What do you mean, son-in-law? I have never been your son-in-law!

LA BARBETTI: But you are Signor Lori, I think?

LORI: Yes, of course I am.

LA BARBETTI: And you married my daughter.

LORI: That is precisely what I meant. Can you possibly fail to realize what an insult to your daughter's memory it is – and an insult I refuse to tolerate – for you to enter my house?

LA BARBETTI: Good gracious me, I thought that was all over years ago!

LORI: No, certainly it was not! In any case, by the time I married your daughter, you had long ceased to be Bernardo Agliani's wife.

LA BARBETTI: I was still Silvia's mother, wasn't I?

LORI: Nonsense! What sort of a mother? You know perfectly well that Silvia refused to think of you as her mother after what happened; and with very good reason.

CARLETTO: Oh, I say, look here, I mean; look here, I mean; look here!

LORI: Who are you?

LA BARBETTI [*coming quickly to her son's defence*]: This is my son . . . [*To* CARLETTO] You be quiet, and let me speak!

CARLETTO: No, stop! Let me say this, sir, that as far as I was concerned I never wanted to come here, and I never would have come –

LORI: And you'd have been quite right!

CARLETTO: I know I would. I said so to mother myself. But that's no reason why you –

LA BARBETTI [*quickly*]: Should speak to me in that tone of voice –

CARLETTO: Without even asking what she's come for –

LA BARBETTI: Yes! What I've come to do for my grand-daughter!

LORI [*struggling against his bewilderment*]: I don't imagine my daughter's feelings about her mother's memory and the respect due to it are any different from my own.

[*At this point* PALMA *is heard in the room on the left.*]

PALMA'S VOICE: Yes, yes, I'll be ready in two minutes!

[PALMA, *in her wedding-dress, comes in from the left. She hurries across to the door on the right, which leads to her bed-room. She is eighteen, and very beautiful. She treats her father with barely-concealed coldness. The moment she appears,* LA BARBETTI *advances upon her with open arms.*]

LA BARBETTI: Here she is, here she is! Oh, my little girl, how lovely you look!

PALMA [*stops in confusion*]: I'm sorry . . . Who are you?

LA BARBETTI: It's grannie! It's grannie, my dear little girl!

PALMA [*at first, dazed more than surprised*]: Grannie! How? [*Then, turning to her father with an air of comic incredulity*] Have I a grannie, too?

LORI: No, no, Palma!

LA BARBETTI [*to* LORI]: What do you mean: no? [*To* PALMA, *emphatically*] I'm mummy's mother: there!

CARLETTO [*to* LORI]: You can't deny that, sir!

LORI: Please don't force me to say things my daughter knows well enough already.

PALMA [*remembering her grandmother's unworthiness but apparently attaching no importance to it and indeed regarding her intrusion rather as a joke*]: Ah, so it's *you*, then! Of course!

LORI: You realize, Palma, that if your mother were here –

PALMA [*annoyed at the unexpectedly embarrassing position into which her father's remark puts her, shrugs her shoulders*]: Yes, but . . . I don't know! What can you do about it now?

LA BARBETTI: He says I did wrong to come!

LORI: Very wrong!

PALMA [*protesting with annoyance*]: Oh, no! Surely there's no need to bother any more *now* –

LORI [*wounded*]: No? Why not?

LA BARBETTI [*sharply and triumphantly*]: There you are! Exactly! It's true, isn't it, my pettikins?

LORI: No need to bother any more about your mother?

PALMA: Yes, of course, about mother, certainly! But, good heavens, now I'm going away –

LA BARBETTI: Quite so, my dear, you're a wife now! He's no right to dictate to you any longer.

LORI: I'm not talking about a right!

LA BARBETTI: And have you any right to prevent me doing what I intend to do for my own granddaughter?

PALMA [*disgusted, begins to move away*]: No, this is too much! Please, don't!

LA BARBETTI [*standing before her, soothingly*]: No, no, my dear, for goodness' sake don't *you* get upset: in your pretty wedding-dress and all.

PALMA: I must go and change: we're just going away.

LORI [*bewildered and unhappy, drawing back*]: Perhaps I went too far . . . I'm sorry.

PALMA: Yes, you did go too far. Never mind. If these things have to happen . . .

LA BARBETTI: I'm sorry if it's any fault of mine –

PALMA [*calm again, and once more seeing the ludicrous side of this unexpected encounter*]: No, no, let's keep a sense of proportion, for Heaven's sake! After all it was a pleasant surprise to find an unexpected grannie waiting here for me.

LA BARBETTI [*rapturously*]: What a lovely girl it is, a precious! [*Turning suddenly to her son for the wedding-present*] Give it me, Charlie, give it me!

PALMA [*not understanding*]: Give you what?

LA BARBETTI: I've brought a little present for you as well!

PALMA [*turning to her father as though to persuade him into a humorous indulgence*]: There, you see? A little present as well!

LA BARBETTI: Come on, come on, Charlie! [*Introducing him to* PALMA] This is my other child.

PALMA: How do you do?

LA BARBETTI [*continuing*]: He'll be . . . yes, he'll be your poor mother's half-brother.

PALMA: I see: a sort of half-uncle, in fact?

CARLETTO: Yes, exactly, a half-uncle. Very pleased to meet you. [*Handing the package to his mother.*] Here it is, mother.

LA BARBETTI [*handing it to* PALMA]: There, take it, take it, my pet!

PALMA [*opening it and admiring it with polite exaggeration*]: Oh, how lovely! How lovely!

LA BARBETTI: Ah, you'll have had lots of things like that!

CARLETTO: With our very best wishes for all future happiness.

LA BARBETTI: Yes, my dear, all the happiness I'm sure you deserve. And don't think that'll be the last thing I shall do for you.

LORI [*unable to contain himself any longer*]: Your grandfather, Bernardo Agliani, returned every penny he'd had from this woman, including the marriage-settlement due to your mother. And your mother was proud and glad he'd done so; and when your grandfather died and she was left an orphan, she preferred to earn her bread and butter by teaching rather than . . . But go on, take it, take it: I'm upsetting your wedding-day and I've no longer even the right to speak, as this lady has said . . .

[*At this point, three gentlemen come in from the left:* SALVO MANFRONI, *the Marchese* FLAVIO GUALDI, *and Conte* VENIERO BONGIANI. *Senator* MANFRONI, *not quite fifty, is tall, upright, and thin. If he had not earned the title of Senator from his scientific and academic distinction, or from his political past, it would have come to him by wealth. In fact he is* the *grand seigneur, a master of other men, and of himself above all.* FLAVIO GUALDI *is thirty-four, still blond, indeed bright blond, but already almost bald; he is pink and shiny, like some exquisite figurine in glazed porcelain.*\* *When he speaks, he affects a certain condescending kindliness which contrasts oddly with the cold, hard look in his blue, almost glassy, eyes.* VENIERO BONGIANI *is about forty; very elegant; a speculator in films, and the founder of one of the wealthiest producing companies.*]

SALVO: What's the matter?

PALMA: Nothing, nothing: a lovely surprise! Look, Flavio!

FLAVIO: Haven't you gone to change?

PALMA: I've found a grandmother, here, waiting to greet me!

FLAVIO ⎫      ⎧ A grandmother!
VENIERO ⎬ [*together*]: ⎨ Splendid!
SALVO ⎭      ⎩ This lady?

FLAVIO [*indicating* LORI]: His mother?

PALMA [*quickly*]: No, fortunately. [*And turning at once to* CARLETTO] And this is ... oh, dear, I'm so sorry – I don't even know your name?

CARLETTO [*starting; politely*]: Ah, Clarino ... [*He bows.*]

SALVO [*amazed, in a tone of reproof*]: What nonsense is this? Palma!

PALMA [*apparently ignoring him*]: Yes, Signor Clarino, my grandmother's son! My half-uncle! [*Suddenly, turning to* LA BARBETTI] Ah! then you're called Signora Clarino now! Are you a widow?

LA BARBETTI: Yes, dear, twice.

PALMA [*turning to* LORI, *almost triumphantly*]: Well, then! She's

\* The original adds here: 'His accent is French rather than Piedmontese.'

Signora Clarino! There's no need to worry about Bernardo Agliani and mummy now, is there? We can all be quite happy. [*She turns to* FLAVIO, *with a look of meaning*] Can't we, Flavio? Especially as we're going away . . .

FLAVIO: Yes, of course, it doesn't matter to me!

LA BARBETTI [*sincerely*]: That's just what *I* said.

LORI [*hurt by* PALMA'S *last words*]: I could have wished it hadn't happened, precisely for that reason, Palma, just as you're leaving here for ever . . .

SALVO [*observing how agitated* LORI *is, and considering this neither the time nor the place for such a display, goes over to him, cutting short his words with*]: No, no, for Heaven's sake, Martino! Whatever's the matter? [*He goes on talking to* LORI *in an angry undertone.*]

PALMA [*to* SALVO, *who appears not to hear her*]: Just as if he'd invited her, isn't it?

[*She goes over to* FLAVIO *and* VENIERO, *who are standing near the door on the left.*]

FLAVIO [*to* PALMA, *with a smile*]: You *will* explain later, I hope?

PALMA: Of course I will! It's terribly funny, actually.

VENIERO: A grandmother, in a very good state of preservation!

PALMA: She's marvellous! You'll have to sign her up for a film! [*To* FLAVIO] I'll tell you all about it later.

FLAVIO: But, my dear, you must hurry.

PALMA: Yes, I'm going . . . But take them in there. [*Indicates the room on the left.*] Offer the son a part as well. [*This is said to* BONGIANI. *Then she leads the two men across to* LA BARBETTI.] Grannie: may I introduce the Marchese Flavio Gualdi, my husband; and Conte Veniero Bongiani. [*She turns to* CARLETTO] And this is Uncle Charles, isn't it?

CARLETTO: Charlie, yes . . .

PALMA: Uncle Charlie! I never thought I would have to do all this in my wedding-dress! Excuse me, please. I must go and take it off. You all go in there, into the drawing-room . . . [*She goes out through the door on the right.*]

LA BARBETTI [*cries after her*]: Sweetheart! Sweetheart! [*Then to* FLAVIO, *as they cross towards the door on the left.*] Oh, I really do feel happy!

FLAVIO [*standing aside to let her pass, at the door*]: Please . . . [*and he follows her out.*]

VENIERO [*to* CARLO, *standing aside in the same way*]: After you . . .

CARLETTO [*holding back*]: Oh, no, I wouldn't dream . . . [*pointing to the door*] After you . . .

VENIERO [*preceding him*]: Quite right: this is almost your home, after all . . . [*He goes and* CARLETTO *follows.*]
  [*They have all gone, except* LORI *and* MANFRONI.]

LORI [*continuing his conversation with* MANFRONI, *passionately*]: I can put all other feelings on one side; but that I can't, I can't! It's the one thing I live by, you know it is!

SALVO [*angrily, almost to himself*]: It's incredible, incredible! [*Then quickly and fiercely*] All right, carry on with your obsession, if you insist: but do at least try and notice how distressing it is for other people to see you being so obstinate, especially when they're only trying to stop you making yourself look ridiculous.

LORI: You think it's ridiculous?

SALVO: Of course it is, my dear fellow: the whole thing's so damned exaggerated. Surely just at the moment when Palma's freeing both herself and you – why, good God Almighty, you might restrain yourself for once!

LORI: I couldn't.

SALVO: I know you couldn't. Exactly! But why must you insist on showing these feelings *now*? I know they served to excuse a great many things in the past; they excused you from taking the care of Palma you should have taken, for example –

LORI: But there was always *you* –

SALVO [*continuing*]: Yes, I naturally looked after the child when I saw she was being neglected.

LORI [*protesting*]: No, that's not true!

SALVO [*angrily cutting him short*]: Oh God, I'm only saying what everyone else says!

LORI [*as though he were gazing far into the past*]: Yes, I know it must have looked like that.

SALVO [*with annoyance*]: Oh, never mind; it was clear to all of us that your grief prevented you from amusing the child as you should have done. [*Loudly, in exasperation*] But we've had enough of it! It's all over now! She's going away! Why lose your temper like this simply because this old scarecrow turns up just as Palma's leaving: you might at least have spared yourself that!

LORI [*with painful indignation, almost in despair*]: After the welcome Palma gave her?

SALVO [*angrier still*]: What welcome? Didn't you see she was determined to enjoy the whole thing? It was the only way she could get out of the embarrassing mess you'd caused by your stupid nonsense.

LORI: She accepted under my very eyes the present they brought her.

SALVO: Did you expect her to refuse it?

LORI: And also the promise of a gift of money her mother would have scorned to accept.

SALVO [*struck*]: She promised her that?

LORI: But I cried her shame in her face!

SALVO [*outraged*]: But you don't see . . . [*He buries his face in his hands.*] My God, don't you see you shouldn't have done that?

LORI: Why not? Palma, thank God . . . [*He corrects himself.*] I say thank God, but it's really thanks to you: Palma has no need of the woman's money.

SALVO: But that's the very reason! [*Almost to himself.*] It's unbelievable!

LORI: What do you mean: that's the reason?

SALVO: What I say! It wasn't your business to say such things!

LORI: Haven't I the right to?

SALVO: No, you haven't! None whatever! This woman is

immensely rich. You're not to know whether or not Palma's
husband –

LORI: But she has the money you've settled on her so gener-
ously . . .

SALVO: Don't be a fool: there can never be too much money.

LORI [*amazed and distressed*]: I see. I'm sorry. I never imagined . . .

SALVO: Imagined what?

LORI: It never occurred to me that you – with all the respect you
used to have, and still have, for Bernardo Agliani's memory –

SALVO [*angered beyond endurance, shrugs his shoulders, and begins
to move to the door on the left*]: Oh, be quiet, for God's sake!
It's really too much!

[*At this point* FLAVIO *returns from the drawing-room.*]

FLAVIO: May I come in?

SALVO: Come in, come in, Flavio.

FLAVIO [*laughing at the thought of* LA BARBETTI]: She's marvellous, marvellous! And the son's even more marvellous
than she is. He's actually agreed to sign up with Bongiani
for a film. Bongiani's having a great time in there with them.
It's fabulous!

SALVO: You know what all this is about, I suppose?

FLAVIO: Yes, of course. It's just a bit of nonsense. [*He corrects
himself with a meaning glance at* SALVO.] Oh, of course I
know it's all the more reason to . . . [*He sketches a gesture
indicating 'to cut things short'.*] . . . ça va sans dire . . .

LORI: No one could have imagined she would have had the
impudence to show herself in this house.

SALVO: You see what you've ruined, my dear fellow? 'A bit of
nonsense.' The bit of nonsense that old peacock came here to
offer us so unexpectedly . . . [*To* FLAVIO] I'll explain later
. . . I must just go in and have a few words with her. You
come with me.

FLAVIO: Right, I'll just tell Palma to hurry up.

[SALVO *goes out to the left.* FLAVIO *goes to the door on the
right, knocks, and stands listening to* PALMA.]

LORI: I'd like to talk to you too . . .

FLAVIO [*annoyed, coldly*]: Excuse me a moment. [*Speaking through the door*] It's me, Palma. [*Pause; he listens; then, with a laugh*] No, no, I don't want to come in. [*Pause.*] Yes, of course, it's getting late. [*Pause.*] But leave that to Gina; she'll do that; hurry up! [*Pause.*] Yes, I'll see to it . . . I'll look after that. [*And he crosses the room quickly to the door at the back.*]

LORI: I wanted to tell you –

FLAVIO: Sorry, I haven't time . . . [*He goes out.*]

[*LORI seems frozen by GUALDI'S open contempt. It does not occur to him that no one believes his feelings to be sincere; he imagines indeed that they are all bored by him and have no consideration for him, now that PALMA, with the protection and support of SALVO MANFRONI, is leaving her modest home, and going with her husband into the world of fashion. He stays there dejectedly staring before him; there is a long pause. Eventually the door to the right opens, and GINA emerges, putting outside bags and hat-boxes, which the PORTER, appearing from the door at the back, takes away a few at a time.*]

GINA [*handing things to the PORTER*]: There's this one, Giovanni. . . . And this! Be very careful with that one . . . No, no, take them a few at a time . . .

[*Finally PALMA comes out too, wearing an expensive travelling costume; she is pulling on her gloves.*]

PALMA [*to GINA*]: Gina, you will remember, won't you, to tell them not to get the bags for the luggage-van mixed up with the ones we want in the compartment?

GINA: Yes, don't worry. Giovanni will go himself.

PORTER: Yes, madam. I'll go. Don't worry.

PALMA [*to LORI*]: Are you coming with us to the station?

LORI: Yes, of course.

PALMA [*to GINA, who is just going out of the door at the back*]: Just a minute, Gina: you're leaving here immediately, aren't you?

GINA: Unless Signor Lori wants me for anything . . .?

LORI: No, thank you, I shall be –

PALMA: Who's staying on here?

GINA: I really don't know – there's the daily woman . . .

LORI: It doesn't matter. Don't bother . . . Palma, my dear –

PALMA: Just a moment, I want to give Gina a few instructions . . .

LORI: Yes, of course . . .

PALMA [*to* GINA]: You'll be back by the end of the month?

GINA: I could come back sooner, if you like . . .

PALMA: No, no, that'll be soon enough. In any case, I'll be writing to you . . .

GINA: Don't worry: by the time you're back, everything will be arranged just as you said.

PALMA: Do remember the little cabinet, won't you? [*To* LORI] And *you'll* see about mummy's jewels, won't you?

LORI: I've already put them on one side for you.

GINA: I shall come and fetch them for you as soon as I get back.

PALMA: Good. So good-bye now, Gina. Give me a kiss.

GINA: Have a lovely time. All my best wishes once more . . .

PALMA: Thank you. But I'll see you again to say good-bye before we leave.

[GINA *goes out at the back.*]

LORI: Palma, I do hope this unpleasant incident –

PALMA: No, don't let's say any more about it. Is she still in there?

LORI: Yes, I think so.

PALMA: It *must* be time we were off.

LORI: Wait one moment . . . I must tell you one thing that distresses me more than anything else . . .

PALMA: But, good heavens, why? I could have understood, before. But why now?

LORI: It *must* be now: now you're going away, my child.

PALMA: But it isn't any longer necessary, surely?

LORI: What! You're leaving this house for ever: do you want me not to tell you before you go, what has been, and still is, my most secret agony?

PALMA [*in a low voice, impatiently, but also realizing the necessity of touching on a very thorny subject which would be better avoided*]: But I know what it is . . .

LORI: You know?

PALMA [*as before*]: Yes, I know. That's why I'm afraid it seems pointless to talk about it to me now.

LORI: It isn't pointless. You don't realize that I've suffered more than you have; you've never guessed what it's cost me to act the part of – [*he pauses a little uncertainly, and adds, with difficulty*] a neglectful father.

PALMA: But surely, *now* –

LORI: Let me speak! It goes back to things that happened long ago, things you can't possibly know about because you were only a baby at the time. I want you to know before you go away.

PALMA [*with a resigned sigh, which does not disguise her impatience*]: Very well, then! Go on.

LORI: The way in which you always treat me –

PALMA: Oh, *please*, don't!

LORI: Let me finish, Palma! I'm not reproaching you for it. The way you always treat me shows me now that your mother was doubly right, and that I was wrong.

PALMA: Do you still have to bring mother into it?

LORI [*sharply*]: Yes! Because she foresaw that this would happen!

PALMA [*a little taken aback by his tone*]: That what would happen?

LORI [*pauses regretfully, and does not answer, for he would have to say: 'that you would never have any consideration for me'. Then he says, with melancholy gentleness*]: Don't think I'm trying to reproach you. But I always hoped I'd be able to prove her wrong: because she never, never wanted . . .

PALMA: Never wanted what?

LORI: She never wanted Salvo Manfroni to come here and take so much interest in you.

PALMA: Well?

LORI: I wanted to earn the right to prove she was mistaken. The years of misery it's cost me, you can never, never have guessed. Ah! Don't say it's not true: because it *is* true. You think I never suffered; you think I'm not suffering now.

PALMA: But who says so, in Heaven's name?

LORI: *That.* The tone of your voice when you ask me.

PALMA: No, no, I'm sorry: if I spoke as I did, it was because I do understand, only too well, the suffering my good fortune has been built on: is that what you wanted me to say? Do you think I don't understand that?

LORI: If you did understand it wouldn't annoy you as it does.

PALMA: It isn't annoyance. It's simply that I don't know why you should want to remind me of it now, when surely it's stopped being a burden: on you, on me, on any of us. . . . That's what's wrong of you: oh, you force me to say it, you make me!

LORI: I've stood aside so much . . .

PALMA: Too much in one way, too little in another!

LORI: What do you mean?

PALMA: But don't you see how useless it is to complain *now*? *Please* don't say any more.

[SALVO MANFRONI *and* FLAVIO GUALDI *return from the drawing-room.*]

FLAVIO [*impatiently*]: Come on, Palma, it's time we were off.

PALMA: I'm ready, yes. Let's go. [*She is about to leave with* FLAVIO.]

SALVO: Wait a moment. [*To* LORI] Look: it'd be better if Palma said good-bye to you here.

LORI [*surprised*]: Why: I'm coming with her to the station.

SALVO: No.

FLAVIO: It's those two in there . . . [*He points to the drawing-room.*]

SALVO: If you come to the station, they'll come too.

FLAVIO: And my sister will be there: and friends of the family.

PALMA [*quickly*]: Oh, no! I'd better say good-bye here, straight away.

LORI: But we can send those two away!

FLAVIO: No, we've already told them –

SALVO: That you're staying behind too. They were getting ready to come with us!

PALMA: That's settled then! We'll say good-bye here!

LORI [*frozen, opening his arms*]: That's settled . . .

PALMA: Well, good-bye, then. [*She kisses him without any show of affection.*]

LORI [*after kissing her on the forehead*]: Good-bye, my dear child. It's all so very sudden. There was so much I'd like to say . . . and I can't say anything. Be very happy . . .

SALVO: Come on, do hurry up.

LORI [*to* FLAVIO, *who holds out his hand*]: Good-bye to you, too; and –

FLAVIO: Excuse me . . . [*He turns to* PALMA] Palma, go and wish them good-bye in there – on the way through.

PALMA: Yes, of course. [*She goes out left.*]

FLAVIO [*to* LORI]: What were you saying?

LORI [*coldly and sadly*]: Nothing. Just good-bye.

FLAVIO: Ah, yes. I've said good-bye. We can go, then . . .

SALVO: Yes, let's go. [*On the way out, left, he turns to* LORI *and says*] See you soon.

[FLAVIO *and* SALVO *go.* LORI *stands for a time, absorbed in his icy disappointment, until* LA BARBETTI *and* CARLETTO *come in from the room on the left, in silence. She is sulking; he seems like an unhooked marionette, dropping with fatigue.*]

LA BARBETTI: Well, well . . . it must be very nice marrying off a daughter to a title.

CARLETTO: I like him making all that fuss because *we* came, and then not even –

LORI: Not even what? It was just because you did come that I've stayed behind.

LA BARBETTI: I dare say! But your daughter –

LORI: My daughter forbade me to create a scandal by throwing you out of the house while her husband was here!

CARLETTO: Her husband was very polite to us.

LA BARBETTI [*promptly seconding him*]: *And* very kind!

CARLETTO: And so was his friend.

LA BARBETTI: And so was Salvo Manfroni. Did you see him talking to me, Charlie?

CARLETTO: Yes, but I wouldn't trust *him* too much, mother.

LA BARBETTI: I don't know what the world's coming to. I can understand a father sacrificing himself for his own daughter's good – but fancy letting somebody take his place like that!

LORI [*controlling his anger with difficulty*]: Will you both kindly leave my house!

CARLETTO: Certainly: we're going. We don't have to be asked.

LA BARBETTI: But between you and me, I don't mind telling you I shall be more welcome in your daughter's house than ever *you* –

CARLETTO: Oh, come on, mother, don't bother with him.

LA BARBETTI: Which is the way out?

CARLETTO [*pointing to the door, left*]: That way. Go on!

LA BARBETTI [*as she goes out*]: What a man! Did you ever see –

CARLETTO [*as he goes out*]: Oh, let him get on with it . . .
[*Just before they go out,* GINA *comes in from the back, her hat on, and a bag in her hand, ready to leave.*]

GINA [*to* LORI]: Would you like me to see them out?

LORI [*with contempt*]: No, leave them!

GINA [*after waiting a moment*]: Well, Signor Lori, if there's nothing I can do for you . . .

LORI: Oh, no, thank you. You go along . . .

GINA: I was wondering if I might take a few of the flowers, as they've left so many of them?

LORI [*as if seeing them for the first time*]: Ah, yes. We must see about those. . . . The house remains behind with me, full of flowers.

GINA: It's not very healthy to have too many of them in the –

LORI: They left them behind for me, here.

GINA: Oh dear ... Some of them are so lovely.

LORI: Take them, take as many as you want.

GINA [*going over to one of the baskets*]: Thank you. I'll only take a few of these.

LORI: Don't you agree that there's no sacrifice too great for a father to make, if it's for the good of his own daughter?

GINA: Ah yes, Signor Lori, when the father is like you ... Oh, do look at these roses! [*She holds them up in the basket from which she is about to take them.*] Look!

LORI: Yes, they're beautiful. Do have them ... I'll take a few with me too. [*He looks at his watch.*]

GINA [*sadly, referring to his daily visit to the cemetery*]: Are you going today as well?

LORI: They wouldn't let me go to the station, because of those two ... I will go and take her a few of her daughter's flowers, and try and tell her what my reasons were. . . . *She* would never listen to me, either.

# ACT TWO

---

*A sumptuous room in the Gualdis' house. The back part of the stage
has a raftered ceiling, lower than that of the rest of the room. In the
far wall there are two glazed doors with small, thick, opaque, leaded
panes. The right door leads to the garden, the left one to part of the
house. Between the two doors is a fireplace, largely masked from
sight by a divan which faces it, its back to the audience. This divan
has the effect of shutting off the back part of the stage into a small
room apart, more intimate, centred on the fire. Against the back of the
divan is a six-legged table, on which there stands a magnificent vase of
flowers. The table is flanked by a pair of standard lamps with large
silk shades. There are various chairs and stools facing the audience.
In the left wall are two other doors: the near one leads to the
billiard-room, the other to the dining-room. Downstage, near the
main entrance (which is in the right wall) is an octagonal table with
a number of illustrated magazines, vases, and other small objects on
it. There is a big leather armchair, with another standard lamp behind
it, matching the other two. Stylish chairs, with many cushions. The
rest of the furniture, disposed between the hall-door and the window,
and in the back part of the room, has a rich, sober elegance indicative
of taste and refinement in the owners of the house. The room is
brilliantly lit.*

> [*At the rise of the curtain, the stage is empty. A few moments
> after,* PALMA *and* SALVO MANFRONI *come in through
> the garden door. They are returning from a drive. They
> are followed by a footman, to whom* MANFRONI *hands
> his hat and overcoat.* PALMA *and* SALVO *are deep in a
> conversation they began as they got out of the motor-car in the
> garden.*]

SALVO [*as the footman takes his coat*]: Yes, yes . . . but there's
always a way, I assure you . . . [*The footman goes out through
the main entrance, downstage right.*] There's always a way of

120

giving people a good opinion of us which at the same time increases their own self-esteem.

PALMA [*promptly, as she slips off her gloves*]: And makes them insufferably conceited!

SALVO: No, my dear, quite the reverse: which turns out to be to *our* advantage too.

PALMA: But I notice so many things nowadays!

SALVO: You don't notice anything. Pay attention to this: Flavio talks to you. You know it's just words, which he says simply for the sake of talking . . .

PALMA: Yes, words without any meaning to them!

SALVO: Quite so. But by the way you listen to them, you can show him they have . . .

PALMA: How? If they just haven't?

SALVO: It's easy! You *give* them a meaning, yourself; you put a meaning into them – whatever meaning best suits you. But you pretend *he's* put a meaning into them. He'll be delighted to find his own words actually making sense. In that way you can gradually make him into exactly what you want him to be; and he'll be under the impression that that's what *he* wants to be. Do I make myself clear?

PALMA: It doesn't sound easy!

SALVO: I know. I'm not saying it's easy. But you can take it from me, it's the way one has to run one's life.

PALMA: It needs such patience, too!

SALVO: Oh, yes, my dear. Above all things: be patient. [*Then, very quietly*] And not only with your husband, either . . . [*He glances round.*]

PALMA [*looks at him for a moment*]: You mean Gina?

SALVO: I always think that young lady has a face like a little fox.

PALMA: She's only become like this since she left the other house.

SALVO: So you've noticed the change as well?

PALMA: There's nothing one can ever actually take exception to: she just watches.

SALVO: She's still very friendly with Martino?

PALMA: Yes. Though, good heavens, she knows as well as –

SALVO: Sh . . .! She's just coming!

[GINA *enters through the house-door at the back. She comes up to* PALMA, *and takes her hat and coat.*]

GINA: Is there anything you want, Signora Marchesa?

SALVO: Ah, good evening, signorina.

GINA: Good evening, Senator Manfroni.

PALMA: No, thanks, Gina, I'm just going to my room for a moment. [*To* SALVO] Excuse me.

SALVO: Please . . . but I imagine you'll have to be going out again, to see your mother-in-law, won't you?

PALMA: Oh, God, what a bore! Again?

SALVO: She has a temperature again.

GINA: Yes, signora! She sent round to say.

SALVO [*attentively, to* GINA]: But nothing serious.

GINA: No more than usual.

SALVO [*to* PALMA]: You'll have to go round . . .

PALMA: 'Above all things: patience.'

[PALMA *goes out through the door at the back.* SALVO *takes up one of the illustrated journals from the octagonal table, and, still standing, idly turns its pages.*]

SALVO: Dear signorina: I'd like you to give me a few lessons some time.

GINA: Lessons? Whatever in, Senator Manfroni?

SALVO [*without looking at her, and still turning the pages of the journal*]: I admire your eyes.

GINA: Really? I never thought they were as nice as all that.

SALVO: They are nice, yes. But quite apart from that, I admire them because they're so very wise.

GINA: Wise?

SALVO: Wise in the sense of watchful, I mean. But watchful without showing it.

GINA: My eyes seem to be watching people all the time, do you mean?

SALVO: No. That's my point. They don't seem to be. But they are. And as I say, I should like to learn from them.

GINA: To learn what?

SALVO: Well, *that*, for example: to be able to ask questions in that way, pretending not to understand something, while you actually understand perfectly well.

GINA [*almost defiantly*]: Ah, you mean the art of looking as though one hadn't understood.

SALVO [*does not reply at once, as though he were intent on the journal; then he shakes a finger in negation, and after a brief pause, goes on*]: No. That's easy enough. You only have to simulate ignorance to do that. No; there's something much more difficult: *not to look as if one had understood*, when other people have seen that we have in fact understood perfectly ... [*then, as though what he had just said was unimportant, he adds lightly*] ... oh, I mean, of course, things that everyone understands anyway ...

GINA: Yes? Well then?

SALVO: Well, then one *really* deceives people! And it needs a naturalness which is far harder to put on than the simulated ignorance which no one expects of us and which would only make us look silly.

GINA: I suppose so. But perhaps it may not *be* an art, Senator Manfroni.

SALVO: No? What else may it be, then?

GINA: Oh ... a painful necessity, perhaps ...

SALVO: Ah, dear signorina, perhaps we only ever learn things thoroughly, when necessity makes us!

[*At this point* FLAVIO GUALDI *and* VENIERO BONGIANI *come in from the hall.*]

FLAVIO: Ah, here he is!

SALVO: I've been here some time.

[GINA *goes out through the door at the back.*]

VENIERO: Illustrious Senator, my warmest congratulations!

SALVO: Thank you, my dear Bongiani.

FLAVIO [*to* SALVO]: Forgive me for asking, but is it an honorary fellowship, or a full one?

SALVO [*as if this were really too much to be asked*]: Why, a full one, of course!

VENIERO: From a foreign academy, and especially from that one! It's wonderful! There must be plenty of honorary fellowships, but only a very few full ones. But will you explain something for me, please, Manfroni . . .

SALVO [*as before*]: Oh, come, Bongiani, *please*, don't go on about it!

VENIERO: Oh, but just one thing about the new honour –

FLAVIO: Yes: it came up at the club this evening. Everyone was wondering if it had really been necessary for you to attribute the credit –

VENIERO: Only part of it –

FLAVIO: Yes, of course, I meant only part of it: but did you have to give the credit for your scientific discovery to Bernardo Agliani?

VENIERO: Since, as they say, the discovery's completely your own!

[*The whole of this conversation has been casual in tone, as if the matter were really unimportant.*]

SALVO: It's quite clear your friends at the club have never seen my book – even from a distance.

VENIERO: That's quite certain!

FLAVIO: Why, do you say in the book – ?

SALVO: Boys, boys! It's just because I took special care in the introduction to the book to give part of the credit to Bernardo Agliani, that they all say I needn't have done so. If I hadn't – !

VENIERO: They'd have said the opposite, I suppose?

FLAVIO: What a brainless lot!

SALVO: No, on the contrary, they're very sensible! Because they know quite well that in Bernardo Agliani's papers there was nothing that gave even the remotest hint of the discovery; they know he simply stated, quite in another connexion certain problems in physics that had occurred to him. But let's drop it! [*Only now does the conversation take on a more seriously interested tone.*] Tell me: has the club finally decided to split in two?

FLAVIO: Why, yes! You never saw such a piece of buffoonery.

VENIERO: The result is they'll all be paying two lots of fees from now on.

FLAVIO: We've already been and put our names down for the new club.

SALVO: Have you really? [*He laughs.*]

VENIERO: Yes, *en masse*. An invasion!

FLAVIO: It's the opening meeting tonight.

VENIERO: You'll come with us, won't you, Manfroni?

SALVO: You must be mad!

FLAVIO: Ah, no! You must come with us!

VENIERO: We promised them!

FLAVIO: Think how awful it would be without you.

SALVO: My dear friends, I'm staying here. [*He sits, or rather stretches out, blissfully, in the leather armchair near the octagonal table.*] Here: as I do every evening.

FLAVIO: Oh, no, you won't! We shall carry you off by force!

SALVO: Carry me off! If you only knew how well I've earned this armchair!

FLAVIO: Oh, nonsense! Just for one evening.

SALVO: Every night I long for the moment after dinner when Giovanni comes in and puts off most of the lights and leaves me here, almost in the dark . . .

VENIERO: But you can't let us down like this!

FLAVIO: Besides, there won't even be Palma here tonight.
    [PALMA *re-enters from the door at the back.*]

PALMA: What's this about me?

VENIERO: Good evening, Marchesa.

PALMA: Good evening, Bongiani. What's the matter?

VENIERO: Will you please help us to persuade Manfroni to come to the opening of our new club tonight?

PALMA: Oh, is it tonight?

FLAVIO [*to* SALVO]: She'll persuade you, you'll see!

SALVO: No one's going to persuade me.

FLAVIO: You are going to see mother again tonight, aren't you, Palma?

PALMA: Do I really have to?

SALVO: But, of course, you must!

FLAVIO: We called in just now, and I promised you'd go round. You needn't stay very long.

SALVO: Exactly. You can go for half an hour, and then come back and keep me company. I can have my nice armchair just as usual!

FLAVIO: Really, you make me angry!

VENIERO: No, he'll come, you'll see.

SALVO: I sha'n't.

PALMA: No, let him stay here.

VENIERO: We can't, we can't!

FLAVIO: They won't let us in, if we go without him.

SALVO: Well, don't *you* go, then!

PALMA: That's a nice piece of selfishness, I must say! You send me off to see –

FLAVIO: Oh God, Palma, it's only for a few minutes.

PALMA: No, thank you; if he's not going to be here when I get back, I might as well stay with your mother all evening. While you go off and enjoy yourselves!

SALVO: Don't worry, my dear, don't worry. You'll leave me here, and you'll find me here.

[*At this point* MARTINO LORI *is heard in the hall.*]

LORI: Are you all in there?

[*There is a reaction of annoyance from everyone.*]

FLAVIO [*groans softly*]: Oh, God!

[*And the conversation drops at once, as* LORI *hesitantly makes his way into the room. A general coldness prevails.*]

LORI: Good evening? Am I in the way?

PALMA: No, not at all.

SALVO: Come in, come in, Martino. Forgive me for not getting up . . .

LORI [*approaching* FLAVIO, *who has drawn* VENIERO *aside to say something to him*]: Good evening, Flavio.

FLAVIO [*hardly turning to him*]: Oh, good evening.

VENIERO: Good evening, Signor Lori. [*He shakes hands with him.*]

PALMA [*to* LORI]: Come and sit down.

SALVO: Come and sit here by me, Martino.

FLAVIO [*in an undertone to* VENIERO]: It couldn't be better: don't you see? He'll come with us, now! [*And they both move towards the second door on the left.*]

SALVO: Where are you two off to?

FLAVIO: We're just going into the billiard-room for a moment.

PALMA: We shall be having dinner almost at once.

FLAVIO: You come too, Palma.

PALMA: What for?

FLAVIO: We want to tell you something. Come on.

PALMA: Excuse me. [*She goes out to the billiard-room, with* FLAVIO *and* VENIERO.]

SALVO [*with a sigh of weariness, as he lies stretched out in the arm-chair*): Well, dear Martino?

LORI [*trying not to show the pain and mortification the departure of the others has caused him: with a slight laugh*]: Here we are . . . [*After a pause.*] Were you saying something you didn't want me to hear?

SALVO: No, no, nothing at all. It's only that they're having the opening meeting of a new club this evening. They're plotting to prevent my taking the evening off. But I'm in retirement. Like you. You from the Council of State; and I from the worries of the great world, my dear friend.

LORI: From those too?

SALVO: From every one of them: the whole lot.

LORI [*with sincere and affectionate regret*]: How awful it is for you. You could have everything you wanted, if you chose . . .

SALVO: Thank you, Martino, I've got everything I want; too much of it. But in order to get anything you have to give, give, give, the whole time. And if you weigh all you've given against what you've received –

LORI: Yes, I know. That's just why I think we shouldn't value the few things we get just for themselves alone.

SALVO: How should we value them then, do you think?

LORI: In proportion to what we've given.

SALVO: Isn't that what I'm saying? Work it out, and you're always short!

LORI: No, I didn't mean that. I meant the value of the little we get comes from how much we've given. God help me, if that weren't so in my case!

SALVO [*annoyed that* LORI *should thus refer the subject to himself*]: Ah, I see. You're talking about something else.

LORI: That, too, has been a question of giving and taking.

SALVO: A father always gives everything!

LORI: And I could hardly get – [*He is about to add; 'less than I do now', when* SALVO, *abruptly and rudely, interrupts and changes the subject.*]

SALVO: Tell me, Martino, I hope they put you on the top rate of pension when you retired?

LORI [*hurt*]: What – what do you mean?

SALVO [*indifferently*]: Oh, nothing. I only wondered.
[*During the following,* LORI *can only with difficulty hold in the distress and anguish provoked by* SALVO'S *efforts to change the tone and subject of their conversation.*]

LORI [*in injured tones*]: You've never, until just lately, allowed your rank or position to come between us . . .

SALVO: Whatever do you mean?

LORI: You've always treated me with the greatest confidence –

SALVO: But of course.

LORI: And friendliness.

SALVO: I hope so.

LORI: Even to the point of embarrassing me a little. Because naturally I've always seen you as my superior as well as my friend.

SALVO: Good God, Martino, what on earth are you talking about?

LORI: No, please let me speak! Can't you see I'm almost choking with wretchedness . . .!

SALVO: But why?

LORI: You ask me why? Is this the way to treat me?

SALVO: But I'm talking to you –

LORI: I don't mean you; I mean the others. I know he received his wife from your hands rather than mine, but still –

SALVO: Oh, really, this is –

LORI: I know: he wouldn't have taken her from my hands. There's too much disparity in our positions; and in character and upbringing.

ALVO: You must have foreseen that!

LORI: Yes, yes, it's only natural. It can't be any pleasure to him to see me there. He snubs me!

SALVO: He doesn't.

LORI: If he doesn't actually snub me, he puts me off by his manner.

SALVO: But, please, please, you ought to realize –

LORI: That my way of life used to be too simple, and now it's too narrow: is that what you mean?

SALVO [out of patience]: But it's the way you behave in everything! Even with me!

LORI: I don't understand you.

SALVO: Let's face it, Martino: there are certain situations one either accepts or doesn't accept, right from the start. If one accepts them, one must be resigned to them. It's the only way of sparing oneself pointless suffering – and sparing others too.

LORI: But I've avoided coming here, as far as I decently can. I still do.

SALVO: Does that seem to you necessary?

LORI: What? To come at all, do you mean?

SALVO: There are times when you look at me like that, when I really think you take pleasure in embarrassing me. Why shouldn't you come here? No one has ever told you not to come. Come: but be easier and more natural about it, so that the others wouldn't find it so hard to cope with you.

LORI: But I think I –

SALVO: You've taken things badly right from the start, I've told you before . . . and I don't see anything to be done about that now! I assure you, it would be a great relief to everyone, including yourself, if only you could behave differently. I'm only saying this, I hope you realize, because I'm anxious to save your self-respect – and this isn't the first time, as you know!

LORI: I'm completely alone now . . . In the old days I did at least have the consolation of your friendship: every day you used to come and see me.

SALVO: But doesn't it seem to you natural that after all I've done, I should come here instead now?

LORI: Yes, but surely, even for the look of things . . . Surely, it's too much, to treat me like that in front of a stranger.

SALVO: Bongiani is not a stranger, he's an intimate friend. My dear Martino, one has to have a clear idea of the causes of things, if one's to appreciate their effects. And you haven't, because you can't see yourself. I *can* see you, and I assure you that it's you who make them behave like that. I agree that to anyone who doesn't know the whole situation, it must appear unpleasant: but Bongiani knows what everyone else knows: and, good God, you know it yourself. That's the reason I'm telling you to make a complete *change*, Martino: circumstances have changed, and so must you.

LORI: But how could I change?

[GINA *enters from the first door on the left.*]

GINA: Excuse me, but they're just going in to dinner, Senator Manfroni.

[PALMA, FLAVIO, *and* VENIERO *come in from the billiard-room.*]

FLAVIO: Hurry up, hurry up, Salvo! We shall have to make haste.

SALVO: Yes, I'm coming. [*He goes towards the dining-room with* FLAVIO *and* VENIERO.]

PALMA [*to* LORI]: Would you like to join us in there . . .? [*She points to the dining-room.*]

LORI: No, I'll stay in here, thank you.

PALMA: Do you still always have supper late?

LORI: Yes. Yes, I do.

FLAVIO [*going into the dining-room with* SALVO *and* VENIERO]: Come on, Palma!

PALMA: I'm coming. Are you staying in here, Gina?

GINA: Yes, I'll stay in here.

[PALMA *goes out with the others through the first door on the left. During the following scene, the mingled voices and laughter of the four diners, the clatter of plates, etc., are occasionally heard.*]

LORI: Please don't stay just for me, if you have things to do.

GINA: No, I've nothing to do.

LORI: I'll wait a little longer. I want to speak to Palma.

GINA [*as though introducing a rather unpleasant topic*]: You've heard about Senator Manfroni's new award?

LORI [*remembering, and reproaching himself for his forgetfulness*]: Oh, of course! I read about it in the papers. And I forgot to –

GINA [*quietly cutting short his self-reproach*]: Signor Lori: you ought to take a great deal more care than you do of a certain bundle of notes you keep in your desk.

LORI [*turning sharply to her, in half-angry, half-frightened amazement*]: How do you know about them?

GINA [*coolly and calmly*]: You remember the day I came to see you at the Ministry, to ask when I might come and collect your wife's jewels, which you'd put on one side for me to bring here?

LORI: Yes: well?

GINA: You gave me the key of the drawer in your desk.

LORI: I know I did. But surely you didn't –

GINA: Forgive me. I was overcome by curiosity.

LORI: But those are the notes, the . . . the first sketches for Agliani's work. You can't have understood much of them.

GINA: I understood everything.

LORI: No, no: they're all formulae, and calculations.

GINA: I read the note in your own handwriting on the outside: 'To Silvia, that she may look down and forgive me'.

LORI [*alarmed at his secret being discovered, and the disastrous consequences this may have for* MANFRONI]: Oh, yes, that note ... I felt the need to ask my wife's forgiveness ...

GINA [*quickly*]: For letting a crime be committed?

LORI [*as though anxious to defend himself*]: No! I said nothing. ... [*But he suddenly cuts short his excuses, and says peremptorily*] And I want you to say nothing either! [*Then, immediately regretting his tone, he pleads*] Please promise me you won't, promise me you won't.

GINA: You're much too generous.

LORI [*more and more agitated, as he implores her*]: No, no! Promise me you'll say nothing: I beg you by whatever you hold sacred!

GINA [*in order to calm him, and looking uneasily towards the dining-room door*]: I promise. But don't let them hear us talking ...

LORI: I said nothing, because if I'd spoken, I would have seemed in my own eyes to have been committing a crime myself, against someone who'd already atoned for his sin against a dead man by the kindness he was showing my daughter. And Agliani was already famous and honoured. ... [*With sudden distress*] I ought to have destroyed those notes!

GINA: You mustn't do that! You mustn't! Salvo Manfroni certainly doesn't know you have them.

LORI: I found them afterwards: after my wife had died; after he'd taken away – though it was against her wishes – all the papers her father left.

GINA: And those he'll certainly have destroyed!

LORI: For God's sake, please realize what I feel about –

GINA: Yes, Signor Lori, I do. But Manfroni is abusing your gratitude horribly, simply because he doesn't know the damage you could do him.

LORI: No, not damage!

GINA: Oh, I know you never would! What I mean is merely that he and the others would never treat you as they do now, if they knew you possessed those notes.

LORI: I'll destroy them!

GINA: No, no, don't!

LORI: I assure you I'd have given them to him myself, if only I hadn't been afraid –

GINA: Of humiliating him?

LORI: Oh, more than that! You can't know what it meant to me when I discovered those notes. It wasn't only that it obliterated straightaway the respect, the unbounded admiration I'd always had for him. No, it wasn't only that. I'm not trying to find excuses for him: but the thought that he was ... deep down ... so weak that he couldn't resist the dreary temptation to profit from all the good he found he had in his hands.

GINA: Oh, that's nonsense! What he did was –

LORI: Horrible, yes, I know! But – can't you see? He gets no enjoyment out of it. He's so tired of everything ...

GINA: That's just a pose.

LORI: I don't think so. And the really serious thing is something else. I mean so far as I'm concerned: the reason I've never said anything, though I know my silence only made me an accomplice in the fraud, in the eyes of my dead wife, who was so jealous for her father's work, and his good name.

GINA: Exactly! For her own sake, you oughtn't to have done this!

LORI: But that's precisely what I'm begging you to try and understand, because it explains everything: my life, my behaviour, everything. I accept it, you see: I accept it as a punishment, a punishment I've deserved, that I'm not allowed to enjoy this happy new life of my daughter's. I've withdrawn from it as much as I possibly could. I almost prefer not to be invited to share in it ...

GINA: Ah, so that's the reason?

LORI: Yes. You see, I should feel even more of an accomplice if I did share in it.

GINA: Yes, I see.

LORI: This punishment, the way they treat me, seems to me my one single excuse – or rather my one means of paying my terrible debt to my wife's memory. That's the reason.

GINA: It may be the reason why you're so tolerant. But it hardly excuses them!

LORI: I know it doesn't. I wish they'd at least try to preserve appearances a little more, so as not to arouse – well, in people like yourself, for example – such contempt.

GINA: It isn't contempt, it's indignation! Especially as it would be perfectly easy for them to –

LORI: Yes, it's what I've said: I said that very thing to him only a few minutes ago. I told him! And I shall say the same to my daughter, certainly I shall. [*Pleadingly, once more*] But please, I beg you –

GINA [*cutting him short*]: Sh . . . ! They're leaving the table. [PALMA *re-enters, turning in the doorway to speak to the others in the dining-room.*]

PALMA: Yes, I'll go at once. And you're going to stay here, aren't you?

SALVO [*off*]: Yes, I'm going to stay in all evening.

FLAVIO ⎱ [*off*]: ⎰No, no! You're not!
VENIERO ⎰          ⎱You're coming with us!

SALVO [*shouting them down*]: I'm not! I'm staying here, I've told you!

PALMA: Good. I'm very glad. [*She crosses the room quickly to the door at the back, saying as she goes*] Will you come with me for a moment, Gina? [*She and* GINA *go out.* LORI *rises.* SALVO, FLAVIO, *and* VENIERO *come in from the dining-room, talking among themselves.*]

SALVO: Yes, it's quite true, we need someone every now and again to cause a little confusion among the learned.

VENIERO: Why confusion?

SALVO: Confusion: to show how thick the dust of old age has

settled on their way of life. But take care the dust you raise doesn't prevent you from seeing the new order you'll have to establish.

FLAVIO: Hear, hear! Excellent!

SALVO: And as for the dust, my dear Bongiani, don't deceive yourself about that either: it'll settle very quickly on your new order, too: because the dust comes from the world, and the world is old [*almost chanting*] and you'd burst your lungs if you tried to blow it away. You'll raise it for a brief while; but back it'll come, and settle down over everything again, inevitably. [*He goes over to* LORI, *and places a hand on his shoulder.*] You're still here?

VENIERO: But don't you see, with a philosophy like that – ?

SALVO: No, stop, Bongiani. Don't let's spoil our digestions.

FLAVIO: Well, let's go then! If you really don't want to spoil yours, I think you'd better – [*He winks furtively in the direction of* LORI.]

VENIERO: Yes, yes. That's much the best thing for you, now that –

SALVO [*as if he had not heard, turning to* LORI]: You know Palma's going out almost at once?

LORI: Are you going with her?

SALVO: I'm not, no.

VENIERO: He's coming with us; it's all settled!

FLAVIO: Yes, come on: let's go!

SALVO: Wait a moment, for God's sake! [*To* LORI] Do you want to speak to her?

LORI: There was something I wanted to say to her.

SALVO: I doubt if she'll have time.

LORI: Oh, I sha'n't keep her long.

SALVO [*turning to the other two*]: You know, I'm almost tempted –

FLAVIO: Of course! Come on, come on, come on!

VENIERO: Entertainment guaranteed, or your money refunded!

SALVO: We shall see about that! [*To* LORI] Would you mind telling Palma I've gone with them?

[*Chilly salutations are exchanged, and* SALVO, FLAVIO, *and* VENIERO *go off through the hall door.* LORI *stands for a moment in indecision, then sits down in the leather armchair in which* SALVO MANFRONI *is accustomed to sit every evening after dinner. There is a brief pause. Then the footman comes in from the dining-room, and begins to switch off the lights, leaving only the three standard lamps still on. It is important that there should now be considerably less light on the stage. The footman withdraws immediately. Eventually* PALMA *returns through the door at the back: she is wearing a hat and coat. She comes down to the armchair, and leans across its back, in order to join her hands under the chin of its occupant.*]

PALMA [*softly and tenderly*]: Daddy . . .

LORI [*at once, impulsively, overcome by gratitude*]: Oh, my own dear Palma!

PALMA [*in surprise at not discovering* SALVO MANFRONI *there, cannot restrain a cry of mingled revulsion and fright, as she draws back*]: Oh! It's you! . . . Why are you here?

LORI [*paling at the realization that the word 'daddy' has not been meant for him*]: I . . . Do you mean you actually call him that when you're alone together?

PALMA [*exasperated, and driven by anger at her own mistake to an extreme boldness*]: Oh, can't we stop all this nonsense? I call him that because it's my duty to call him that!

LORI: Because he's always behaved like a father to you?

PALMA: No! Don't be ridiculous! Can't we put an end to this idiotic play-acting once and for all? I'm sick of it!

LORI: Play-acting? What do you mean?

PALMA: Yes, play-acting! I'm sick of it, I tell you! You know perfectly well he is my father; why should I call anyone else by that name?

LORI [*as though stunned, unable to make head or tail of this*]: Salvo! Your father? What . . . what are you talking about?

PALMA: Are you still trying to pretend you don't know?

LORI [*seizing her by the arm, still bewildered, but already with a mounting sense of outrage and fear*]: What do you mean? What do you mean? Who's told you so? Has *he*?

PALMA [*freeing herself*]: Of course he has! Let me go! Don't!

LORI: He told you you were his daughter?

PALMA [*firmly and sharply*]: Yes; and that you knew I was.

LORI [*astounded*]: I did?

PALMA [*arrested by the amazement in his voice*]: Wh – What do you mean?

LORI: He said that I knew? [*Her bewilderment makes him almost reel and he seems to clutch at his own words for support.*] Oh God! . . . Oh God! . . . Whatever has happened? . . . [*Grasping her arm again.*] What did he tell you? Tell me what he said to you?

PALMA: What do you think he said to me?

LORI: I want to know! I want to know!

PALMA [*with almost fearful regret, but yet almost trying not to believe the evidence*]: But . . . do you *really* not know?

LORI: I know nothing! He told you your mother . . .? Answer me! Answer me!

PALMA: I don't know. . . . He made it clear that –

LORI: That she – Tell me! Tell me!

PALMA: But I know nothing about –

LORI: He said she had been his mistress?

PALMA: No . . .

LORI: No? What do you mean, no? If he said you were his daughter? Whether that's true or not, if he could say that to you, it shows she must have been. . . . Oh, God, oh God. . . . Is it possible, is it possible? She! Silvia! No! He was lying, lying! He was lying! Because . . . because it isn't – no, no, it's impossible that she – [*A terrible idea flashes on him.*] Ah, God! But if . . . no, no, good God, unless it was when –! But how, how, afterwards, could she have . . . No, it isn't possible! Silvia! Silvia! Silvia! [*The thrice-repeated name seems to reflect three different visions of horror: he collapses into the armchair, and bursts into convulsive weeping.*]

PALMA [*distressed, approaching him*]: Forgive me, oh please forgive me. . . . I didn't know. I thought . . . He assured me you knew everything. And you, too – because of how you've always *been* towards me . . . and all you've let happen – I was sure you . . .

LORI [*suddenly, as though these last words contained a ray of hope*]: Ah, but perhaps that's the reason? He said it, because I always let him treat you as a daughter? [*He stares at* PALMA, *and sees that this cannot be.*] No? He said you were really his daughter? [*In an instinctive wish to offend her at once*] And so you were proud of your mother's disgrace? Because it means she was his mistress! And *that* – that's the reason you've all treated me like this?

PALMA: But we thought you knew!

LORI: Knew? Knew this? You think I could know all this, and still bear to be treated as I have been? And Salvo . . . Oh, God . . . it must have been then. Yes, yes . . . it must have been *then*. Yes. She wanted to go back to teaching again. She used to say I couldn't have opinions, because I had no nerves. That was the reason for the hell of that first year! She fell in love with him at first sight, when she came from Perugia after her father died; she fell in love at first sight with her young Member of Parliament. . . . Yes, that must have been the reason she was blushing when she came with him into my office at the Ministry, to be introduced and recommended by him. He'd been her father's pupil; now he was in Parliament. She fell in love with him at first sight . . . and she married *me*! Yes . . . yes, that was it, that was why he took me with him when he was made a Minister. And I was dazzled, dazzled by two glories: Silvia's father, so great and famous; and Salvo, my own chief. I saw nothing! I saw nothing! And then those papers of her father's appeared – because of this! Because of this! . . . But she'd already repented! She'd already repented! By the time you were born, she'd regretted it. She was mine, she was mine! From then on, she was mine alone; from your birth to her death, she belonged to me, as no woman has ever belonged to any man.

That's why I've been like this ever since. I noticed nothing before you were born; how could I possibly have noticed after! She wiped it out herself, with her love for me, wiped away every trace of betrayal. And her love was so great that it kept me from discovering, even after her death. . . . [*After a pause*] But how . . . how could you have believed I knew? Every day since you were a baby, you've seen me go every day to her grave!

PALMA: Yes . . . but that was just the reason I –

LORI: The reason you what?

PALMA: I never concealed from you –

LORI: Your contempt. No, you none of you ever concealed it. So that was the reason? You all thought I knew, and that I was keeping my mouth shut? But why – tell me, tell me *why* should I have kept quiet if I'd known you were not my daughter? Why should I have pretended not to notice the scorn you all showed? Yes, I can see it now: I can see how you all despised me. But if I'd known you weren't my daughter, I couldn't have pretended to have been concerned for you and for your future, could I? Why, why should I? Why? [*Suddenly, a terrible fear assails him, which he can hardly bring himself to put into words: in a whisper*] Unless . . . unless you thought I was doing it . . . to help myself in my career . . .? Good God! Did you all think me capable of that? Did you think I could really go there to her grave every day . . . to act out a farce? [*He sinks back into the chair, and buries his face in his hands. Then, leaping to his feet*] What filthy creature have you all taken me for?

PALMA: No, that's not true! It's not true!

LORI: Cowardly and filthy!

PALMA: No, no, we only thought you were pretending to –

LORI: Yes, yes. You've all told me often enough that I 'kept it up' too long; you all said I overdid it. Yes, you've always been quite frank with me, all of you! And I still didn't understand . . . I must give you every credit for your frankness. You've shown in every possible way how much you all despised me! [*As though he suddenly felt cut off from everyone*] And where have I been? What have I been? Oh, God! Then I've never been in a real life at all. . . . No one has betrayed me! No one has deceived me! It's just that I've never seen – there are so many things I've never seen. Oh God! But now . . . now . . . I can see them. They all come back to me now. . . . [*He is overcome once more by grief, and the thought of how cruelly he has been betrayed.*] And I've mourned for her, I've mourned for sixteen years, for that woman. [*He bursts into tears again.*]

PALMA [*trying to comfort him*]: No, no, don't. Try and remember –

LORI: She dies for me in this moment, dies for me in this moment, killed by her own betrayal! Don't you see I've nothing in the world to cling on to now? Where am I now? What am I doing here? You're not my daughter. I know now that you're not. You knew it long ago, and you and the others have shown me all along how pointless it was for me to keep on coming here. . . .

PALMA: No. I wanted –

LORI: I don't believe you! You've got your husband now, and him – your father – you can have him here, now, openly. Yes. He told me himself half an hour ago that I oughtn't to keep coming here. And I suppose you call him father now in front of everyone?

PALMA: No . . . no . . .

LORI: Then it certainly wasn't out of any thought for me. . . . Oh, God, I've been more than blind, more than blind. I've never been anything, I'm nothing now, I have nothing, not even that dead woman, nothing! [*Overcome again, and almost absently*] I've lived in an illusion with nothing to support me! Because you were all forever snatching my support away from me, because it seemed to you pointless. You left me alone, in contempt and derision, clinging to that dead woman, play-acting . . . and over-doing even that. [*With a burst of rage*] But at least you could have told me!

PALMA: Please . . .

LORI: Perhaps you did tell me?

PALMA: Not openly, ever, but –

LORI: It's even possible that you all did tell me and I never understood. You all thought there was nothing to hide from me, because I knew everything . . .

PALMA: Surely you can see that if it had even crossed my mind for a second that you didn't know –

LORI: If it had ever occurred to you I wasn't that despicable –

PALMA: Please . . . please don't say that any more!

LORI: But how did he come to tell you you were his daughter? How could he have the impudence to insult your mother to your face?

PALMA: He only told me he was my father, when it couldn't possibly offend me any more. You'd left the way open for him to show that he was my father.

LORI: Ah, yes, it's true . . . I even made it easy for him. And now . . . now it's all over, isn't it? Now . . . I'm dismissed?

PALMA: No, no. Why? Everything's different now.

LORI: What's different?

PALMA: If you never knew –

LORI: Does that *make* you my daughter?

PALMA: No, but don't you see that it changes – it's already changed – everything I feel towards you!

LORI: But don't you know that *now* I can – I can – Yes, there are things I can do, now. I can –

PALMA: Can do what?

LORI: Things I . . . don't even know myself yet. It's as if I were . . . emptied. I have nothing left inside me. And when I leave here, I don't know what may spring up inside me, I don't know . . . I . . .

PALMA: But sit down, sit down . . . here. . . . You're shaking all over. Sit down. [*She makes him sit in the armchair, and crouches beside him solicitously and compassionately.*) Perhaps I can still be for you something I've never been before.

LORI [*sharply*]: And what about *him*?

PALMA: Why should you want to do anything against him, now?

LORI: Because he's paid me, do you mean?

PALMA: No!

LORI: Yes. He's paid for my wife; and paid for my daughter.

PALMA: No . . . no . . .

LORI: What do you mean, no? Think of my devotion to him! He seemed to me like the sun in Heaven!

PALMA: I meant that after all these years . . .

LORI [*suddenly shaken by a recollection from the distant past*]: You don't know what I can see. . . . Listen. She was dead. I was like a madman. She was dead within three days: it was her own fault, because she'd wanted to take you – you were only three – to a circus. It was winter; she caught a chill out in the open, and she was dead in three days . . . at the time when she was already mine, all mine; she no longer wanted him to come to the house; she was angry with me because I hadn't the courage to tell him not to. But what was I to do? He'd been my chief. . . . And then she died! I was . . . oh, like I am now . . . empty. Well, he drove me out of the room where she lay dead, and forced me to come and see you, because you were crying for your mother. He said he would stay and watch. I let him send me away. But then during the night I crept back like a shadow to her room. He was there, with his face buried in the pillow, where she lay with the four candles round her. At first I thought he'd been overcome by sleep, and had let his head drop on the pillow without meaning to. Then I could see him more clearly, and I saw that his body was shaken with stifled sobs. [*He turns to look at* PALMA, *astounded still at the memory of* MANFRONI'S *presumption.*] He was crying for her, weeping for her, there under my very eyes. And I didn't understand. I was so very sure of the love of both of them. Until that moment, my own tears had refused to flow, but when I saw him there, I burst out crying too. And suddenly he got up, and as I went forward to put my arms round him, he pushed me back, angrily, hitting me on the chest. I sank back in bewilderment again, and I thought it was the violence of remorse, and that he couldn't bear to see me weep because of the harm he'd caused me. Ah, but he shall pay for his tears! He shall pay for them, now! [*Furiously, he gets up to go.* PALMA *restrains him. Their next speeches follow each other with mounting agitation.*]

PALMA: Now?

LORI: Now I know what to do!

PALMA: But surely it's absurd after all these years to want to – Where are you going?

LORI [*wildly*]: I don't know!

PALMA: What are you going to do?

LORI [*trying to free himself*]: I don't know.

PALMA: Please stay here.

LORI: No . . . no . . .

PALMA: Yes, stay and talk to me.

LORI: To you? What more is there to say?

PALMA: I can still perhaps be what you thought I was.

LORI: Because you're frightened?

PALMA: No!

LORI: Because you're sorry for me?

PALMA: No!

LORI: You are nothing to me, and I am nothing to you, nothing . . . and never shall be. [*He frees himself, and pushes her from him.*] And if you only knew how clearly I see now, all at once, how many years of nothing I've had to live through!

# ACT THREE

---

*A large writing-room in* SALVO MANFRONI'S *house, decorated with austere magnificence. The door to the hall is on the left. The same night as Act Two, a few hours later.*

> MARTINO LORI *is alone on the stage as the curtain rises. His face is like a dead man's: the eyes fixed, and as though unseeing. He has been waiting for a long time, in the silence of the house. From time to time his face reflects the feelings that are fighting inside him. Every now and then he shakes himself and mutters a few unintelligible words to himself, accompanied by rapid gestures. Occasionally he also unconsciously loses himself in some distraction which appears at once strange and perfectly natural: for example, he goes across to the desk to examine very attentively some object on it which has aroused a childish curiosity in him, simply because his glance happens to have fallen on it. But as soon as he reaches the desk, he stops, dazed, no longer knowing why he has risen; and gripped once more by his inner anguish, he begins soundlessly talking to himself again; but the object on the desk once more attracts his attention, and he picks it up, almost without knowing that he does so, and looks at it as if he could not quite see it, and still holding it in his hand, pursues his tormented thoughts; then he places the object down and returns to his former place.*]

> [MANFRONI'S *old* MANSERVANT *comes in from the hall.*]

MANSERVANT: Ah, you're still waiting, Signor Lori. I don't know why Senator Manfroni isn't back yet. He's usually in long before this, at his reading or writing. It's almost midnight.

LORI: Oh, yes, I've just remembered: he went – where was it? He did tell me . . . just before he went out. [*He remembers that* MANFRONI *had asked him to tell* PALMA *that he was going out with* GUALDI *and* BONGIANI; *but it seems useless to go on.*]

... To a meeting ... with his ... [*He has almost said 'son-in-law'; with a faint smile which is almost a sob.*] Yes, yes ... and the other one ... Bongiani.

MANSERVANT: To a meeting?

LORI: The opening meeting of some new club, I think it was. He didn't want to go, but his ... [*Again he almost says 'son-in-law' but simply adds*] his ... [*And he looks once more at the* MANSERVANT: *then he begins to smile again, as though the sight of the old man sends a chilling thought across his mind, and he points a finger towards him.*] You must have been here with him a long time?

MANSERVANT: With Senator Manfroni! Oh, yes ...

LORI: From the time he first went into Parliament?

MANSERVANT: For about twenty-five years, sir.

LORI [*with a horrible smile, winking*]: You'll have seen her here then, I suppose?

MANSERVANT [*astonished*]: What did you say, sir?

LORI: Aha! Adventures, eh? A young politician's adventures.

SERVANT [*evasively*]: Women, you mean, sir?

LORI: Too many to count, no doubt!

MANSERVANT: Perhaps, when he was younger ...

LORI: Young, newly-married women. And later on, when he became a Minister, the young wives of his subordinates. [*He observes that the* MANSERVANT *is disturbed by this, and at once adds, slyly*] I was his office-chief, and I know. ... Confidential posts! You don't get those, except at a certain well-known price. [*Pale and laughing, he makes the well-known gesture indicating a cuckold. The* MANSERVANT *looks at him in amazement. A pause.*]

MANSERVANT [*sighing*]: That was all years ago, Signor Lori.

LORI: Yes, we're getting old, aren't we? It's all a long time ago! [*Pause. The* MANSERVANT, *more than ever bewildered, looks at him once more. But he is lost in thought, as though he could see his young wife before him, there in the writing-room: he is speaking almost to himself*] She was lovely. ... Her eyes, when she spoke ... She seemed irradiated. [*Uttering the words distinctly*] Shining, bright ... [*Then, with love, as though caressing some distant, secret memory of her*] She wanted to impress you with her intelligence. But when a woman is so beautiful, you watch her eyes and mouth. You smile at her lips when they speak, without noticing what they're saying. She used to notice all of a sudden and get angry with me. ... Then – like a woman – she'd smile at you for smiling: it was as if she were responding to the kiss your eyes had laid on her lips. And then ... [*He pauses, lost in thought; then shakes his head and asks*] But was it for me alone? [*Suddenly turning, transfigured, to the* MANSERVANT] Who knows how often he must have held her in his arms and kissed her, in this very room?

MANSERVANT [*genuinely disturbed*]: Signor Lori ...

LORI: But what's it matter? It's all past and done with, isn't it? We all know that!

[*At this moment* SALVO MANFRONI *appears in the doorway, still with his hat and coat on.*]

MANSERVANT [*with a start*]: Ah, here is the Senator ...

SALVO: What, you here, Martino? What's the matter? [*Alarmed*] Has anything happened?

LORI: No. I've got to talk to you.

SALVO [*remembering their earlier scene that evening; annoyed*]: Again? At this time of night?

LORI: No. Only a couple of words. Just to get things clear. [*Meanwhile the* MANSERVANT *has taken* MANFRONI'S *coat, hat, and stick; he goes out on* LORI'S *last words.*]

SALVO [*crossing the room with outstretched hand*]: Well then?

LORI [*pushing his hand brusquely aside*]: No. We won't shake hands.

SALVO [*stopping short*]: What do you mean?

LORI: Wait a bit. When we've got things straight, then I'll shake hands with you.

SALVO: But what's the matter?

LORI: Nothing! Nothing! By the grace of God, there's no need for explanations. The facts are clear and undeniable.

So much so that you and everyone else were quite certain I knew; so there's no need to argue.

SALVO: But please, whatever are you talking about?

LORI: I've simply come to bring you two pieces of news, and to satisfy a curiosity.

SALVO [*watching his movements*]: Why . . . I can hardly recognize you, Martino.

LORI: Of course not! I've become a different man in the last three hours.

SALVO: But whatever's happened?

LORI: Nothing. Everything's been turned upside down, that's all. The world suddenly becomes a different place, something one never thought was possible. I've opened my eyes at last!

SALVO: Have you been talking to Palma?

LORI [*nods several times: then*]: You'll be amazed! [*He detaches the words from each other, deliberately*] I – knew – nothing – at – all!

SALVO [*astounded*]: You . . . you didn't know?

LORI: Not a thing. Either that my wife had been your mistress, or that Palma was your daughter . . .

SALVO: *She* told you?

LORI: *She* told me. That you'd told *her*: that she was your daughter; and that I knew.

SALVO: Well, isn't it true?

LORI [*simply*]: No. It isn't true. I knew nothing at all. [*Then, as* MANFRONI *stares at him in astonishment*] Yes! It's incredible. For the last three hours I've been asking myself: *how?* How could they have made it plainer than they did? They've *sung* it to you in every way they knew; shown you clearly, every day, in every way! How can you have imagined that a Member of Parliament, who never even knew you, could have taken you up, a humble office secretary; and when he became a Minister of State, could put you at the head of his office staff, simply because you'd married the daughter of his former teacher? And then, when your wife died, could be so kind to your daughter, and bring her up almost as if she were his own, and find her a husband, and give her an enormous dowry? I believed in that woman's honesty, d'you see? I believed she died too soon! But even if she'd lived for ever, I'd never have noticed anything, don't you see? Because – oh, yes, it's unbelievable, isn't it – to me she was honest! And I believed in your friendship too: in the great sun's light you brought into the house, illuminating me, blinding me. . . . I believed in your reverence for your old teacher, even though I'd had the proof that it was something far different from reverence you felt!

SALVO [*abruptly*]: What do you mean?

LORI: That's the other piece of news I have for you! Wait! I must tell you the whole story. When I had that other proof, it was worse.

SALVO [*as before*]: Proof? What proof?

LORI: The proof – the proof that complicated everything, because it showed me that my own simplicity was lying on a bed of thorns, thorns that pricked it on all sides and made it bleed, made it suffer! But oh, how boldly you gathered the thorns up, and took them, and made a hair-shirt out of them for me: something I had to learn to wear, and understand in a new way! But it was still something that simplicity *can* understand – as we all know! [*The telephone rings on the desk.*] Ah, yes! They're calling you on the telephone.

SALVO: They? [*He moves to take up the receiver.*]

LORI [*holding his arm*]: No. Wait. Tell them to come here.

SALVO: Here? Are you mad? Why?

LORI: Because I want them to! [*The telephone rings again.*]

SALVO: At this time of night?

LORI: It won't take them two minutes in the car.

SALVO: But what do you want them to come here for? [*Telephone.*]

LORI: You hear how urgent it is. It's Palma. She wants to tell you about her conversation with me. [*Telephone.*] Answer it. Go on.

SALVO: No. Not if you don't tell me why you want them to come.

LORI: I want us to clear things up, all four of us.

SALVO: What things? Isn't everything cleared up already!

LORI: No. There's the future. There are many things to be arranged.

SALVO: We can do that tomorrow, if necessary!

LORI: No! Tonight! [*Telephone.*]

SALVO [*picking up the receiver*]: Hello? [*Pause.*] Yes, Palma . . .

LORI: Tell her I'm here.

SALVO [*into the telephone*]: Yes . . . I know . . . I know . . . [*Pause.*] What? [*Pause.*] Yes. Listen . . . He's here with me.

LORI: Tell them to come at once, now.

SALVO [*into the telephone*]: Yes, unfortunately . . . Look . . . [*Pause.*] What? [*Pause.*] Yes, yes . . . But it'll be best if you come round. [*Pause.*] Yes, of course. Straight away. [*Pause.*] To talk about it. [*Pause.*] With Flavio, yes. What?

LORI: Doesn't she want to come?

SALVO [*to* LORI]: No, she says she doesn't know if the car – [*Breaks off, to speak into the telephone.*] Yes. Yes, all right. I'll expect you, then. Come as soon as you can. [*He replaces the receiver.*] What is it you want the four of us to talk about?

LORI: You and I shall talk first. I want to know when it was!

SALVO: Be quiet!

LORI: No. Answer me. Immediately after we were married? [SALVO *shrugs his shoulders.*] Answer me. Had you already fixed it up, as soon as she came from Perugia?

SALVO: No! I never even thought of it, then!

LORI: Perhaps *she* thought of it?

SALVO: No, no! [*More mildly*] At least, I don't know. I don't think so.

LORI: Then was it when she began to make so much fuss about wanting to take up teaching again?

SALVO [*in order to stop his questions*]: Yes! Yes!

LORI: The day I didn't find her at home?

SALVO: What's the use of brooding over it now?

LORI: She wanted to do what her mother had done. She wanted to go away. To come away with you. Ah, but you had your political career to think of!

SALVO: Stop it, please stop!

LORI: And you persuaded the wandering lamb to return to the fold!

SALVO: I don't know what pleasure you get from –

LORI: But it's still tormenting me! It's still tormenting me!

SALVO: I know, I know. But think how long it's been over and done with. She's dead.

LORI [*in a coarse, horrible outburst, as the wish for revenge rises in him*]: She hated you, she hated you, when she came back to me! She realized your ambition meant more to you than she did, and she hated you!

SALVO: Yes, I know she did.

LORI: And she hated the fruit of her love, inside her, too. She never wanted to be a mother, she never wanted to, I know. She was my mistress, far more than she was ever Palma's mother. And even when I was happy, I was distressed at that. For the child's sake, the child I thought was mine, born of our reconciliation.

SALVO: Don't say any more, Martino, please!

LORI: No more? My dear Salvo, this is only the beginning!

SALVO: The beginning of what?

LORI: You'll soon see. It's taken me nineteen years to grasp all this. Now it's all over, you say, very politely, like any well-bred gentleman –

SALVO: But, please –

LORI: – Like all people who know the right way to behave – now it's all over, you think there's nothing more to say. The wife's been dead sixteen years, the daughter's married – that's all there is to it, you think. There's the door: good luck! Oh, no! Now it's my turn. I understand everything now. I've gone over the whole thing.

SALVO: Can't you see all this is crazy?

LORI: No. I'm quite clear in my mind. I've thought it all out. I can see it all. I'm speaking and behaving like this because I can't help it. I'm like a runaway horse. Everything keeps darting out from the shadows at me, on all sides, lashing out at me. But I know at last what I'm going to do. And you can look out! [*Seizing him by the arm.*] First of all: are you convinced at last that I'm not the despicable thing you all made me out to be?

SALVO: Of course! That's why I can't see –

LORI: What more is there to be done? There's nothing, you think? I must have known from the start, and been the lowest of the low to profit from the situation: that's what you thought, isn't it? But I didn't know: so now, you think, after nineteen years . . . But you're wrong!

SALVO: Would you want to profit from it now?

LORI: No! You're wrong, because if I'd known at the time, I'd never have profited! I'd have killed you!

SALVO: You're not thinking of killing me now?

LORI: No, I know there's nothing I can do now! Nothing – [*He breaks off as a new and agitating idea flashes across his mind.*] But wait! Profit from it now, you said? And . . . and how could I – how could I, after all this time?

SALVO [*hesitatingly*]: I don't know, I . . . I could still do something for you, perhaps . . .

LORI [*after a terrifying glance at him, almost leaps at his throat, making him fall into an armchair, and clutching at his coat*]: You! By God, you deserve to be killed now for saying that! [*He lets go of him. His earlier thought recurs to him.*] Get up. Pull yourself together. Perhaps, perhaps there is a way of profiting . . . [PALMA *and* FLAVIO *come in at this moment, from the hall, anxious and apprehensive. Seeing them*] Ah, here they are!

PALMA: What's the matter? What's happened?

LORI: Nothing, nothing, Palma! We've cleared it all up, the whole thing's quite straight now. I recalled a few facts and a few precise dates, and he's had to admit he made a mistake. It's not true you're his daughter. You're *my* daughter: *my* daughter, Palma! [*To* SALVO] Go on, tell them, say it out loud, here, to both of them! You had to admit it, didn't you?

SALVO: Yes, it's true.

[*There is a moment's silence.*]

LORI: It's true. [*To* FLAVIO] You understand what that means?

FLAVIO [*a mere murmur*]: I understand.

LORI: No, what I mean is that the respect that is naturally due to your wife's father, will in future be due to me: because I'm her father. I'm her father!

FLAVIO [*as before*]: Yes, very well . . .

LORI: And in future you won't dare to treat me as an intruder, like someone who never knew the proper way to play the various parts you cast him for! You made me play them without knowing what I was supposed to be doing, all of them: the complaisant deceived husband; the friend; the widower; the father-in-law. I played them all very badly. Yes! I didn't know how they ought to be played, did I? But now I do know, now I do know: you'll see! [*He has been so carried away by a tide of passion that he does not realize that he has overstepped the mark, and that it has become apparent that he has been pretending, since the arrival of* PALMA *and* FLAVIO.]

PALMA [*as she realizes, in amazement*]: What?

FLAVIO [*also astonished, turning to* SALVO, *who is standing aloof*]: What does he mean?

LORI [*recovering*]: What do I mean? [*He turns to* PALMA.] I mean . . . I mean your mother – oh yes, her betrayal still remains, alas – but the other outrage doesn't. No! That outrage isn't true, it's not true! [*There is a long silence.* SALVO MANFRONI *and* FLAVIO *stand looking at the ground.* PALMA *looks bewildered, in anxious suspense.* LORI *looks at the two men; then at* PALMA. *He observes her perplexity, and understands it; and he too feels, as it were, a sudden dismay at the effect on her of his own reiterated assertion, and at the fabrication he is stubbornly trying to keep up. Nevertheless, almost in defiance of*

*his own feelings, he repeats his last words, going tenderly up to
her, in a different voice, almost suffused with irony at the transient
satisfaction it has given him.*] It isn't true! Though perhaps
that displeases you? Does it? Tell the truth: you're not glad,
are you?

PALMA: Yes ... Yes, I am ...

LORI [*looking into her eyes, unable to believe her*]: You are?

PALMA: Yes.

LORI: Glad that *I'm* your father?

PALMA: Yes.

LORI: I, and not him?

PALMA: Yes, I tell you.

LORI: Even though I'm a poor man whom you despised till a
short time ago ...?

PALMA: Yes, for that very reason!

LORI: Someone who'll always be despised by everyone – because I shall never be able to make anyone believe I didn't
know: you realize that? If I tell them, they'll only laugh!

PALMA: But *I* believe you! I believed you the minute you told
me. I'm even more ready to believe you, now you tell me
that what he [*she indicates* MANFRONI] thought was wrong!

LORI [*moved, shivering, almost horrified by the abyss this seems to
open before him*]: You see? You see? It's frightful! You learn
something: and everything changes, changes immediately.
It was like that with me, a few hours ago. I thought I was
your father: and you despised me, because you knew you
weren't my daughter. But now that you begin to think I *am*
your father, and are completely changed towards me, I
can't, I can't take you in my arms again, because I know, I
know you're *not* my daughter, and that I'm only play-acting
in front of him, in front of your husband and you!

PALMA [*stupefied*]: Play-acting?

FLAVIO: But, for heaven's sake ...!

LORI [*nervously, harshly, almost with a malign effort to protect himself against the depth of his feelings*]: Play-acting! I did it well,
didn't I? So well that for a moment you were all taken in!

[*With a bitter ghost of a laugh*] Haha! So was I, even without
meaning to be. [*He passes a hand across his eyes, and shows it
to them.*] Look! I've even been crying! [*Turning to* FLAVIO]
No, don't worry! Don't worry!

FLAVIO: Then . . . it's not true?

LORI: It's not true. I've tried; but I can't. It revolts me. It
makes me weep . . .

SALVO: Then let's stop all this, for God's sake!

LORI [*turning sharply on him*]: You don't like it? Yet *this* farce
at least ought to have gone on. The drama passed into my
life before I realized; and now I can't keep it up any longer!
But don't you worry either. I can't even play-act any more.
I know! If I hadn't told them, you'd have gone round there
tomorrow and explained that you'd had to pretend to accept it all in front of them, because you were sorry for the
state I was in; and you'd have persuaded them to accept me
as well. . . .

SALVO: No! Why do you think that?

LORI [*violently*]: Because I'm not a fool!

SALVO: Who said you were?

LORI: Ah, you were all quite happy to think I was merely
contemptible! But, no, I was a fool as well. But I could only
go on being a fool so long as I went on believing in pure
and sacred things: honesty, friendship! And I don't any
more! And even if I could still submit to being the despicable creature you made me think I was, I couldn't go on
being humble and timid and shy – the poor devil who used
to go and behave like a clown every day at the cemetery. Do
you realize that? It's obvious! So . . . so I . . . I . . . [*He gazes
round in perplexity, as though looking for, and not finding, some
way of escape: sketches a vague, empty gesture in the air: and
buries his face in his hands.*] Oh God, how . . . how am I to
go on living?

SALVO: Stop! Why must you talk like this?

PALMA: And if it's all over . . .

LORI: But that's just the reason! It's because it's all over that

can't go on living! If it's all over . . .! If I can't destroy the
thing I was to other people! It's here – in *my own body* – in
my own eyes, which used to look out and never see what I
was to other people; in this hand I used to stretch out to
people without ever realizing it was the hand of someone
they all laughed at or despised! How can I ever look at people
now; or offer them my hand? *I'm* the one who feels contempt and loathing now: yes, for my own self! – the self I
see and feel myself to be: *someone who isn't me, someone who
never has been me* – and someone I long to be rid of, to be rid
of! [*He indicates, as he says this, that he wishes to leave.*] To be
rid of . . .!

SALVO [*barring his way*]: What are you going to do?

LORI [*looks at him, as though in a dream – then, as he remembers*]:
Ah, yes: there's something else, isn't there? I was forgetting.
The one thing I can do against you. And I'll do it: not because it matters to me, but I'll do it to show you I'm not a
fool. I'm going to take my revenge, in cold blood, in the
one way left to me: by making of you what you've made of
me: leaving you alive, as you left me, with no one to respect
you any more; showing that you're the one to be despised.
Yes, you! *This* is the man [*he turns to* PALMA *and* FLAVIO]
to despise: this man you were so proud to have as a father,
this is the man to despise, not only because of what he did
to me, but because he's a thief!

SALVO [*threateningly standing over him*]: What?

LORI [*boldly facing him*]: A thief! A thief! [*Turning to the other
two*] He's a thief, because he stole from Bernardo Agliani!

SALVO [*bursts into a deep laugh*]: Hahaha!

LORI [*looks at him for a time, then turns to* PALMA *and* FLAVIO]:
It makes him laugh. I've proof of it at home!

SALVO: Have they made you believe that, too? Did they make
the proof up for you at Perugia?

LORI: No. It's in Agliani's own handwriting.

SALVO [*pointing to his desk*]: But I've got all Agliani's papers
here.

LORI: No, not all of them.

SALVO: Yes, all of them.

LORI: No, not all.

SALVO [*disconcerted at* LORI'*s reiteration*]: Unless . . . unless you have some others I'm unaware of.

LORI: You're confused now, aren't you?

SALVO: No!

LORI: You went pale. And now you're beginning to blush!

SALVO: Well, because, naturally, I wouldn't like it if Agliani, in some other, later, notes –

LORI: No: they're earlier: the very first! The first draft of the copy you have.

SALVO: But in the papers of Agliani's that I have here, there's nothing that –

LORI: You haven't got all of them!

SALVO: I have! All of them!

LORI: Yes, all you saw fit to preserve. The rest you'll have destroyed!

SALVO: That's a slander!

LORI: I can prove it to you.

SALVO: Prove what? All you'll be able to prove – is that – is that the same idea may also have occurred to Agliani in connexion with his own problems.

LORI: Yes: excellent. But not to Agliani *also*. To him *alone* You appropriated it for yourself. [*He turns to* PALMA *and* FLAVIO.] I've the notes at home: a pile like this!

SALVO: All right! Prove it to me then, that in these notes I have in here [*he beats furiously on the desk*] there's the slightest suggestion of that idea! Prove it!

LORI: Ah, you don't deny it any more: you challenge me!

SALVO [*contemptuously*]: Why should I challenge anyone like you? Who do you think is going to take your word against mine, if I swear that I've never known – and it's quite true – about these new notes of Agliani's, and if I produce the papers of his I have here?

LORI: Quite so! If it weren't for your book . . .

SALVO [*once more disconcerted*]: My book?

LORI: They'll have to believe *that*. Not me, no; but your book, yes. The proof's there!

SALVO [*as before*]: In my book?

LORI [*turning to the others*]: How do you think anyone as ignorant as I am could understand anything at all in those formulae and calculations? The evidence of the theft sprang right out at me, without even being looked for, when I compared those notes with your book.

SALVO: You're not worth answering!

LORI: I discovered it long ago – and I kept silent for her sake [*pointing to* PALMA] – for the kindness you showed my daughter, because I never knew about your other crime, of which this is perhaps only the accidental consequence. Because *you* have never felt any *genuine* passion, have you? These papers of Agliani's were only, to begin with, a means of hiding your intrigue: an excuse for being in my house, with her! If you've nothing to fear, would you like me to publish the notes I have at home, just as they are? I'd have come and brought them to you –

SALVO [*at once*]: Give them to me, and I'll publish them myself, acknowledging before everyone –

LORI: What? Your unadmitted appropriation?

SALVO [*violently*]: That it never was! And no one will ever believe it was!

LORI: Quite. . . . Your word against mine. . . . [*Turning to* PALMA, *and noticing her expression of mingled scorn and dejection*] Look! It'll be enough for me if *she* believes me – if she takes my word: the word of someone who's kept quiet for her sake – someone who'll say no more, after tonight! What do you think your book matters to me? Or who's written it! Or you! [*He grasps* PALMA'S *arm, and looks into her eyes.*] Do you believe me?

PALMA: Yes!

LORI: You believe me, and not him?

PALMA: Yes! Yes!

LORI: Then that's all I want! I won't publish anything! I won't do anything! I came here meaning to do God knows what against him, against everyone. My weapons have all dropped from my hands. What weapons? I have none! Not so much as a pin. And what good would it do? What I've done is little, and petty, and nasty.... I'm ashamed of it myself, now.... [*He turns again to* PALMA] You do believe me?

PALMA: Yes! Yes!

[*A pause.*]

LORI: That's all I want. Good-bye.

PALMA [*distressed, running to him and throwing her arms round him, to keep him from going*]: Ah, no, no! I shan't let you go! You've got to live! To live! That's all that must matter to you!

LORI: No ... no ...

PALMA [*urgently*]: What do you mean: no? When you have all my respect and affection now! [*She gestures to* FLAVIO *to come closer and join them.*] The respect of everyone ...

FLAVIO [*going to them*]: Yes, of course you have.

LORI [*gloomily, almost harshly*]: The only person I can ever be reconciled with now, without being cheated, is the one who was sorry for her sin, and atoned for it with her love. The only real, living thing I had, after the crime. All the rest has been a sham. The one who cheated me most, cheated me least. I could never join in your life again, without feeling disgust for myself and for the rest of you.

PALMA: No, no! Why disgust? Don't feel disgust! When you said that he [*she indicates* SALVO] had deceived everyone about me –

LORI: But I wasn't telling the truth!

PALMA: But I believed you at once, the minute I came in with Flavio. And everyone else will believe it as well. I shall make them believe it, all of them, because they'll all see how much we respect you and care for you –

LORI: You? But you surely can't tell people –

PALMA: There'll be no need to tell them anything! They'll see me with you, near you, round you, as they've never seen me before! And they'll all agree then that –

LORI [*in a last effort to oppose her kindness, which surrounds and disturbs him, and is almost more than he can bear*]: But . . . But *I* can't believe it!

PALMA: But you will! You will believe it! You'll have to; they'll make you!

LORI [*as before*]: Make me? How?

PALMA: Why, because it's real, don't you see? My affection for you is a *real* affection, now! There's no pretence about it! My affection and respect for you are a *reality*, in which you can live. It will force itself on everyone, even on you!

FLAVIO: It's true! It's true! It *will* be like that.

LORI [*exhausted, weary, and almost broken by so much excitement, leans on* PALMA'S *arm; then looks up wanly, and almost stammers*]: It . . . it'll be play-acting then?

PALMA: Not at all! There'll be no play-acting! They'll see how *really* fond of you I am.

FLAVIO: Of course they will. It *will* be like that.

LORI [*to* FLAVIO]: And it'll all be for the best?

PALMA [*affectionately, embracing him, and almost holding him up*]: Come. Come away now. You must be so tired! Let's go. We'll take you back home.

FLAVIO: Yes, it's getting very late.

PALMA: The car's down below; it won't take us long. . . .

LORI: Home . . . in a car. . . . Ah, yes . . . all for the best . . . all for the best. . . . [*He begins to move away with* PALMA, *almost childishly, followed by* FLAVIO. *After a few paces he stops, turns, looks at* SALVO MANFRONI, *and, pointing at him, says to* PALMA.] And . . what about him?

PALMA [*watching him, uncertainly*]: What do you mean?

LORI: We must say goodnight to him, mustn't we? [*He waves a hand in salutation to* SALVO, *and also makes a slight bow in his direction; then, turning back to* PALMA] All for the best. . . .

# HENRY IV

*Enrico Quarto*

TRANSLATED BY FREDERICK MAY

F

This play, translated by Edward Storer, was first presented professionally in English at the Everyman Theatre, London, on 15 July 1925, with the following cast:

| | |
|---|---|
| . . . . . (HENRY IV) | Ernest Milton |
| THE MARCHIONESS MATILDA SPINA | Nancy Price |
| FRIDA | Beatrice Filmer |
| MARQUIS CHARLES DI NOLLI | Ronald Nicholson |
| BARON TITO BELCREDI | Frank Vosper |
| DOCTOR DIONISIO GENONI | Stanley Lathbury |
| LANDOLPH | Grosvenor North |
| HAROLD | Robert Glennie |
| ORDULPH | Godfrey Winn |
| BERTHOLD | Geoffrey Wincott |
| ATTENDANTS | Herbert Anstey |
| | Dennis Hosking |
| JOHN | Geoffrey Dunlop |

Produced by A. E. Filmer

Frederick May's version was first presented by the University of Leeds Theatre Group at the Riley-Smith Theatre, Leeds, on 10 March 1953, with the following cast:

| | |
|---|---|
| . . . . . (HENRY IV) | Malcolm Rogers |
| THE MARCHIONESS MATILDA SPINA | Maureen Laird |
| FRIDA | June Melling |
| MARQUIS CHARLES DI NOLLI | Geoffrey Morley |
| BARON TITO BELCREDI | Barrington Black |
| DOCTOR DIONISIO GENONI | Cyril Jacob |
| LANDOLPH | Arthur Cockerill |
| HAROLD | Eric Buchanan |
| ORDULPH | Derek Boughton |
| BERTHOLD | Raymond Whiteley |
| ATTENDANTS | Derek Esp |
| | Gerald Bolton |
| JOHN | Jim Frankland |

Produced by Tim Evens

# CHARACTERS

..... (HENRY IV)

The Marchioness MATILDA SPINA

Her daughter FRIDA

The young Marquis CHARLES DI NOLLI

Baron TITO BELCREDI

Doctor DIONISIO GENONI

The four make-believe Privy Counsellors:

     The first, LANDOLPH (LOLO)

     The second, HAROLD (FRANCO)

     The third, ORDULPH (MOMO)

     The fourth, BERTHOLD (FINO)

Two LACKEYS (RETAINERS) in costume

The old manservant JOHN

SCENE: A lonely villa in the Umbrian countryside
TIME: The present (1921)

# ACT ONE

*A large hall in the villa, which has been decorated and furnished so as to provide as nearly as possible an exact reconstruction of the throne-room of Henry IV in the imperial palace at Goslar. But in the midst of the antique furnishings are two modern full-length, life-size portraits in oils. They stand out boldly from the wall back, a little above the level of the stage, and are held in position by a ledge of carved wood running along the bottom of them and continuing the whole length of the wall. This ledge juts out somewhat – it is, in fact, rather like a very long bench, and sufficiently wide to be used as a seat. The portraits stand on the right and left of the throne, which is placed in the middle of the wall back and breaks the line of the ledge. The imperial seat has a low-hanging baldachin over it. The two portraits represent a young lady and a young gentleman dressed up in carnival costumes, she as the Marchioness Matilda of Tuscany, he as Henry IV. There are doors left and right.*

[*When the curtain rises, the two* LACKEYS, *as if caught unawares, jump down from the ledge on which they have been lying, and go and stand like statues, halberd in hand, at the foot of the steps leading up to the throne – one to the left, one to the right. Shortly after, through the second door on the right, there enter* HAROLD, LANDOLPH, ORDULPH, *and* BERTHOLD, *young men employed by the* MARQUIS CHARLES DI NOLLI *to play the parts of 'privy counsellors' – royal vassals drawn from the lower aristocracy – at the Court of Henry IV. They are dressed, therefore, as German knights of the eleventh century. The last mentioned,* BERTHOLD – *whose real name is* FINO – *is just taking up his duties for the first time. His three companions are telling him what he has to do and deriving a great deal of fun from the process. The whole scene should be played with great liveliness: vivacity touched by fantasy is its keynote.*]

LANDOLPH [*to* BERTHOLD, *as if in the middle of an explanation*]:
And this is the throne-room!

HAROLD: At Goslar!

ORDULPH: Or, if you prefer it, at the Castle in the Hartz!

HAROLD: Or at Worms!

LANDOLPH: According to what bit we're playing, it jumps
about with us. Now it's one place, now another.

ORDULPH: Saxony!

HAROLD: Lombardy!

LANDOLPH: On the Rhine!

FIRST LACKEY [*without moving, his lips scarcely parting*]: Psst!
Psst!

HAROLD [*turning at the sound*]: What's the matter?

FIRST LACKEY [*in a low voice, still as a statue*]: Is he coming in
here or not? [*He is alluding to* HENRY IV.]

ORDULPH: No, no! He's asleep. You can take it easy.

SECOND LACKEY [*relaxes his pose, takes a deep breath and lies
down again on the ledge*]: God, man, you might have told us!

FIRST LACKEY [*who has also relaxed, going up to* HAROLD]:
Have you got a match, please?

LANDOLPH: Hey! You can't smoke a pipe in here!

[HAROLD *meanwhile has struck a match.*]

FIRST LACKEY: No, only a cigarette. [*Lights his cigarette at the
match which* HAROLD *is holding. Then he too goes and lies down
again on the ledge, smoking away.*]

[*Meanwhile* BERTHOLD *has been walking round the room and
has been watching this little scene, torn between amazement and
perplexity. The more he studies his own costume and that of the
others, the longer he looks at the throne-room, the more amazed
and perplexed he becomes.*]

BERTHOLD: I say ... This room ... And these clothes ...
Which Henry IV is it? ... You've got me flummoxed. ...
Is it Henry IV of France or isn't it?

[*At this question* LANDOLPH, HAROLD, *and* ORDULPH
*burst into noisy laughter.*]

LANDOLPH [*his voice suffused with laughter*]: Henry IV of

France, he says! [*As he says this, he is pointing to* BERTHOLD, *as if inviting his laughing companions to make fun of him too.*]

ORDULPH [*laughing away, gesturing in the direction of* BERTHOLD]: He thought it was Henry IV of France!

HAROLD: My dear fellow, it's Henry IV of Germany! The Salian Dynasty!

ORDULPH: The great and tragic Emperor!

LANDOLPH: You know, the one at Canossa! Here, day after day, we carry on a truly terrible war between Church and State! Ho, ho!

ORDULPH: The Empire against the Papacy! Ho, ho!

HAROLD: Anti-popes against Popes!

LANDOLPH: Kings against anti-kings!

ORDULPH: And war against the Saxons!

HAROLD: And all the rebel princes!

LANDOLPH: Against the Emperor's own sons!

BERTHOLD [*putting his hands over his ears to protect himself against this avalanche of information*]: I get it! I get it! Of course, I couldn't work out what it was all about at first! You know, I was quite right! I *knew* there was something wrong the moment I came in here. I looked at myself dressed up like this, and I said to myself, 'These costumes don't belong to the sixteenth century!'

HAROLD: Sixteenth century be damned!

ORDULPH: At this moment and in this room we are some-where between the year 1000 and the year 1100!

LANDOLPH: You can work it out for yourself. . . . If on the 25th of January 1077 we are before Canossa . . .

BERTHOLD [*more dismayed than ever*]: Oh, my God! What a mess I've made of it!

ORDULPH: I'll say you have, if you thought we were at the French Court!

BERTHOLD: But all that historical stuff I swotted up . . .

LANDOLPH: We, my dear boy, are four hundred years earlier! To us you're a mere babe in arms!

BERTHOLD [*anger coming into his voice*]: Hell, they might have

told me it was the German one and not Henry IV of
France! They gave me a fortnight to mug the part up! God
only knows how many books I've sweated through!

HAROLD: But didn't you know that poor Tito's job here was
to be Adalbert of Bremen?

BERTHOLD: Adalbert! I ask you! How the hell should I know
who Adalbert was?

LANDOLPH: No, of course not. But you see how it is. . . .
When Tito died, the young Marquis di Nolli . . .

BERTHOLD: Yes, that's the chap! It's all *his* fault! It wouldn't
have hurt him to have told me . . .

HAROLD: But perhaps he thought you knew already!

LANDOLPH: He didn't want to take on any one else to fill his
place. He thought the three of us who were left could quite
well manage by ourselves. But then *he* began. . . . He'd suddenly cry out, 'With Adalbert driven away . . .' Because,
you see, it didn't occur to him that poor Tito was dead. . . .
He thought that as Bishop Adalbert he'd been driven from
the Court by his rivals, the Bishops of Cologne and Mainz.

BERTHOLD [*burying his head in his hands*]: But I don't understand a word of all this rigmarole!

ORDULPH: Then you've had it, dear boy!

HAROLD: The trouble is, *we* don't know who you are either.

BERTHOLD: You don't . . .? D'you mean to say that not even
you know who I'm supposed to be?

ORDULPH: Hum! 'Berthold'.

BERTHOLD: Berthold! Why *Berthold*? *Which* Berthold?

LANDOLPH [*clearly he is imitating* HENRY IV]: 'They've driven
Adalbert away! So they've deprived me of Adalbert, have
they? Very well then, I want Berthold! I want Berthold!'
There he stood, shouting for Berthold.

HAROLD: And there *we* stood, all three of us, looking at
one another. . . . Wondering who this Berthold might be.

ORDULPH: And here you are, my dear fellow. . . . 'Berthold'!

LANDOLPH: I'm sure you'll make a dashing Berthold!

BERTHOLD [*rebelliously, making as if to leave*]: Oh, no! Not on your life! Thanks very much, but you won't catch me doing Berthold! I'm off! I'm getting out of here!

[HAROLD *and* ORDULPH *restrain him: all three are laughing.*]

HAROLD: Hang on a bit! Calm down! Don't get so worked up about it!

ORDULPH: After all, you don't have to be like Berthold in the fairy-story!

LANDOLPH: And if it's any comfort to you, *we* don't know who *we* are either! He's Harold. . . . He's Ordulph. . . . And I'm Landolph. That's what *he* calls us. We've got used to it now. But who are we? Names of the time. Well, yours is probably a name of the time, too. 'Berthold.' There was only one of us . . . poor Tito . . . who had a real part. . . . One that you can read about in the history books. . . . He was the Bishop of Bremen. He looked just like a bishop, too! He was a damned fine actor was Tito, poor devil! He had a magnificent line in bishops!

HAROLD: Yes! Look at the books he got through! He had a chance to mug up *his* part!

LANDOLPH: Why, he even ordered His Majesty about! He opposed his views, guided him, advised him in everything. . . . He was like a kind teacher and counsellor. We're 'coun- sellors' too, '*privy* counsellors'. But . . . well, you know what I mean . . . he was something special, and we're just the or- dinary, everyday article. Because it's written in the history books that Henry IV was hated by the upper aristocracy for having surrounded himself at Court with young men drawn from the lesser aristocracy.

ORDULPH: That's us!

LANDOLPH: Yes, petty royal vassals . . . devoted to the Em- peror . . . a little dissolute . . . light-hearted . . .

BERTHOLD: Have I got to be light-hearted too?

HAROLD: Of course you have! Just like us!

ORDULPH: And, let me tell you, it's none too easy!

LANDOLPH: It's a great pity really . . . because, with these costumes and with these superb sets, we could put on a magnificent historical show. The audiences simply lap them up these days. There's any amount of material for a play in the story of Henry IV, any amount! Why, you could make half a dozen tragedies out of his life, let alone one! Oh, well! There's nothing doing! We four and those two wretches there [*with a gesture in the direction of the lackeys*], when they come to attention and stand stiff and erect at the foot of the throne . . . well, we're . . . we're . . . just like that . . . with nobody to put us on, nobody to produce us in a scene or two. We're . . . how shall I put it? . . . form without content. We're worse off than the real privy counsellors of Henry IV . . . because . . . oh yes, they hadn't been given a part to play either. . . . But at least they didn't know that they were supposed to be playing a part. They played their part because they were playing their part. And it wasn't a part in their case. It was their *life*. They looked after their own interests at the expense of others. They sold investitures . . . and God only knows what else besides! We, on the other hand . . . well, here we are, dressed up like this, in this magnificent Court . . . and to do what? Nothing. . . . We're just like six puppets hung up on the wall, waiting for someone to come and take them down . . . waiting for someone to make them move like this or like that, and give them a word or two to say.

HAROLD: Oh no, dear boy! That's not quite true! We've got to give the right answers, you know! We've got to know what he's talking about! There's all hell let loose if he says something to you and you don't give him the kind of answer he wants!

LANDOLPH: Yes, that's true enough! Yes, it's only too true!

BERTHOLD: And you said there was nothing to do! How the devil am I going to give him the right answers if I've swotted up Henry IV of France, and now *he* turns out to be Henry IV of Germany?

[LANDOLPH, ORDULPH, *and* HAROLD *burst out laughing again.*]

HAROLD: You'd better get down to remedying that at once! If not sooner!

ORDULPH: Don't you worry, we'll help you out!

HAROLD: We've got hundreds of books on the subject in there! All you'll need to begin with is a quick run through the main points.

ORDULPH: You probably know all about it vaguely anyway. . . .

HAROLD: Look at this picture! [*He turns him round and shows him the picture of the Marchioness Matilda which is in the niche in the wall back.*] Who's that, for instance?

BERTHOLD [*looking at the picture*]: Who's that? Well, the first thing I'd like to say is . . . they're a bit out of place, aren't they? A couple of modern pictures in the middle of all this respectable antiquity. Or have I said the wrong thing?

HAROLD: Oh no, you're quite right! As a matter of fact, they weren't here to begin with. There are two niches there behind those paintings. There were to have been two statues in them, sculptured in the style of the time. When they were left empty, they filled them in with those two canvases.

LANDOLPH [*interrupting and continuing the story*]: It certainly would be a bit of a howler if they really were paintings.

BERTHOLD: What are they, then? *Aren't* they paintings?

LANDOLPH: Yes! Just you go up there and touch them! They're paintings all right! But for *him* . . . [*he points mysteriously to the right, alluding to* HENRY IV] . . . who *doesn't* touch them . . .

BERTHOLD: No? And what are they for *him*, then?

LANDOLPH: They're . . . But, mind . . . I'm only giving you what I *think's* the explanation of the way things are! But I'm willing to bet I'm not far out in my guess. They're images. The sort of images a mirror throws back at you. . . . Do you get my meaning? That one there [*pointing to the portrait of Henry IV*] represents *him* . . . the living man whose throne-room this is. . . . And, mind you, this throne-room's exactly in period . . . as it should be, of course. So what's there to be so amazed at? If they shoved a mirror in front of you here and now, wouldn't you see yourself in it as a modern, living man dressed in a period costume? Well, it's just as if there were two mirrors there, casting back living images in the midst of a world which . . . Oh, don't you worry, my dear fellow! . . . You'll see. . . . You'll see. . . . After you've lived here with us for a bit . . . it'll begin to come alive for you too.

BERTHOLD: Oh, no! Look . . . I've got no particular desire to go mad here!

HAROLD: Go mad be damned! You'll have a wonderful time!

BERTHOLD: But, I say . . . how have you all managed to become so learned?

LANDOLPH: My dear fellow, you can't go back through eight hundred years of history without picking up some kind of experience!

HAROLD: Now, come on! Let's get on with your education! You'll see, you'll have it all off pat in next to no time!

ORDULPH: At our school you too can become wise and learned!

BERTHOLD: Well, for heaven's sake, give me all the help you can! And pretty soon too! At least give me the main outlines!

HAROLD: Just you leave it to us! A bit here . . . a bit there. . . . He'll tell you this . . . I'll tell you that . . .

LANDOLPH: We'll put your wires on you and make sure you're in good working order . . . like a first-class and thoroughly accomplished marionette. Come on, let's get going! [*Takes him by the arm and starts to lead him out.*]

BERTHOLD [*stopping and looking towards the portrait on the wall*]: Wait a minute! You haven't told me who that is! Is she the Emperor's wife?

HAROLD: No. The Emperor's wife is Bertha of Susa, the sister of Amadeus II of Savoy.

ORDULPH: The Emperor can't stand her! He wants to be

young ... Like us! So he's thinking of putting her away.

LANDOLPH: That's his most ferocious enemy, Matilda, Marchioness of Tuscany!

BERTHOLD: I've got it. ... Wasn't she the one ...? Wasn't the Pope staying at her castle ...?

LANDOLPH: Dead right! At Canossa!

ORDULPH: Pope Gregory VII.

HAROLD: Our *bête noire*! But, come along! We must get moving!

[*All four are moving towards the right, so as to go out through the same door as they came in by, when the old retainer,* JOHN, *enters left, wearing butler's dress.*]

JOHN [*comes in hurriedly, and when he speaks there is a note of anxiety in his voice*]: Hey! Psst! Franco! Lolo!

HAROLD [*stopping and turning*]: What do you want?

BERTHOLD [*astonished at* JOHN'S *entry and at his coming into the throne-room in tails*]: Oh, I say! This is the last straw! He ... but I mean to say ... dressed like that ... in here ...

LANDOLPH: Out upon you, man of the twentieth century! [*And mock-menacingly he rushes over to him, accompanied by the other two, as if intent on throwing him out.*]

ORDULPH: Messenger of Gregory VII, away!

HAROLD: Away! Away!

JOHN [*defending himself from their onslaught*]: Oh, stop playing the fool! [*There is annoyance in his voice.*]

ORDULPH: Never! You shall not set foot in here!

HAROLD: Out! Out with the invader!

LANDOLPH [*to* BERTHOLD]: You see ... It's sheer magic! He's a demon conjured up by the Wizard of Rome! Out with your sword, man! Out with your sword! [*And he too claps his hand to his sword and starts to draw it.*]

JOHN [*shouting above the din*]: Oh, have done! Stop this fooling about, I tell you! The Marquis has arrived with some friends ...

LANDOLPH [*rubbing his hands*]: M'm! Good oh! And are there any ... um ... *ladies*?

ORDULPH [*also rubbing his hands*]: Old ones? Young ones?

JOHN: There are two gentlemen.

HAROLD: Yes, yes! But what about the ladies? The ladies, man! Who are they?

JOHN: The Marchioness and her daughter.

LANDOLPH [*in amazement*]: What did you say? The *Marchioness*?

ORDULPH [*similarly amazed*]: The Marchioness! Did you say the *Marchioness*?

JOHN: Yes! The Marchioness! The *Marchioness*!

HAROLD: And who are the gentlemen?

JOHN: I don't know.

HAROLD [*to* BERTHOLD]: You see, they've come to give us the content to go with our form!

ORDULPH: They're all messengers from Gregory VII! Now there'll be fun and games!

JOHN: Will you let me speak, or will you not?

HAROLD: Fire away! Fire away!

JOHN: I fancy that one of the two gentlemen is a doctor.

LANDOLPH: Oh, I get you, one of the usual sort!

HAROLD: Three cheers for Berthold! You've brought us luck, old man!

LANDOLPH: Just you wait and see how we manage him! We'll fix the doctor!

BERTHOLD: It looks to me as if I'm going to land myself in trouble right up to my neck, and very soon, too!

JOHN: Listen to what I've got to say! They want to come in here, into the throne-room.

LANDOLPH [*amazement and consternation mingling in his voice*]: What? She wants... The Marchioness wants to come in here?

HAROLD: We look like getting our content with a vengeance, if *she* comes in here!

LANDOLPH: We'll have a real tragedy on our hands!

BERTHOLD [*his curiosity aroused*]: Why? Tell me, why?

ORDULPH [*pointing to the portrait*]: Don't you realize that that's *her* portrait?

LANDOLPH: Her daughter's engaged to the Marquis.

HAROLD: But what have they come here for? Are we allowed to know?

ORDULPH: If he catches sight of her! Whee! there'll be trouble!

LANDOLPH: Perhaps he'll no longer be able to recognize her.

JOHN: Your job is to keep him in there, should he wake up.

ORDULPH: Oh, yes? I suppose that's your idea of a joke! And *how*, may I ask, am I to do it?

HAROLD: You know perfectly well what he's like!

JOHN: Oh, good Lord! You're to use force if you have to! Those were my orders! So go on! Off you go!

HAROLD: Yes, we'd better get going. He might be awake already, for all we know! It's late enough!

ORDULPH: Come on, then! Let's get going!

LANDOLPH [*to* JOHN, *as he goes off with the others*]: But afterwards you've got to tell us what all this is about!

JOHN [*shouting after them*]: Lock the door behind you, and hide the key! And this other door too! [*Pointing to the other door on the right.*]

 [LANDOLPH, HAROLD, BERTHOLD, *and* ORDULPH *exeunt through the second door on the right.*]

JOHN [*to the two lackeys*]: *And* you two! Go on! Off you go! That way! [*Pointing to the first door on the right*] Lock the door again behind you! And take the key away with you!

 [*The two lackeys exeunt through the first door on the right.* JOHN *goes to the door left and opens it to admit the* MARQUIS DI NOLLI.]

DI NOLLI: Have you done what I told you? Do they know what they've got to do?

JOHN: Yes, my Lord. Everything will be all right.

 [DI NOLLI *goes out again for a moment and returns with the others. First of all* BARON TITO BELCREDI *enters, accompanied by* DR DIONISIO GENONI. *Then the* MARCHIONESS

MATILDA SPINA *comes in with her daughter, the young* MARCHIONESS FRIDA. JOHN *bows and exit.*

[DONNA MATILDA *is about forty-five. She is still beautiful, and still has a good figure. There are only too evident signs of her having sought to repair the inevitable ravages of time by means of make-up – but for all the, one might say,* violence *of that make-up, it is extremely skilfully done. As a result, her head puts you in mind of the proud head of a Valkyrie. Her make-up stands out in a kind of relief, and there is a profoundly disturbing conflict to be observed in her mouth, where extreme beauty and extreme sorrow are commingled. She has been a widow for many years and she now has as her lover* BARON TITO BELCREDI, *whom neither she nor anyone else has ever taken seriously. At least, that is how things appear on the surface. What, at bottom,* TITO BELCREDI *really is for her, he alone knows. He can therefore afford to laugh if his mistress finds she needs to pretend not to know what their relationship is. And so he is always able to respond with a laugh to the jests which the Marchioness makes at his expense, and good-humouredly to meet the mocking laughter which her sallies prompt among their acquaintance. He is slim, prematurely grey, a little younger than she, and his head is curiously bird-like in shape. He would be a very vivacious person if his litheness and agility – which have made him a redoubtable swordsman – were not sheathed in a somnolent, Arab-like sloth, which manifests itself particularly in his strange nasal drawl.*

[FRIDA, *the* MARCHIONESS'S *daughter, is nineteen. She is a sad person because her imperious and too beautiful mother rather over-shadows her. Her life is saddened, too, by the facile gossip which her mother's behaviour provokes not only to her own detriment, but also to the detriment of her daughter. Fortunately for her, however, she is engaged to the* MARQUIS CHARLES DI NOLLI. CHARLES DI NOLLI *is a stiff young man, very indulgent in his attitude to other people, but reserved and very firmly fixed in his assessment of his own slight worth and position in the world. Deep down within himself, however, he is none too sure of what they may be. He is, at all events, deeply concerned by the great weight of responsibility which he believes rests on him. And so it is that he looks upon the world as a place in which others may laugh and talk and enjoy themselves. . . . Oh, yes! Lucky people! But he . . . No, he cannot. Not because he doesn't want to. . . . No, it's just that he may not. He is dressed in deep mourning for his mother, who has recently died.*

[DOCTOR DIONISIO GENONI *has the bold, unabashed rubicund face of a satyr, protruding eyes and a little, pointed, shining silvery beard. His head is almost completely bald. His manners are elegant.*

[*They enter in some trepidation, almost as if afraid. All except* DI NOLLI *look curiously round the room, and at first, when they speak, they keep their voices low.*]

BELCREDI: Oh! Magnificent! Magnificent!

DOCTOR: How extremely interesting! Even in the most minute details. . . . Everything around him fitting in with his particular delusion! It is indeed magnificent! Yes, you are quite right, my dear Baron, it *is* magnificent!

DONNA MATILDA [*has been looking round for her portrait. Now she sees it and goes over to it*]: Ah, there it is! [*She stands back a little from it and studies it. A variety of emotions stirs within her.*] Yes . . . Yes . . . Look . . . Oh, God! [*Calling her daughter*] Frida! Frida! . . . Look!

FRIDA: Oh! Your portrait, you mean . . . ?

DONNA MATILDA: No! Look at it! That's not me. . . . That's you up there!

DI NOLLI: There you are, you see! Didn't I tell you so?

DONNA MATILDA: You did indeed. But I should never have believed it could be so. . . . [*She trembles as if a shudder had run down her spine.*] My God, what a strange feeling it gives you! [*Then, looking at her daughter*] What's the matter, Frida? [*She draws her to her and slips her arm round her waist.*] Come along! Can't you see yourself in that picture of me up there?

FRIDA: Well, to tell you the honest truth, I . . .

DONNA MATILDA: You can't? But why . . .? I don't see how you can help being struck by . . . [*Turning to* BELCREDI] Tito, *you* have a look! *You* tell her!

BELCREDI [*without looking*]: Oh, no! I'm not looking at it! As far as I'm concerned, *a priori* you must be mistaken!

DONNA MATILDA: What a fool the man is! He thinks he's paying me a compliment! [*Turning to* DOCTOR GENONI] You tell her, Doctor! *You* tell her!

[*The* DOCTOR *makes a movement towards the picture.*]

BELCREDI [*keeping his back turned and pretending to attract his attention surreptitiously*]: Psst! No, Doctor! For heaven's sake, Doctor, have nothing whatever to do with it!

DOCTOR [*with a bewildered smile*]: And why shouldn't I?

DONNA MATILDA: Oh, don't pay any attention to him! Come over here, Doctor! He's insufferable!

FRIDA: Didn't you know, he's always playing the fool! It's his *vocation*!

BELCREDI [*to the* DOCTOR, *seeing him go over to the* MARCHIONESS]: Watch your step, Doctor! Watch your step! And do mind where you're going! Your feet, you know . . .

DOCTOR [*the same bewildered smile*]: My feet? What about my feet?

BELCREDI: Your shoes are made of iron.

DOCTOR: My shoes are . . .?

BELCREDI: Yes, Doctor! And they are going to meet four little feet that are made of glass.

DOCTOR [*with a loud laugh*]: No! No! You're quite wrong! After all, I can see nothing surprising in a daughter's looking like her mother . . .

BELCREDI: Crash! Bang! Wallop! Now you've done it!

DONNA MATILDA [*coming down towards* BELCREDI, *simply beside herself with rage*]: What do you mean 'Crash! Bang! Wallop!'? What has he done? What did he say?

DOCTOR [*ingenuously*]: Well, don't you think I may be right?

BELCREDI [*replying to the* MARCHIONESS]: He said there was nothing surprising about it, while all the time you've been shrieking about how astounded you were. Why should you be, if the whole thing strikes you now as being so simple and natural?

DONNA MATILDA [*even more angrily*]: Oh, you idiot! You idiot! It's precisely because it *is* so natural! It's precisely because that *isn't* my daughter there! [*Pointing to the canvas*] That is *my* portrait! It was finding my daughter there . . . instead of myself . . . that was what astounded me! And when I say astounded me, please believe that I'm sincere! I forbid you to doubt that! [*After this violent tirade there is a moment's awkward silence.*]

FRIDA [*quietly, wearily*]: My God! It's always the same! Scenes . . . scenes . . . rows over nothing . . .

BELCREDI [*quietly, apologetically . . . his tail, you feel, almost between his legs*]: My dear, I wasn't doubting anything. [*Then, to* FRIDA] I noticed how, right from the moment we came in here, you didn't share your mother's astonishment. . . . Or, if you were at all surprised, it was because she saw such a *striking* resemblance between you and the portrait.

DONNA MATILDA: Naturally! Of course she would be surprised! Because she cannot recognize herself in me as I was at her age. Whereas, when I look at that picture, I can quite well see myself in her as she is now!

DOCTOR: Exactly! Because a portrait is always there. . . . Fixing for ever one particular moment in time. For the young lady it's something far far away. It has no memories for her. For the Marchioness, however, it can bring back so much . . . the memory of a gesture, a glance, a smile, a movement. . . . The memory of so many things that aren't in the picture. But things that . . .

DONNA MATILDA: How right you are, Doctor! How right you are!

DOCTOR [*turning to her and continuing*]: And you, quite naturally, can now see all those things living once again in your daughter.

DONNA MATILDA: He always manages to spoil everything for

me! The moment I show the slightest sign of real feeling . . . He does it just to annoy me!

DOCTOR [*dazzled by the light he has managed to cast on things, he adopts a professorial tone and, turning to* BELCREDI, *resumes his discourse*]: Resemblances, my dear Baron, often spring from imponderable things! As a matter of fact, that is how one explains . . .

BELCREDI [*cutting short the lecture*]: Why it is that someone could even discover a resemblance between you and me, my dear Professor!

DI NOLLI: Oh, let's have done with all this arguing! Do stop it! Please, everybody! [*He makes a gesture in the direction of the doors right, to warn them that there is someone in there who can hear.*] We've wasted too much time as it is, coming in here and . . .

FRIDA: As one might expect with *him* about! [*She is alluding to* BELCREDI.]

DONNA MATILDA [*immediately*]: That's why I didn't want him to come in the first place!

BELCREDI: But what a wonderful time you've had making fun of me! There's ingratitude for you!

DI NOLLI: Tito! Please! Stop it! We came here on a very serious mission. You know how important it is to me. Dr Genoni has come along with us, to . . .

DOCTOR: Quite so, my dear Marquis. Quite so. First of all, I'd like to get one or two points quite clear. Forgive my asking, but . . . This portrait of yours, Marchioness, how does it come to be here? Did you make him a present of it?

DONNA MATILDA: No! Oh, no! By what right could I possibly have given it to him? I was a girl like Frida at the time. I wasn't even engaged. I handed it over three or four years after the accident. [*With a gesture in the direction of* DI NOLLI] *His* mother begged me, implored me, to let her have it for him.

DOCTOR: His mother . . . that's *his* sister. [*He is alluding to* HENRY IV. *He gestures in the direction of the doors right as he says 'his'.*]

DI NOLLI: Yes, Doctor. And our coming here like this is the fulfilment of a promise.... It's something I owe my mother. She died a month ago. If things had been otherwise she [*a gesture towards* FRIDA] and I would certainly not be here now.... We should in fact have been on our honeymoon.

DOCTOR: And preoccupied in quite a different way, h'm?

DI NOLLI: Hum!... She died firmly believing that her adored brother was just about to be cured.

DOCTOR: You can't tell me, can you, on what she based this belief?

DI NOLLI: It seems to have been based on ... on some peculiar remarks that he made very shortly before Mother died.

DOCTOR: Remarks? H'm! H'm! You know, it would be extremely helpful ... *extremely helpful* ... if I could know just what he said! It would indeed!

DI NOLLI: Ah, I'm afraid I don't know! All I know is that my mother was frightfully upset when she came back from seeing him that time.... It was the last time she ever saw him. It seems that he had shown unusual tenderness.... Almost as if he were foreseeing her imminent death. On her deathbed she made me promise that I would never neglect him.... That I'd see that people went to visit him.... That he had the right doctors ...

DOCTOR: Yes! Ye-es! Good! Let me see! Let me see!... The first thing ... So often it's the slightest of causes ... This portrait, then ...

DONNA MATILDA: For heaven's sake, Doctor, I don't think you ought to attach too much importance to it. It affected me the way it did because it's so many years since I last saw it.

DOCTOR: Please, my Lady! Please! Now if you'll only be patient ...

DI NOLLI: Yes! Yes!... It must have been here quite fifteen years ...

DONNA MATILDA: Oh, longer than that! It's more than eighteen, now!

DOCTOR: Forgive my interrupting, but ... please let me go on! I haven't yet had a chance to tell you what it is I'm try-ing to get at. I attach a great deal of importance to these two portraits, which must have been painted, I imagine, before the famous – and most unfortunate – pageant. Am I right?

DONNA MATILDA: Oh, yes! You most certainly are!

DOCTOR: That is to say, when he was completely in his right mind. That was what I meant! Was it he who suggested to you that you should get yours painted?

DONNA MATILDA: Why no, Doctor! Many of us who took part in the pageant had ours done. You know, as a souvenir of the occasion.

BELCREDI: I had mine done too ... as Charles of Anjou!

DONNA MATILDA: They were done as soon as the costumes were ready.

BELCREDI: Because there was some idea, you see, of collecting them all together, and hanging them in the drawing-room of the villa where the pageant was to be held. As a record ... you know, a sort of permanent exhibition to commemorate ... But when it came to the point, everybody wanted to keep his own picture.

DONNA MATILDA: And, as I told you, this portrait ... *my* portrait, that is ... I gave him ... without very much re-gret ... because *his* mother. . . . [*A gesture in the direction of* DI NOLLI.]

DOCTOR: You don't know whether it was he who asked for it?

DONNA MATILDA: No, I'm afraid I don't! Perhaps ... Or it may have been that his sister wanted to help him by ... Out of her love for him, she may have ...

DOCTOR: And one thing more! One further point! This pageant. . . . Was it *his* idea?

BELCREDI [*immediately*]: No! No! It was *my* idea! The idea was mine!

DOCTOR: Please ...

DONNA MATILDA: Don't pay any attention to him. It was poor Belassi's idea.

BELCREDI: Belassi be damned!

DONNA MATILDA [*to the* DOCTOR]: It was Count Belassi . . . who died, poor man, two or three months afterwards.

BELCREDI: But I tell you Belassi wasn't there when . . .

DI NOLLI [*irritated by the threat of another argument*]: Forgive me, Doctor, but is it absolutely essential for us to establish whose idea it was originally?

DOCTOR: Well . . . *yes*. . . . It would help me to . . .

BELCREDI: But I tell you it was my idea! Good grief! You surely don't think I'm glad that I thought of it! It's hardly the sort of thing to boast about, when you consider how it all ended up! Look, Doctor, I can remember very clearly how the whole thing started. It was one evening at the beginning of November. I was at my club, leafing through a magazine. It was one of those German illustrated weeklies. I was just idly looking at the pictures, because I don't understand German. One of them was of the Kaiser visiting some university town where he'd been a student.

DOCTOR: Bonn, Bonn.

BELCREDI: Yes, that's right, Bonn. He was on horseback, dressed up in one of those outlandish traditional costumes worn by the ancient student guilds they have in Germany, and followed by a procession of other noble students, also in costume and on horseback. It was that picture which gave me the notion of . . . You see the idea had been mooted at the club that we should get up a really good fancy dress show of some sort for the forthcoming Carnival. . . . So I suggested that we should put on this historical pageant on horseback. Historical! H'm! A Tower of Babel pageant might be a more apt description! Each one of us was to choose a historical character from any century he liked . . . a king or an emperor or a prince . . . and he was to ride along. . . . Everybody was to be on horseback, of course . . . with his lady . . . his queen or his empress . . . by his side. Even the horses were to have period harness and saddles and so forth. My suggestion was immediately accepted.

DONNA MATILDA: It was Belassi who sent me *my* invitation.

BELCREDI: If he told you that it was his idea, then I'm afraid he wasn't telling the truth. I repeat, he wasn't even at the club that evening, when I suggested that we should hold the pageant. . . . Just as *he* wasn't there either. [*He is alluding to* HENRY IV.]

DOCTOR: And he chose the character of Henry IV, then?

DONNA MATILDA: He chose it because I . . . thinking of my own name, and not really attaching very much importance to my choice . . . said that I should like to be the Marchioness Matilda of Tuscany.

DOCTOR: I don't . . . er . . . I don't quite see the connexion. . .

DONNA MATILDA: I don't suppose you do! Neither did I at first. I was completely mystified when he said that in that case he would be at my feet, just like Henry IV at Canossa. Oh yes, I'd heard of Canossa, of course! But . . . Well, to tell you the honest truth, I had only the haziest of memories of what it was all about. And I remember I got a most curious sensation when I was reading up the stuff on my part, and found that I was the completely devoted and zealous friend of Pope Gregory VII, and carrying on a ferocious struggle against the German Empire. It was then that I understood very clearly why, since I had chosen to play the part of his implacable enemy, he wanted to be by my side in the pageant . . . as Henry IV.

DOCTOR: Ah! Because, perhaps . . .?

BELCREDI: Good heavens, Doctor, it was because he was in passionate pursuit of her at the time, and quite naturally she . . . [*With a gesture in the direction of the* MARCHIONESS.]

DONNA MATILDA [*flaring up, stung by his words*]: Naturally! Of course it was natural that I should . . .! And at that time more so than ever!

BELCREDI [*pointing to her*]: You see . . . she couldn't stand the man!

DONNA MATILDA: No, that's not true! I never really disliked him. Quite the contrary! But . . . Oh, when a man begins

to make demands . . . when he wants me to take him seriously . . . well . . .

BELCREDI [*finishing it for her*]: He gives you the clearest proof
of his stupidity!

DONNA MATILDA: No, my dear Tito! Not in his case. You
see, he was never a fool . . . as you are.

BELCREDI: Well anyway, I've never asked you to take me
seriously.

DONNA MATILDA: Yes, I know that only too well! But you
couldn't make a joke of things with him. [*Her tone changes
and she says to the* DOCTOR] One of the many misfortunes
which happen to us women, Doctor, is to see before us,
every so often, a pair of eyes which are gazing at us with a
contained intense promise of eternal devotion. [*Bursts into
noisy laughter*] There's nothing more comic! If only men
could see themselves when they've got that look of eternal
fidelity in their eyes! I've always thought it comic . . . then
even more so than now. But I must make a confession. I can
make it now, now that twenty years and more have gone
by. When I laughed at him like that, it wasn't only because
he amused me. . . . No. . . . I was afraid of him, too. Perhaps
because there was a promise in those eyes that you could
believe in. But it would have been very dangerous to have
believed in it.

DOCTOR [*with lively interest, pondering*]: H'm! Ah! H'm! I should
be very interested to know . . . ! Very dangerous, did you say?

DONNA MATILDA [*lightly*]: Yes . . . and precisely because he
wasn't like the rest of them! And then I'm . . . well, I'm . . .
what shall I say? . . . I'm just a little . . . No, to be perfectly
honest, more than a little . . . [*Trying to find a suitably moder-
ate word*] intolerant . . . Yes, intolerant of everything that's
too intellectual and tedious. But I was too young at the time
. . . and I was a woman. I had to have my fling! I had the bit
between my teeth and . . . oh, it would have taken more
courage than I felt I possessed! So I laughed at him, too. But
rather . . . oh, remorsefully! And I hated myself thoroughly

for doing it. Since I could see my laughter mingling with
that of the rest of them. . . . All those fools who were making fun of him!

BELCREDI: Which is my own plight . . . more or less.

DONNA MATILDA: You make people laugh at you, my dear,
because of your trick of always humiliating yourself. But
he, on the contrary . . . Oh, there's a world of difference
between you! And besides, as far as you're concerned . .
Well, people laugh at you to your face!

BELCREDI: Which is better than having them laugh at me behind my back!

DOCTOR: Don't let's wander from the subject! Let's get back
to what we were talking about! Well, then . . . He was
already somewhat excited . . . if I'm understanding you
aright.

BELCREDI: Yes, but in a somewhat curious manner, Doctor.

DOCTOR: How do you mean?

BELCREDI: Well, I'd be inclined to say . . . Somehow cold-
bloodedly . . .

DONNA MATILDA: Nonsense! He wasn't at all cold-blooded.
It was like this, Doctor. He was a little strange, certainly.
But it was because he was so tremendously full of life. . . .
Inspired, slightly fantastic . . .

BELCREDI: I'm not saying that he was pretending to be excited. Quite the contrary. He'd very often get really,
genuinely excited. But I'd be willing to swear, Doctor, that
the moment he reached that state of exaltation he would
immediately see himself as being in it. That's what I meant
just now. And it's my belief that this happened to him quite
inevitably, even when he was acting most spontaneously. I'd
like to say, moreover, that I'm quite certain that it must have
made him suffer. Sometimes he'd break out into the most
comical fits of rage against himself!

DONNA MATILDA: That's true!

BELCREDI [to DONNA MATILDA]: And why did he? [To the
DOCTOR] As I see it . . . it was because the immediate

lucidity that comes from playing a part . . . from portraying some emotion . . . at once put him out of touch with the very emotion he was feeling. The intimate bond he had with that emotion was at once snapped, and the thing he was feeling seemed to him . . . not exactly false . . . because it was, after all, sincere . . . but like something to which he had immediately, there and then, to give some sort of a value. I don't know. . . . He had to make it an act of intelligence, to compensate for the warmth of sincerity which he felt it to be lacking. And so he would improvise, exaggerate, let himself go. . . . So as to be able to take his mind off things, to forget himself. He appeared inconstant, fatuous, and . . . well, we might as well say it . . . even ridiculous at times.

DOCTOR: And . . . tell me . . . would you say that he was *unsociable*?

BELCREDI: Oh, no! Not at all! He was the most sociable of men! He was famous for getting things up! *Tableaux vivants*, dances, charity shows. . . . All for the fun of the thing, of course. He was an excellent actor, you know.

DI NOLLI: Madness has made a superb actor of him. . . . And a positively terrifying one.

BELCREDI: But he always was! So you can imagine that when the awful thing happened, after he'd fallen from his horse . . .

DOCTOR: He hit the back of his head, didn't he?

DONNA MATILDA: Oh, it was horrible! He was riding next to me! I could see him down there under the horse's hooves . . .! The horse was rearing . . .!

BELCREDI: At first we didn't think it was at all serious. Oh yes, the procession was held up for a few moments. There was a bit of confusion. People wanting to know what had happened. But they'd already picked him up and taken him back to the villa.

DONNA MATILDA: There wasn't a sign of a wound! Nothing at all! Not a single drop of blood, even!

BELCREDI: We all thought he'd merely fainted.

DONNA MATILDA: And when, about a couple of hour
later....

BELCREDI: Yes! He reappeared in the drawing-room of the
villa.... That was what I meant when ...

DONNA MATILDA: My God! His face! I saw in a flash what
had happened!

BELCREDI: No! No! That's not true! Nobody realized anything at all, Doctor! Believe me!

DONNA MATILDA: No! because you weren't in a fit state to
realize anything! You were all behaving like a lot of madmen!

BELCREDI: Everybody was fooling about, pretending to be
the character he was dressed up as! It was absolute Pande-
monium!

DONNA MATILDA: You can just imagine, Doctor, how terrified we all were when we realized that he, unlike the rest
of them, was playing his part in deadly earnest ...

DOCTOR: Ah, you mean ... because he too then started ...?

BELCREDI: Yes! He plunged straight into our midst! We
thought he'd recovered and was fooling about like the rest
of us ... only he was doing it rather better because ... as I
was telling you ... he was an extremely good actor! We
thought in fact that he was just playing a joke on us!

DONNA MATILDA: They began to hit him ...

BELCREDI: And then ... being a king, he was armed, of
course ... he drew his sword and hurled himself at two or
three of us. It was a terrible moment for all of us!

DONNA MATILDA: I shall never forget that scene.... All our
masked faces, hideous with terror, gazing at the terrible
mask of his face. But it was a mask no longer.... It was the
face of Madness itself!

BELCREDI: He had become Henry IV! He *was* Henry IV! In
person! In a moment of fury!

DONNA MATILDA: Of course he had been obsessed by the
part.... He'd been working on it for the past month and
more.... And I should say myself that his mind had been

affected by the work he'd done on it. But then, he was like that. Whatever it was he was doing, he became absolutely obsessed with it.

BELCREDI: The amount of work he put in! His preparation was most careful. . . . He made sure that everything was perfect, right down to the last tiny detail. . . .

DOCTOR: It all seems quite simple and straightforward to me. When he fell from his horse and hurt his head, he became fixed in what had formerly been purely a temporary obsession. The damage to his brain resulted in his being fixed, once and for all, in the rôle he was then playing. Some people are made imbecile by such falls, others merely become insane.

BELCREDI [to FRIDA and DI NOLLI]: You see the kind of joke that life can play on us, my dears. [To DI NOLLI] You were four or five years old at the time. . . . [To FRIDA] And you . . . Well, your mother thinks that you've taken her place up there in the portrait. And yet, you know, when that portrait was painted she hadn't the remotest idea that she would be bringing you into the world. My hair is already grey . . . And he . . . Well, look at him. . . . [Pointing to the portrait] Whoomph! A knock on the head and he never moves again! There he is, up there . . . Henry IV for ever!

DOCTOR [during this speech he has been lost in thought, brooding upon what he has heard. Now he spreads his hands wide, as if to focus the attention of the others, and settles himself to deliver his scientific explanation]: Well then, ladies and gentlemen . . . it comes, we may say, to this . . .

[But suddenly the first door on the right opens (that is to say, the door nearer the footlights) and BERTHOLD comes in, his face contorted with anger.]

BERTHOLD [rushing in like a man at the end of his tether]: May I come in? I'm sorry, but . . . [He stops short, however, when he sees into what dismay and confusion his appearance has immediately thrown the others.]

FRIDA [with a shriek of terror, looking for somewhere to hide]: Oh, my God! Here he is!

DONNA MATILDA [*retreating in dismay and flinging her arm across her face, so as not to see him*]: Is it him? Is it?

DI NOLLI [*immediately*]: No! No! Of course it isn't! Now, don't get so worked up!

DOCTOR [*astonished*]: Who is it, then?

BELCREDI: A refugee who's made his escape from our masquerade!

DI NOLLI: It's one of the young men we employ here to help keep up the illusion for him. . . .

BERTHOLD: I beg your pardon, my Lord . . .

DI NOLLI: Pardon be damned! My orders were that the doors were to be kept locked, and that no one was to come in here!

BERTHOLD: Yes, sir, I know! But I can't stand it any longer! I've come to ask you to let me leave at once!

DI NOLLI: Ah, you must be the new man who was due to start this morning . . .

BERTHOLD: Yes, sir. And I tell you I can't stand it any longer . . . !

DONNA MATILDA [*excitedly to* DI NOLLI, *consternation in her voice*]: Then he's not so calm as you said he was!

BERTHOLD [*immediately*]: Oh no, madam! It's not him! It's the other three. . . . The chaps I'm supposed to be working with! You said my job was to help him, Marquis. Help be blowed! Those fellows don't do much helping! They're the ones who're barmy! I come in here . . . never seen the place before in my life . . . And instead of helping me, Marquis . . .

[*Enter* LANDOLPH *and* HAROLD *anxiously, hurriedly, through the same door right. They stop short at the threshold, however, before coming into the room.*]

LANDOLPH: May we come in?

HAROLD: May we come in, your Lordship?

DI NOLLI: Come in! But what the devil *is* all this? What are you all doing?

FRIDA: Oh, God! I'm frightened! I'm going to run away! I'm going to run away! [*And she makes for the door left.*]

DI NOLLI [*immediately restraining her*]: No, Frida! You mustn't!

LANDOLPH: My Lord, this idiot . . . [*Pointing to* BERTHOLD.]

BERTHOLD [*protesting*]: Oh, no! Thanks very much, my dear friends! I'm not stopping here! I'm not having anything more to do with this lark! I'm off!

LANDOLPH: What do you mean, you're not stopping here?

HAROLD: He's ruined everything, my Lord, running away in here like this!

LANDOLPH: He's made him simply furious! We can't keep him in there any longer. He's given orders for him to be arrested. He intends to try him at once from the throne! What are we to do?

DI NOLLI: Shut the door! Shut the door! Quickly! Go and shut that door!

[LANDOLPH *goes and shuts it.*]

HAROLD: It won't be possible for Ordulph by himself to keep him in there. . . .

LANDOLPH: I've got an idea, your Lordship. If we could only announce your visit to him, it would distract him. If you ladies and gentlemen have thought about who you're going to be . . . I mean, what costumes you're going to appear in . . .

DI NOLLI: Yes, yes! It's all been arranged. [*Then, to the* DOCTOR] If you think, Doctor, that it would be a good idea for you to see him immediately. . . .

FRIDA: I don't want to see him! I don't want to see him, Charles! I'm going into the other room! And Mummy . . . please, Mummy! . . . You come too! Come with me! *Please!*

DOCTOR: There is just one . . . Um . . . He's not *still* armed, I suppose . . . by any chance . . . ?

DI NOLLI: *Armed*, Doctor? Why, of course not! Of course not! [*Then, to* FRIDA] You know, Frida, it's very childish of you to be so afraid! You wanted to come. . . .

FRIDA: Oh no, I didn't! It was Mummy's idea!

DONNA MATILDA [*resolutely*]: And I am quite ready to see him! Now then, what is it we have to do?

BELCREDI: Sorry if it's the wrong question, but ... do we really have to disguise ourselves in some sort of rigout?

LANDOLPH: Oh yes, sir! It's absolutely essential! Absolutely essential! Yes, unfortunately.... As you can see ... [*showing him his own costume*] there'd be awful trouble if he were to see you ladies and gentlemen as you are now, dressed in modern clothes!

HAROLD: He'd think it was some diabolical disguise.

DI NOLLI: Just as *they* seem to be in fancy dress to *you* ... so *we*, wearing the clothes we have on now, would appear to be in fancy dress to *him*.

LANDOLPH: That probably wouldn't matter so much, my Lord, if it weren't for the fact that it would be bound to look like the work of his mortal enemy to him!

BELCREDI: Pope Gregory VII?

LANDOLPH: Precisely! He says he was a pagan!

BELCREDI: The Pope? That's not bad!

LANDOLPH: Yes, sir! And he says that he used to call up the dead! He accuses him of all the diabolical arts. He lives in terrible dread of him.

DOCTOR: Persecution mania!

HAROLD: He'd be simply furious!

DI NOLLI [*to* BELCREDI]: You know ... There's no need for you to be present. We'll go and wait in there. It'll be quite sufficient for the doctor to see him.

DOCTOR: On my own ... do you mean?

DI NOLLI: But they'll be there, too! [*He points to the three young men.*]

DOCTOR: No! No! That wasn't what I meant.... I should say that if the Marchioness ...

DONNA MATILDA: Of course! I certainly mean to be present! Oh yes, I intend to be present! I want to see him again!

FRIDA: But why, Mummy? Please ... I beg you .... come in there with us!

DONNA MATILDA [*imperiously*]: Leave me alone. This is what I came for! [*To* LANDOLPH] I shall be Adelaide, *her* mother

LANDOLPH: Yes, that's an excellent idea! The mother of the Empress Bertha! Excellent! Then all you'll have to do, my Lady, is to put on the ducal coronet and a cloak that covers all your other clothes completely. [*To* HAROLD] Off you go, Harold! Off you go!

HAROLD: Hang on a bit! What about the gentleman? [*With a gesture in the direction of the* DOCTOR.]

DOCTOR: Ye-es! M'm! ... I think we said ... the Bishop ... Bishop Hugh of Cluny.

HAROLD: The gentleman means the Abbot, doesn't he? Very good ... Hugh of Cluny.

LANDOLPH: He's already been here quite a number of times. ...

DOCTOR [*in utter astonishment*]: What! He's been here before?

LANDOLPH: Don't be alarmed! I mean that ... Well, being an easy sort of disguise ...

HAROLD: We've made use of it on several occasions.

DOCTOR: But ...

LANDOLPH: There's no risk of his remembering. He pays more attention to the dress than to the person wearing it.

DONNA MATILDA: That's fortunate for me, then.

DI NOLLI: We'll go, Frida! You come with us, Tito! Come along!

BELCREDI: Oh, no! If she's staying, I'm staying too. [*He points to the* MARCHIONESS.]

DONNA MATILDA: But I haven't the slightest need of your company!

BELCREDI: I'm not saying that you *have*! It so happens that I too should very much like to see him again. Mayn't I?

LANDOLPH: Yes, perhaps it would be better if there were three of you.

HAROLD: Well then, what shall we do about the gentleman?

BELCREDI: Mind you dig out an easy disguise for me, too!

LANDOLPH [*to* HAROLD]: Yes. H'm! ... I've got it! He can be a Cluniac.

BELCREDI: A Cluniac? What on earth is that?

LANDOLPH: A monk. . . . You'll wear the habit of a Benedictine monk from the Abbey of Cluny. You'll be part of
Monsignor's retinue. [*To* HAROLD] Go on! Get going! [*To*
BERTHOLD] And off with you, too! And make yourself
scarce for the rest of today! [*But hardly do they begin to go
out.*] Wait a minute! [*To* BERTHOLD] He'll give you the
clothes, and you bring them in here. [*To* HAROLD] And
you go immediately and announce the visit of the 'Duchess
Adelaide' and of 'Monsignor Hugh of Cluny'. Got it?

    [HAROLD *and* BERTHOLD *go out through the first door
right.*]

DI NOLLI: We'll leave you now. [*Goes out with* FRIDA *through
the door left.*]

DOCTOR [*to* LANDOLPH]: Shall I be *persona grata* with him in
my rôle of Hugh of Cluny? I imagine I shall.

LANDOLPH: Oh yes, very much so! You need have no fears on
that score. Monsignor has always been received here with
the greatest of respect. And you too, Marchioness, he will
be very glad to see. He never forgets that it was due to your
intercession, and that of Monsignor, that, after waiting two
days out there in the snow, and when he was almost frozen
to death, he was admitted to the castle at Canossa and to the
presence of Gregory VII, who had been so unwilling to
grant him an audience.

BELCREDI: And what about me?

LANDOLPH: You will stand respectfully on one side.

DONNA MATILDA [*is all on edge, and says irritatedly*]: It would
be much better if you were to go away altogether!

BELCREDI [*in a low voice, spitefully*]: How terribly worked-up
you are!

DONNA MATILDA [*proudly*]: I am what I am! Leave me
alone!

    [BERTHOLD *comes back with the costumes.*]

LANDOLPH [*catching sight of him as he comes in*]: Ah, here are
the costumes! This is for you, Marchioness. [*Hands her the
cloak.*]

DONNA MATILDA: Wait just a minute! Let me take off my hat! [*Does so and hands it to* BERTHOLD.]

ANDOLPH: Don't forget to take that out with you when you go.... [*Then, to the* MARCHIONESS, *offering her the ducal coronet*] Shall I put this on for you?

DONNA MATILDA: Good Heavens! Isn't there any kind of a mirror in here?

ANDOLPH: There are several in the other room. [*He points to the door left.*] If the Marchioness would rather do it herself...

DONNA MATILDA: Yes, yes, it would be better. Give it to me. I'll go and put it on. I shan't be a moment. [*She retrieves her hat and goes out with* BERTHOLD, *who carries the cloak and coronet. In the meantime the* DOCTOR *and* BELCREDI *dress themselves as best they can in the Benedictine habits.*]

BELCREDI: Well, I must confess that I never expected to finish up as a Benedictine monk. You know, this crazy business must cost a pretty penny!

DOCTOR: Oh well, it's not the only kind of madness that does that...

BELCREDI: Of course, when you've got a handsome fortune to draw on to help you keep up your illusion...

ANDOLPH: In the other room we've got a whole wardrobe full of costumes of the period. They're beautifully made, and perfect copies of the genuine thing. It's my particular job to look after that side of things. I get them from the best theatrical costumiers. It's an expensive business.

[DONNA MATILDA *comes back in, wearing the cloak and coronet.*]

BELCREDI [*immediately, in admiration*]: Oh magnificent! My dear, you look every inch a queen!

DONNA MATILDA [*she catches sight of* BELCREDI *and bursts out laughing*]: Oh, God! No! No! Take it off! You're impossible! You look like an ostrich dressed up as a monk!

BELCREDI: If you think *I'm* funny, take a good look at the Doctor!

DOCTOR: I don't think I look too bad, do I? Just let me . . .

DONNA MATILDA: No, of course you don't! You look quite nice, Doctor! But *you're* too funny for words!

DOCTOR [*to* LANDOLPH]: Am I to infer that you have a great number of audiences of this sort?

LANDOLPH: Oh, it all depends. He'll often order So-and-so to be summoned to his presence. . . . Or demand to see the Prince of Thingummy, or the Bishop of Whatsitsname. . . And then we have to find somebody to play the part. Then there are the women . . .

DONNA MATILDA [*hurt by this, but trying to hide the fact*]: Oh! Women too?

LANDOLPH: Yes, at first . . . hordes of them.

BELCREDI [*laughs*]: Oh, what a wonderful notion! In costume? [*Points to the* MARCHIONESS.] Like the Marchioness?

LANDOLPH: Oh well, sir, you know what . . . well . . . women of the sort who . . .

BELCREDI: Who lend a helping hand . . . Who yield . . .! I take your meaning! [*Treacherously, to the* MARCHIONESS] Look out, my dear! Mind you don't run yourself into danger!

[*The second door on the right opens, and* HAROLD *comes in. He makes surreptitious signals to the people in the throne-room to stop talking, and then solemnly announces*:]

HAROLD: His Majesty the Emperor!

[*The two* LACKEYS *enter first. They go over and take up their positions at the foot of the throne. Then* HENRY IV *enters, flanked by* ORDULPH *and* HAROLD, *who respectfully remain slightly behind him. He is nearly fifty and very pale. The hair on the back of his head is already grey. That at the temples and over his forehead, on the other hand, appears fair — an all too evident and almost childish piece of dyeing. On his cheeks, and conflicting sharply with his tragic pallor, are crude, doll-like daubs of rouge. Over his regal habit he is wearing a penitent's sackcloth such as the emperor wore at Canossa. In his eyes there is a fixed, anxious, terrifying expression which is in striking con-*

*trast with his bearing. Clearly he wishes to appear penitent and humble, and the more he feels that his being demeaned in this way is unmerited, the more he strives to achieve that appearance.* ORDULPH *is carrying the imperial crown in both hands;* HAROLD, *the eagle-headed sceptre and the orb and cross.*]

HENRY IV [*bows first to* DONNA MATILDA, *then to the* DOCTOR]: My Lady ... Monsignor ... [*Then he looks at* BELCREDI *and is just about to bow to him too when he turns to* LANDOLPH, *who is now close by, and asks him in an undertone full of mistrust*] Is that Peter Damiani?

LANDOLPH: No, your Majesty, he is a monk from Cluny. He's with the Abbot.

HENRY IV [*looks again at* BELCREDI *with increasing mistrust, and, noticing that he appears embarrassed and in suspense, and that he keeps on glancing at* DONNA MATILDA *and the* DOCTOR, *as if seeking their advice, he stands upright and cries*]: It is Peter Damiani! It's no use, Father, your looking for help from the Duchess! [*Then, turning instantly to* DONNA MATILDA, *as if to avert some danger.*] I swear that my heart is changed towards your daughter! I swear it! I confess that if he [*pointing to* BELCREDI] hadn't come in the name of Pope Alexander and prevented me from doing it, I'd have repudiated her! Yes! Oh, yes! There were plenty of people who were only too ready to favour her repudiation! The Bishop of Mainz for one! He'd have done it for the trifling consideration of a hundred and twenty farms. [*A little dismayed, he shoots a sideways glance at* LANDOLPH *and immediately adds*] But this isn't the moment for me to speak ill of the bishops. [*He turns again to* BELCREDI *and says humbly*] I am grateful to you ... believe me, I am grateful to you, Peter Damiani, for preventing me from doing it! My life has been one long series of humiliations ... my mother ... Adalbert ... Tribur ... Goslar ... and now this sackcloth which you see me wearing! [*Suddenly, unexpectedly, the tone of his voice changes, and he speaks like a man who, in a parenthesis of astuteness, is running over his part.*] It doesn't matter! Clarity of ideas ...

perspicacity . . . steadfastness and patience in adversity . . . those are the things that matter! [*Then he turns to them all and says with contrite gravity*] I know how to make amends for the errors that I have committed. And even before you, Peter Damiani, I can humble myself! [*Bows profoundly to him, and remains for a moment with his body still bent. It is as if the dawning of some odd, oblique kind of suspicion keeps him in that position. Now it impels him to add, almost against his will, and in a menacing tone*] Was it not you who started that obscene rumour that my holy mother Agnes had had illicit relations with Bishop Henry of Augusta?

BELCREDI [*his hands to his breast, denying the charge*]: No . . . No . . . it wasn't I who . . .

  [*While* BELCREDI *has been stammering out his reply,* HENRY IV *has remained bent before him, his finger pointed menacingly up at him. Now he straightens up.*]

HENRY IV: So, it's not true? You didn't . . . Oh, infamy! [*Looks him straight in the face for a moment and then says*] I didn't think you were capable of doing such a thing! [*Goes over to the* DOCTOR *and lightly plucks his sleeve. Then with a sly, knowing wink he says*] It's always *they* who start these rumours! Always the others, Monsignor!

HAROLD [*aside, with a sigh, as if prompting the* DOCTOR]: Ah yes, the rapacious Bishops.

DOCTOR [*turning to* HAROLD, *and manfully striving to keep it up*]: Oh, yes! The others. *Them!* Oh, yes!

HENRY IV: They were utterly insatiable! . . . I was a little boy, Monsignor . . . an unhappy little boy. . . . But you pass the time . . . playing . . . even when, without knowing it, you're a King. I was six years old, and they tore me away from my mother, and made use of me against her, without my knowing anything about it. They even made use of me to attack the very powers of the Dynasty itself! They sullied everything with their profaning hands. Always stealing! Always stealing! One greedier than the other! Hanno worse than Stephen! Stephen worse than Hanno!

LANDOLPH [*sotto voce, persuasively, trying to recall him to a proper sense of where he is and what he is saying*]: Your Majesty!

HENRY IV [*turning immediately*]: Yes, you're right! This isn't the moment for me to speak ill of the Bishops. But this infamous attack on my mother, Monsignor, is quite unforgivable! [*He looks at the* MARCHIONESS *and tenderness comes into his voice.*] And I can't even weep for her, my Lady! I appeal to you . . . for you must know what it is to have a mother's heart and a mother's feelings! She came here from her convent to see me about a month ago. And now they tell me she is dead. [*There is a sustained pause, charged with emotion. Then, smiling very sadly, he says*] I cannot weep for her because, if you are here now, and I am dressed like this [*he shows her the sackcloth he is wearing*], it means that I am twenty-six years old.

HAROLD [*softly, almost sotto voce, comfortingly*]: And that she, therefore, is still alive, your Majesty.

ORDULPH [*the same softly comforting tone*]: And still in her convent.

HENRY IV [*turning to look at them*]: Yes, of course she is. So I can postpone my grief until another time. [*Then, almost coquettishly, he shows the* MARCHIONESS *where he has dyed his hair.*] Look, my hair is still fair. . . . [*Then, confidentially lowering his voice*] It's for you that I've done this. There'd be no need for me to do it for myself. But it's useful to have these outward and visible signs. Terms in the language of time, if you take my meaning, Monsignor! [*He goes up to the* MARCHIONESS *again and, noticing the colour of her hair, says*] Ah, but I see that . . . you too, Duchess . . . [*he gives a slight wink and makes an expressive gesture with his hand*] in the Italian manner, I observe. [*Which is as much as to say, 'spoof'—though without the slightest suspicion of contempt. On the contrary, there is a note of malicious admiration in his voice.*] God forbid that I should show disgust or surprise! Oh, the fantastic notions we get into our heads! No one cares to recognize that obscure and fateful power which sets limits to our will. But, I tell you, man *is* born and man *does* die! Birth. . . . Did *you* want to be born, Monsignor? *I* didn't! And between our being born and our going out of the world . . . and our will is powerless at both events . . . so many things happen to which we must with grudging hearts resign ourselves . . . but which we would to God had never happened!

DOCTOR [*feeling rather strongly that he must say* something, *and studying him intently all the while*]: Ah, yes! Unfortunately . . .

HENRY IV: It's like this. . . . When we are not resigned, out come all our fantastic desires. . . . A woman wants to be a man. . . . And an old man wants to be young again. . . . And we're all in deadly earnest, not one of us is lying or pretending to himself! There's not much you can say, for we're every one of us fixed in all good faith in a wonderful conception of ourselves. However, Monsignor, even while you're standing there, so firm and so solid, holding on tight with both hands to your holy habit, something is slipping down your sleeve. . . . There! . . . Slipping away . . . slithering away like a serpent . . . something you don't even notice . . . *Life*, Monsignor! And there are surprises in store for you when suddenly you catch sight of it . . . out there . . . sitting in front of you, after it's made its escape. . . . And it has a whole host of shapes . . . contempt and anger against you yourself . . . and remorse . . . yes, remorse, too! Oh, if you only knew how often that haunting face of remorse has flashed before my eyes! It was my own face, but so twisted and horrible that I could hardly recognize it! [*He goes up to the* MARCHIONESS *again.*] Has that sort of thing never happened to you, my Lady? Do you really remember yourself as always having been one and the same person? But wasn't there that day when . . .? Oh, my God! How could you . . . How could you possibly have done what you did? [*And he looks so fixedly into her eyes as almost to make her go pale.*] Yes! Precisely! I see you know what I mean. . . . What you did that day . . .! Oh, don't worry! I shan't tell anybody what

it was. And you, Peter Damiani, how could you be a friend
to that man?

LANDOLPH [*the same persuasive tone*]: Your Majesty!

HENRY IV [*immediately*]: No, no! I shan't say what his name is!
I know it'll offend him if I do! [*Turning very quickly to* BEL-
CREDI] What was *your* opinion of him? Tell me, what did
*you* think of him? . . . But, quite regardless of what the
opinions of other people may be, each one of us holds on tight
to the conception he has of himself. . . . Just as the man who
is growing old dyes his hair. What does it matter if, for you,
this dye I've used completely fails to deceive you as to the true
colour of my hair? You, my Lady, certainly don't dye your
hair to deceive other people, or even yourself! But just to . . .
well . . . just to cheat your reflection in the mirror a little. Oh,
a *very* little! I do it for a joke. You do it in all seriousness.
But I assure you, my Lady, that for all your seriousness, you
too are wearing a mask. Oh, I'm not talking about the
venerable coronet on your head . . . before which I bow . . .
or your ducal robes . . . I'm speaking only of the memory
that you wish artificially to fix in yourself . . . the memory
of your fair complexion as you saw it one day, and which
you found so very pleasing. . . . Or your dark complexion,
if you were dark. . . . The fading image of your youth. To
you, on the other hand, Peter Damiani, the memory of
what you have been, and of what you have done, appears
now as the recognition of past realities that remain within
you like a dream. That *is* so, isn't it? And that's how things
are with me, too. It's all a dream. So many realities, when
you come to think back. . . . So many, and so inexplicable.
Oh, well! . . . It's not really so surprising, Peter Damiani . . .
The life of today is the dream of tomorrow! [*Suddenly he
becomes furious. Snatching at his sackcloth, he cries*] And this
sackcloth . . . [*With a joy which is almost ferocious he makes as
if to tear it off. Terrified,* HAROLD *and* ORDULPH *immediately
rush over, as if to prevent him from doing so.*] Oh, my God!
[*And he draws back, tears off the sackcloth and shouts at them*]

Tomorrow at Bressanone twenty-seven German and Lombard bishops will sign with me the act of deposition of Pope Gregory VII! He is no true Pontiff! Merely a false monk! [HAROLD, ORDULPH, *and* LANDOLPH *try to quieten him.*]

ORDULPH: Your Majesty! Your Majesty! In God's name . . .

HAROLD [*trying to coax him into putting the sackcloth on again*]: Be careful what you say, your Majesty! [*Holds out the sackcloth.*]

LANDOLPH: Monsignor and the Duchess are here to intercede in your favour, your Majesty! [*Unseen by* HENRY IV, *he makes urgent signals to the* DOCTOR *to say something immediately.*]

DOCTOR [*in dismay*]: Ah, yes! . . . M'm! . . . That is . . . We are here to intercede . . .

HENRY IV [*immediately he becomes penitent, almost terrified. He lets the three young men put the sackcloth back over his head and, clasping it about him with convulsively twitching hands, says*]: I beseech your pardon. . . . Yes. . . . Yes. . . . I beseech your pardon, Monsignor! And yours too, my Lady! I swear . . . I swear I feel the full weight of the anathema! [*He bends forward, taking his head in his hands, as if in expectation of something which must inevitably come and crush him. He stands for a while like this but then, in a different tone of voice, yet without changing his position or attitude at all, he says quietly, confidentially, to* LANDOLPH, HAROLD, *and* ORDULPH]: I don't know why, but today I find it quite impossible to be humble before that man! [*And, almost surreptitiously, he gestures in the direction of* BELCREDI.]

LANDOLPH [*sotto voce*]: But, your Majesty, it's because you *will* persist in believing that he's Peter Damiani, when he's not!

HENRY IV [*timidly peeping at him*]: He's not Peter Damiani?

HAROLD: Why, no! He's a poor monk, your Majesty!

HENRY IV [*sorrow in his voice, yet with a sigh of exasperation*]: Ah, none of us can truly evaluate what he does when he does it by instinct. . . . Perhaps you, my Lady, can understand me better than the others . . . because you are a woman.\* [This is a solemn and decisive moment. I could, you see, at this very moment, whilst I am speaking to you, accept the help of the Lombard bishops, and get control of the Pope by besieging him here in this Castle. Then I could rush to Rome and elect an Anti-Pope, stretch out the hand of alliance to Robert Guiscard, and Gregory VII would be lost! I resist the temptation and, believe me, I am wise in so doing. I sense the spirit of the times and I can fully appreciate the majesty of one who knows how to be what he must be . . . a Pope! Do you feel like laughing at me now, seeing me humiliated like this? You would be just so many fools if you did . . . because you would be revealing how little you understood the political wisdom which counsels me to wear this penitential garb. I tell you . . . tomorrow the rôles might quite well be reversed! And what would you do then? Would you by any chance laugh at the Pope when you saw him a prisoner? No! We'd have got even with one another. Today you see me in the mask of the penitent. . . . Tomorrow you would see him in the mask of the prisoner. But woe to the man who does not know how to wear his mask, be it the mask of King, or that of Pope! Perhaps in what he is doing to me at the moment he is a little too cruel. . . . Yes, he is.] Just think, my Lady . . . Bertha your daughter . . . for whom, I repeat, my feelings have changed. . . . [*He turns unexpectedly on* BEL-CREDI *and shouts in his face, just as if he had said 'No'*] Yes! *Changed!* . . . Changed! . . . Because of the affection and of the devotion of which she has given me proof in these terrible days! [*He stops, convulsed by his angry outburst, and makes efforts to restrain himself. We hear the sob of exasperation in his throat. Then he turns again with a sweet and sorrowing humility to the* MARCHIONESS.] She came with me, my Lady! I can see her, down there in the courtyard. She insisted on following me here, like a beggar. And she is very cold. Her body is frozen with the cold. Two nights she has spent out there in

___

\* As it is essential that the action should proceed rapidly, the following 22 lines (in square brackets) are probably best omitted in performance. (Author's note.)

the open, out there in the snow! You are her mother! Doesn't it touch your heart to pity? Won't you have compassion on me, and join him [*pointing to the* DOCTOR] in imploring the Pope to pardon me? In begging him to grant us audience?

DONNA MATILDA [*trembling, and speaking in a scarcely audible voice*]: Yes! Of course I will! Yes! At once . . .

DOCTOR: We will indeed! Yes, indeed we will!

HENRY IV: And one other thing! One other thing! [*He calls them around him and says quietly, with an air of great secrecy:*] It's not sufficient that he should grant me an audience. You know . . . he can do *anything* . . . *anything*, I tell you! He can even call up the dead! [*He taps his chest.*] And here am I! Look at me, and you will see a man who is no better off than one who is dead. There's no magic art that's unknown to *him*. Well, Monsignor, my Lady . . . my real punishment is this . . . or rather *that* . . . Look! [*He points to his portrait on the wall, almost fearfully*] I cannot free myself from the magic of that painting! I am a penitent now, and such I shall remain. . . . I swear it. . . . I shall remain here until he grants me an audience. But when the ban of excommunication has been taken off, you must. . . . Both of you must implore the Pope to do this thing for me. . . . The thing that he and he alone can do. . . . Free me from *that* [*points to the portrait again*] and let me live my life fully . . . my poor wretched life . . . the life from which at present I'm shut out. . . . You can't always be twenty-six, my Lady! And I ask you to do it for your daughter's sake too . . . so that I may love her as she deserves to be loved. For now I am well disposed towards her. I feel a great tenderness for her, because of the compassion for me that she has shown. Well! That is what I wish to ask of you. . . . I am in your hands. . . . [*He bows.*] My Lady! Monsignor! [*And he starts to go out, bowing his way towards the door through which he entered. But he suddenly perceives that* BELCREDI, *who has been standing to one side in order to hear better, has turned to look upstage. He leaps to the conclusion that* he means to steal the imperial crown from him – it has been put down on the throne during the preceding scene. Instantly he dashes back and picks it up, amidst the astonishment and dismay of everyone on stage. He hides it under his sackcloth and then, with a very cunning smile in his eyes and on his lips, he moves towards the door again, and, bowing repeatedly, disappears. The MARCHIONESS is so deeply affected that she falls suddenly to a sitting position, almost fainting.]

# ACT TWO

---

*The scene is another large room in the villa, adjoining the throne-room. Its furniture is antique and austere. To the right of the stage is a rostrum about eighteen inches high. It has a wooden balustrade all round save where, at one side and at the front, a couple of steps provide access to it. It's rather reminiscent of the choir stalls in a church. On the rostrum are a table and five large, period chairs – one at the head of the table, and two on either side. The principal entrance is back. Left are two windows which look out on to the garden. Right is a door which leads into the throne-room. It is late in the afternoon of the same day.*

[*When the curtain rises* DONNA MATILDA, *the* DOCTOR, *and* TITO BELCREDI *are on-stage. They are in the middle of a conversation.* DONNA MATILDA, *however, is standing a little apart from the others. She is looking rather gloomy and is clearly very annoyed by what the other two are saying. She cannot help listening to them, however, because in her present state of disquietude everything interests her in spite of herself, and even though it prevents her from fully developing a plan that is stronger than she, a plan which has flashed into her mind and which is now tempting her. The talk of the others attracts her attention because at this moment she feels instinctively the need to be held by something.*]

BELCREDI: You're probably right. . . . It's probably just as you say, my dear Doctor. . . . But that was certainly *my* impression.

DOCTOR: I shan't presume to contradict you. . . . But, believe me, it's only . . . well, just as you yourself said . . . an *impression.*

BELCREDI: But, my dear fellow, he actually said as much! Quite clearly! [*Turning to the* MARCHIONESS] Didn't he, Marchioness?

DONNA MATILDA [*turning round, her line of thought broken in upon*]: What did he say? [*Then, disagreeing*] Oh, yes! . . . But not for the reason you think.

DOCTOR: He was referring to the costumes we'd put on. . . . Her cloak . . . [*With a gesture in the direction of the* MARCHIONESS.] Our Benedictine habits. . . . There's something very childish . . . *childlike* . . . about it all.

DONNA MATILDA [*rounding on him abruptly, indignantly*]: Childish? Childlike? What do you mean, Doctor?

DOCTOR: From one point of view it *is*! No, Marchioness, let me go on! And yet, on the other hand, it's much more complicated than you can possibly imagine.

DONNA MATILDA: As far as I'm concerned, the whole thing's perfectly clear.

DOCTOR [*with that smile of compassion which the experts so often bestow upon those unlearned in their specialism*]: Of course, my dear Marchioness! But it is necessary to understand the special psychology of the madman. It gives him . . . and I would particularly emphasize this point . . . it gives him a peculiar keenness of observation. He can, for instance, quite easily detect the true identity of anyone who appears before him in disguise. We can be absolutely sure of that. He can, in fact, clearly distinguish it *as* a disguise and yet, at the same time, *believe in it*. Just as children do. For them dressing up is not only play. . . . It is reality too. That is why I said it was 'childish' or 'childlike'. But the thing is also extremely complicated. It's complicated in this sense. . . . He must be perfectly conscious of being for himself. . . . In his own eyes he must inevitably *be* . . . an Image . . . a picture in his own imagination . . . *that* picture in there. [*He is alluding to the portrait in the throne-room, and he points, therefore, to his left.*]

BELCREDI: That's what he said, in fact.

DOCTOR: Very well, then! An image, before which other images . . . our images . . . have appeared. Do I make myself quite clear? Now he, in his acute and perfectly lucid state of delirium, was able immediately to detect a difference between his image and ours. . . . That is, he could tell at once that we . . . our images . . . were not what we pretended to be. . . . We were fictitious. And so he mistrusted us. All madmen are armed with a special kind of mistrust which remains constantly on the alert. It's all quite simple really. Naturally he couldn't see the compassion implicit within our acting, as we played out our little game around his world of make-believe. And this world of his revealed itself to us as more and more tragic the more he . . . well . . . how shall I put it? . . . he almost seemed to be challenging us. . . . That was because he mistrusted us. . . . Yes, the more he tried to show us up for the mummers that we were, the more tragic he seemed. . . . Coming to greet us like that . . . Oh yes, he was acting out a part too! . . . With his hair dyed at the temples . . . rouge on his cheeks . . . and telling us he'd done it on purpose . . . as a joke!

DONNA MATILDA [*impatiently*]: No! You're wrong, Doctor! It's not like that at all! You're quite, quite wrong!

DOCTOR: And why am I wrong, may I ask?

DONNA MATILDA [*a decisive, throbbing note in her voice*]: I am absolutely certain that he recognized me!

DOCTOR: No . . . it's impossible . . . utterly impossible.

BELCREDI [*at the same time*]: My dear, how on earth could he have done?

DONNA MATILDA [*speaks almost convulsively but even more decisively than before*]: I tell you, he recognized me! When he came up close to speak to me . . . when he looked into my eyes . . . deep into my eyes . . . he recognized me!

BELCREDI: But he was talking about your daughter!

DONNA MATILDA: That's not true! He was talking about me! He was talking about me!

BELCREDI: Yes, perhaps . . . when he talked about . . .

DONNA MATILDA [*immediately, letting herself go*]: . . . About my hair being dyed! But didn't you notice how he added at once, 'Or the memory of your dark complexion, if you were

dark'? He had remembered perfectly that I . . . in those days
. . . had dark hair.

BELCREDI: Nonsense, my dear! Utter nonsense!

DONNA MATILDA [*not bothering to listen to him, and turning to
the* DOCTOR]: My hair, Doctor, is really dark . . . just like
my daughter's. That's why he started talking about her!

BELCREDI: But he doesn't even know your daughter! He's
never so much as set eyes on her!

DONNA MATILDA: Precisely! Oh, how stupid you are! When
he was talking about my daughter he meant *me*! Me as I was
at that time!

BELCREDI: Oh, God! This is catching! This lunacy is catching!

DONNA MATILDA [*in a low voice, contemptuously*]: It's not
lunacy! Don't be a fool!

BELCREDI: Forgive me, my dear, but were *you* ever his wife?
In this mad world of his it's your daughter who's his wife –
Bertha of Susa.

DONNA MATILDA: Of course she is! Because I'm no longer
dark as he remembered me . . . but 'like this' . . . fair . . .
and I presented myself to him as 'Adelaide', her mother.
My daughter doesn't exist for him. . . . He's never even
seen her. . . . You said so yourself. So how can he know
anything at all about whether she's fair or dark?

BELCREDI: But he said dark because . . . Well, it was a
generalization . . . My God! It was like someone wanting
somehow to fix the memory of youth by the colour of the
hair! It didn't matter whether it was dark or fair! And you
. . . as usual . . . let your imagination run riot and build up
all sorts of fantastic theories! And *she* says *I* shouldn't have
come! H'm, Doctor! *She's* the one who shouldn't have
come!

DONNA MATILDA [*for a moment or so this observation of* BEL-
CREDI's *disheartens her, and she stands there, absorbed in thought.
Then she resumes, but rather furiously, because now she is half in
doubt*]: No! No! He was talking about me! All the time he

was talking to me . . . with me . . . and about me . . .

BELCREDI: Good Lord! He didn't give me a moment's breathing space, and you say that he was talking about you all the time! Maybe you think he was referring to you when he was talking to Peter Damiani!

DONNA MATILDA [*her manner challenging, almost breaking through all restraint of decorum*]: Who knows? Can you tell me why . . . from the very first moment . . . he felt such an aversion for you . . . and for you alone? [*The tone in which she asks the question makes the reply, which must in fact come in answer to it, almost explicit – 'Because he realized that you are my lover!' BELCREDI realizes this so well that he is immediately plunged into confusion by her words. He stands there in silence, an empty smile playing upon his lips.*]

DOCTOR: Forgive my breaking in, but the reason for *that* may quite well be that he had only had announced to him a visit from the Duchess Adelaide and the Abbot of Cluny. So, finding a third person before him, someone who hadn't been announced to him, his suspicions were immediately aroused!

BELCREDI: Precisely! You're absolutely right, Doctor! He felt mistrustful, and immediately he saw in me an enemy . . . Peter Damiani! But she's got it so firmly fixed in her head that he recognized her . . .

DONNA MATILDA: There's no doubt at all about it! His eyes told me that he'd recognized me, Doctor! You know, there's a way of looking that . . . well, it leaves no room whatsoever for doubt! It may only have been for a split second. . . . But would you have me deny what I believe to be true?

DOCTOR: It's a possibility that mustn't be overlooked. . . . A lucid moment . . .

DONNA MATILDA: There you are! Perhaps that's what it was! And then everything he said seemed to me, every word of it, to be full of regret for that time when he and I were both young. . . . Regret born of the terrible thing that happened to him. . . . The thing that fixed him there, fixed him in

that mask from which he has been unable to free himself!
And he longs . . . oh, how he longs to free himself from
it!

BELCREDI: Of course he does! So that he can start making love
to your daughter! Or, as you prefer to believe, now that
your compassion has aroused his tenderness, so that he can
start making love to you.

DONNA MATILDA: My compassion for him is very great. . . .
Please believe that.

BELCREDI: That is obvious, my dear Marchioness! In fact a
miracle-worker would be quite confident that it would work
a miracle for him!

DOCTOR: May I say a word now, please? I do not indulge in
miracles, because I am a doctor, and not a miracle-worker.
I have paid great attention to what you've been saying, and
I repeat that it is very evident that that particular analogical
elasticity, which is specific to every systematized state of
delirium, is in his case very much . . . how shall I put it? . . .
very much relaxed. To put it succinctly, the elements of his
delirium no longer hold together to form a coherent pattern.
It seems to me that he now has great difficulty in maintaining the equilibrium of his second personality. Sudden
recollections drag him back . . . and this is most comforting!
. . . Not from a state of incipient apathy, but rather from a
morbid tendency to subside into reflective melancholy which
shows a . . . um . . . er . . . yes . . . really considerable cere-
bral activity. Most comforting, I repeat. Now, if by means
of this violent device which we have planned . . .

DONNA MATILDA [*turning towards the window, her voice the
fretful voice of a sick person*]: Why hasn't the car come back
yet? It's three and a half hours since . . .

DOCTOR [*bewildered*]: What did you say?

DONNA MATILDA: The car, Doctor! It's been gone more than
three and a half hours!

DOCTOR [*taking out his watch and looking at it*]: H'm! More
than four by my watch!

DONNA MATILDA: It could have been back a good half-hour ago! As usual, however ...

BELCREDI: Perhaps they can't find the costume.

DONNA MATILDA: But I told them exactly where it was! [*She is now thoroughly impatient.*] It's much more probable that Frida ... Where *is* Frida?

BELCREDI [*leaning out of the window a little*]: Perhaps she's in the garden with Charles.

DOCTOR: He's probably trying to make her see how silly she is to be frightened of ...

BELCREDI: But she's not frightened, Doctor! Don't run away with that idea! She's just fed up with the whole business!

DONNA MATILDA: Doctor, please do me the kindness of not asking her to help in any way. ... I know what she's like.

DOCTOR: I think we must wait patiently to see how things turn out. In any case, it will all be over in a moment or so ... and we must wait till it's evening anyway. As I was saying, if we can succeed in shaking him in his belief in what he is at the moment ... if at one fell swoop we can break the threads ... and already they are slackening ... the threads which still bind him to the fiction which he has created for himself, and in which he lives ... and at the same time give him back what he himself has asked for ... didn't he say, 'You can't always be twenty-six, my Lady'? ... that is to say, he was asking to be freed from this punishment which he is undergoing ... he himself feels that it is a form of punishment ... Well, to sum up ... if we can get him to recover, at one bound, the sensation of the distance of time ...

BELCREDI [*immediately*]: ... He'll be cured! [*Then, lingering ironically on each syllable*] We'll free him for you, Doctor!

DOCTOR: We may hope, then, to set him going again, just like a watch that has stopped at a certain time. Yes, it'll be just as if we were standing here watch in hand, waiting for that time to come round again, and then ... we give it a shake ... and let's hope it'll start to tick again, and tell the

right time once more, after having stopped for so long.
[*At this point the* MARQUIS CHARLES DI NOLLI *comes in by the main door.*]

DONNA MATILDA: Ah, Charles! . . . And Frida? . . . Where is she?

DI NOLLI: She's in the other room. She'll be here in a moment.

DOCTOR: Has the car come?

DI NOLLI: Yes.

DONNA MATILDA: Oh, it *has* come? And have they brought my dress?

DI NOLLI: Oh, yes! It's been here some time.

DOCTOR: Oh, excellent! Excellent!

DONNA MATILDA [*trembling*]: But where is it? Where is it?

DI NOLLI [*shrugging his shoulders and smiling sadly, like a man who is lending himself reluctantly to a joke which he regards as rather unseemly*]: Oh! . . . You'll see. . . . Any minute now . . . [*And pointing to the main entrance*] Here it comes . . .

[BERTHOLD *appears on the threshold and solemnly announces*]:

BERTHOLD: Her Highness the Marchioness Matilda of Canossa!

[*And immediately* FRIDA *enters. She looks magnificent and very beautiful. She is dressed in the old costume which her mother wore as 'The Marchioness Matilda of Tuscany', and so appears as the living embodiment of the portrait in the throne-room.*]

FRIDA [*she passes quite close to* BERTHOLD – *who bows – and says to him with contemptuous haughtiness*]: Of Tuscany! Of Tuscany, *please*! Canossa is just one of my castles!

BELCREDI [*admiringly*]: Just look! Just look at her! She looks exactly like someone else!

DONNA MATILDA: She looks like me! My God, can't you see? Stand still a moment, Frida! There. . . . Do you see? She's the living image of me as I was when that portrait was painted!

DOCTOR: Oh, yes! Yes! It's absolutely perfect! Absolutely perfect! As you say, Marchioness, the portrait to the life!

BELCREDI: Yes. . . . Oh, there's no if or but about it! She's

you to the life, my dear! Look at her, everybody! Just look!
Quite superb, isn't she?

FRIDA: Don't make me laugh, *please*, or I shall burst! What a
tiny waist you had, Mummy! It was a terribly tight squeeze
getting into it!

DONNA MATILDA [*she is deeply moved*]: Just a moment, Frida.
. . . Stand still. . . . These creases . . . Is it really so tight on
you? [*While she is speaking she arranges the dress a little.*]

FRIDA: I can hardly breathe! Oh, do be quick, Mummy! And
do let's get it over quickly!

DOCTOR: Oh . . . um! We must wait until it's dark!

FRIDA: No! No! I can't possibly hold out till then! I just can't!

DONNA MATILDA: Why did you put it on so soon, then?

FRIDA: Oh, the moment I saw it . . . well, the temptation was
irresistible . . .

DONNA MATILDA: You might at least have called me and let
me help you with it. . . . It's still all crumpled. . . . Oh, dear!
Oh, dear!

FRIDA: So I saw, Mummy! And they're old creases. . . . They
won't come out very easily. . . .

DOCTOR: That doesn't matter, Marchioness. The illusion is
perfect. [*Then he goes up to* DONNA MATILDA *and asks her to
come forward and stand a little in front of her daughter, without
masking her, however.*] Please, Marchioness . . . would you
be so good as to . . . yes . . . like that . . . m'm! . . . just here
. . . so that there's a slight distance . . . that's it, a little bit
further forward . . . m'm!

BELCREDI: To get the sensation of the distance of time.

DONNA MATILDA [*turning slightly – Oh, so slightly! – in his
direction*]: Twenty years after! A disaster! M'm?

BELCREDI: Oh, come! Don't let's exaggerate!

DOCTOR [*embarrassedly trying to save the situation*]: Oh, no! No.
I was . . . er . . . I was referring to the dress . . . I wasn't
thinking about . . . you . . . Marchioness . . . I meant that I
wanted to see . . .

BELCREDI [*laughing*]: But if you were referring to the dress,

Doctor ... well, it's much more than twenty years! It's more like eight hundred years! An abyss! And do you really want to give him such a terrific shove that he'll leap them in one sudden jump? [*Points first to* FRIDA, *then to the* MARCHIONESS.] From there to here? Why, you'll have to pick up the pieces afterwards in a basket! Ladies and gentlemen ... No, this is serious! ... Do think what you're doing. For us it's a matter of a mere twenty years ... a couple of dresses ... and a masquerade. But if, as you say, Doctor, time has stopped for him ... and if he lives *there* [*pointing at* FRIDA] ... with her ... eight hundred years ago ... well, let me tell you something. ... The jump he'll have to make will leave him so giddy that, finding himself suddenly among us ... [*The* DOCTOR *shakes his finger in disagreement.*] You don't think so?

DOCTOR: No, my dear Baron, I don't. Because life, you see, can pick up its own rhythms again. This life of ours will ... if we do what I suggest ... will at once become as real for him as it is for us. And it'll pull him up short, suddenly tear him out of the grip of the illusion which holds him, and reveal to him that the eight hundred years you're talking about are in fact a mere twenty! You see, it'll be like one of those tricks that ... Well, take the leap into space in the Masonic rites, for example. ... It feels as if it's heaven knows how far, and in point of fact it's only a drop of a few inches or so.

BELCREDI: But what a wonderful discovery! Yes! Yes! Look ... look at Frida and the Marchioness, Doctor! Which of them is the more advanced in time? We old people, Doctor! Everybody thinks it's the young people who're more advanced. No! Not a bit of it! We're the ones who're more advanced ... because time belongs more to us than to them.

DOCTOR: Ah, if only the past didn't estrange us so!

BELCREDI: But it doesn't! And anyway, estrange us from what? If they [*pointing to* FRIDA *and* DI NOLLI] have still to do what we have already done, Doctor. ... That is, grow old and repeat more or less the same stupid mistakes that we've made, Doctor. . . . You know how we all believe that we come forward through a door into life. . . . But that's only an illusion. . . . It's not true at all! As soon as one is born, one begins to die, and the man who began first is the most advanced of all. And the youngest of us is old father Adam! Look at her [*pointing to* FRIDA], she is eight hundred years younger than any of us. . . . The Marchioness Matilda of Tuscany! [*And he gives her a deep bow.*]

DI NOLLI: Tito! Don't play the fool! Please! *Please!*

BELCREDI: Oh, so you think I'm playing the fool, do you?

DI NOLLI: Yes, I do! My God, you've done nothing but fool about and make silly jokes ever since we got here!

BELCREDI: Well, I'm . . .! Why, I even went so far as to dress up as a Benedictine monk, just to . . .

DI NOLLI: I know you did! But that was for a serious purpose!

BELCREDI: Well, there you are, then! And it really has turned out seriously for some of you, hasn't it? For Frida, for example. . . . [*Then, turning to the* DOCTOR] I give you my word of honour, Doctor, I still don't understand what it is you're trying to do!

DOCTOR [*crossly*]: You'll see! Just leave me to arrange things in my own way! Of course you don't understand . . . ! At the moment you see the Marchioness still dressed in modern clothes . . .

BELCREDI: You mean, then, that she's going to . . .?

DOCTOR: Of course! Of course! I've got another costume in there for her . . . all ready for the moment when it comes into his mind that it is the Marchioness Matilda of Canossa that he sees before his eyes . . .

FRIDA [*hears the* DOCTOR *make this mistake, and interrupts the conversation which she has been carrying on in an undertone with* DI NOLLI]: Of Tuscany! Of Tuscany!

DOCTOR [*crossly*]: It's the same thing!

BELCREDI: Ah, I understand! Instead of one Marchioness, he'll find himself confronted by two, eh?

DOCTOR: Exactly! . . . By *two*! And then . . .

FRIDA [*calling him over*]: Doctor! Come here a moment! There's something I want to say to you! [*He goes up to the two young people and pretends to explain things to them.*]

BELCREDI [*in a low voice, to* DONNA MATILDA]: My God! This is getting out of hand! Look, my dear . . .

DONNA MATILDA [*turning to him, her face set*]: What?

BELCREDI: Does it really interest you as much as all that? To make you willing to take part in . . .? It's a terrifying undertaking for a woman!

DONNA MATILDA: For an *ordinary* woman . . . Yes!

BELCREDI: No, my dear, there I must disagree with you! It's a terrible experience to ask *any* woman to undergo! Why, it's a total denial of one's own . . .

DONNA MATILDA: I owe it to him!

BELCREDI: Don't lie, my dear! You know quite well you won't be sacrificing any of your self-respect . . . . Not a scrap!

DONNA MATILDA: Well, then? Where does the self-denial come in?

BELCREDI: You'll do just as much as is necessary to prevent you from losing caste in other people's eyes, and just enough to insult me.

DONNA MATILDA: But who's thinking of you at the moment?

DI NOLLI [*coming forward*]: Yes! I quite agree! That's excellent! Yes! That's what we'll do! [*Turning to* BERTHOLD] Oh, you! Go and call one of the others!

BERTHOLD: Yes, sir. At once! [*And exit* BERTHOLD *by the main door.*]

DONNA MATILDA: We shall first of all have to pretend to say good-bye.

DI NOLLI: Exactly! And that's why I've sent for someone to announce that you're about to leave. [*Then, to* BELCREDI] There's no need for *you* to say goodbye! You stay in here.

BELCREDI [*shaking his head ironically*]: Oh, no! There's no need . . . No need for me to say goodbye!

DI NOLLI: You do understand, don't you? We don't want to arouse his suspicions again.

BELCREDI: Of course, I understand. I'm a . . . how shall I put it? . . . a *quantité négligeable!*

DOCTOR: We must convince him . . . utterly convince him . . . that we've left. He must be absolutely certain of that!

[LANDOLPH *enters right, followed by* BERTHOLD.]

LANDOLPH: May we come in?

DI NOLLI: Yes. . . . Yes, do come in! Now, then. . . . You're Lolo, aren't you?

LANDOLPH: Lolo or Landolph, just as you like!

DI NOLLI: Good! Now, look! The Doctor and the Marchioness will say good-bye now. . . .

LANDOLPH: Very good. All we'll have to say is that they've persuaded the Pope to grant him the favour of an audience. He's there in his room at the moment, moaning and groaning, repenting everything he said, in an absolute state lest the Pope should refuse to grant him an audience. If you'd be so kind as to . . . Would you mind just putting these costumes on again . . .?

DOCTOR: No, of course not! Come along, then! Come along . . .

LANDOLPH: Oh, just one moment! May I make a suggestion? Why not add that the Marchioness of Tuscany has joined you in imploring the Pope graciously to grant him an audience?

DONNA MATILDA: There, what did I tell you? You see, he *did* recognize me!

LANDOLPH: I'm afraid not, my Lady! Forgive me, but . . . you see, he lives in such fear of the Marchioness, with whom, as you know, the Pope was staying at the time of Canossa. It's all very strange. . . . As far as I can see . . . I'm afraid my history's a bit weak, and you'll certainly know this much better than I do . . . isn't there a legend that Henry IV was secretly in love with the Marchioness of Tuscany?

DONNA MATILDA [*immediately*]: No . . . Nothing of the kind!

There's no such legend! In fact, they were deadly enemies!

LANDOLPH: Well, that's what I thought! But he says that he loved her. . . . He keeps on saying it. . . . And now he's panic-stricken lest her disdain for this secret love of his should do him harm with the Pope.

BELCREDI: We must make him realize that this aversion for him no longer exists!

LANDOLPH: Ah, it would be an excellent thing if we could do that!

DONNA MATILDA [to LANDOLPH]: Yes, an excellent thing! [Then, to BELCREDI] Because, so the history books tell us . . . just in case you didn't know . . . the Pope did in fact only yield when begged to do so by the Marchioness Matilda and the Abbot of Cluny. And I may say, my dear Belcredi, that I intended to take advantage of this fact then, at the time of the pageant, in order to show him that I no longer felt as hostile towards him as he imagined.

BELCREDI: But how wonderful, my dear Marchioness! Your devotion to history is most touching! Pray continue with your devotions. . . .

LANDOLPH: Well then! In that case we needn't worry about . . . the Marchioness can save herself the bother of a double disguise and present herself with Monsignor [a gesture in the direction of the DOCTOR] as the Marchioness of Tuscany.

DOCTOR [immediately, forcefully]: No! No! That would never do! It would ruin everything! The impression he gets from the confrontation must be a sudden one. . . . It must give him a tremendous shock! No! No, Marchioness! Now let's go and get changed! You will appear again as the Duchess Adelaide, mother of the Empress. And we'll take our leave of him. The most important thing is that he should know that we've left. Now come along! We must get on. . . . We mustn't lose any more time. . . . There's still a great deal to be done before we're ready for this evening.

[Exeunt the DOCTOR, DONNA MATILDA, and LANDOLPH right.]

FRIDA: I'm beginning to feel terrified again!

DI NOLLI: Again, Frida?

FRIDA: It would've been better if I'd seen him the first time.

DI NOLLI: There's nothing to be frightened of! *Really!*

FRIDA: He's not dangerous, is he?

DI NOLLI: Why, of course not! He's quite calm!

BELCREDI [*with ironical sentimental affectation*]: In the depths of melancholy! Didn't you hear that he loves you!

FRIDA: Thank you very much! It's because of that that I'm afraid!

BELCREDI: He won't hurt you. . . .

DI NOLLI: And it'll only take a moment or so. . . .

FRIDA: Yes . . . perhaps . . . but there in the dark . . . alone with him . . .

DI NOLLI: But only for a moment! And I'll be there, too . . . ever so near you . . . and everybody else will be hiding behind the door . . . ready to rush in at the crucial moment. The instant he sees your mother standing before him, your part will be over. . . . See?

BELCREDI: It's something altogether different that I'm afraid of. . . . I'm afraid myself that we're just wasting our time!

DI NOLLI: Now, don't you start! I think the idea's quite a good one . . . and I think it'll come off.

FRIDA: And so do I! So do I! I can feel it in my bones! Oh dear, I'm trembling all over!

BELCREDI: But, my dear young people, mad folk . . . though they don't know it, alas! . . . are blessed with a peculiar kind of happiness which we never take into account . . .

DI NOLLI [*irritated, interrupting him*]: Good God, man! What are you talking about now? What kind of happiness?

BELCREDI [*forcefully*]: They don't think logically!

DI NOLLI: But what the devil has logic got to do with what we're talking about?

BELCREDI: What? Can't you see that that is precisely what he'll need when he catches sight of her [*pointing at* FRIDA] and her mother? Don't you see that he'll have to think logically if your plan is to come off? Remember, the whole thing is the product of *our* thinking, not of his!

DI NOLLI: Oh, rubbish! What the devil do you mean? Logic be damned! What we're doing is presenting a double image of his own fiction to him! Oh, you heard yourself what the Doctor said!

BELCREDI [*suddenly, unexpectedly*]: You know, I've never understood why they take degrees in medicine!

DI NOLLI [*bewildered*]: Who?

BELCREDI: Psychiatrists.

DI NOLLI: What the . . .? What ought they to take their degrees in, then?

FRIDA: But if they want to be psychiatrists what else should they . . .?

BELCREDI: Precisely! Why in law, of course, my dear! Talk! Talk! Talk! And the more you talk the more famous you are! 'Analogical elasticity'! 'The sensation of the distance of time'! And then the first thing they tell you is that they don't work miracles . . . when a miracle's the very thing you need! But they know quite well that the more they say they're not miracle-workers, the more people are impressed by their seriousness. Oh no, they don't work miracles! But somehow they always manage to land on their feet! Which is rather nice for them, I should think!

[BERTHOLD *meanwhile has been spying through the key-hole of the door right.*]

BERTHOLD: They've just . . . ! Oh look, they're . . . ! Oh, it looks as if they're coming in here!

DI NOLLI: Are you quite sure?

BERTHOLD: M'm! It looks as if he wants to come with them. . . . Yes! Yes! . . . He's coming towards the door!

DI NOLLI: We'd better go then! We'd better get out of here at once! [*When he reaches the door, he turns and says to* BERTHOLD] You stay here!

BERTHOLD: Must I?

[*Without bothering to reply,* DI NOLLI, FRIDA, *and* BEL-

CREDI *make their escape through the main door, leaving*
BERTHOLD *in an agony of dismay and suspense. The door
right opens and* LANDOLPH *comes in first. He stands bowing
at the door and* DONNA MATILDA *enters, wearing the cloak
and ducal coronet that she wore in the first act. She is accompanied by the* DOCTOR, *who is dressed as the Abbot of Cluny.*
HENRY IV, *dressed in his emperor's robes, walks between them.*
ORDULPH *and* HAROLD *bring up the rear.*]

HENRY IV [*continuing to speak on a subject upon which one is to
suppose they had embarked while in the throne-room*]: I ask you,
how can I possibly be so astute, if I'm as pig-headed as they
make out?

DOCTOR: Why, no . . . you're not at all pig-headed!

HENRY IV [*smiling, pleased at the* DOCTOR'S *reply*]: So, according to you, then, I'm really rather astute?

DOCTOR: No! No! Neither pig-headed nor astute!

HENRY IV [*stops and, in the tone of one who is quite benevolently,
but not without a certain irony, indicating that such a state of
affairs just cannot be, exclaims*]: Monsignor! If pig-headedness
is not a vice which may go hand in hand with astuteness, I
had hoped that in denying me it, you would at least have
been kind enough to allow me a little astuteness. I assure
you I stand in very great need of it! But if you want to keep
it all for yourself . . .

DOCTOR: But, what makes you think that I . . .? Do I strike
you as being an astute sort of man?

HENRY IV: Oh no, Monsignor! What an extraordinary
question! I don't think you're at all astute! [*Breaks off and
turns to* DONNA MATILDA.] By your leave, a word in confidence with the Duchess . . . here on the threshold. . . . [*He
leads her a little to one side and asks her very earnestly, making
a great show of secrecy*] Is your daughter really very dear to you?

DONNA MATILDA [*in dismay*]: Why, yes. . . . Certainly. . . .

HENRY IV: And do you wish me to reward her with all my
love? . . . With all my devotion? So that I may right all the
wrongs I have done her? Though you mustn't believe all

those stories my enemies have been spreading about my being dissolute. . . .

DONNA MATILDA: No! No! I don't believe them! I never have believed them. . . .

HENRY IV: Well, then . . . is it your will that . . .

DONNA MATILDA [*dismay in her voice*]: . . . That what?

HENRY IV: . . . That I should once again love your daughter? [*He looks at her, and adds immediately in a mysterious tone, in which warning and dismay are mingled.*] You mustn't be friends with the Marchioness of Tuscany! You must never be that woman's friend!

DONNA MATILDA: But, as I've already told you, she has been no less persistent than we in begging the Pope . . . in beseeching him . . . to grant you pardon. . . .

HENRY IV [*immediately, softly – he is trembling all over*]: You mustn't tell me that! You mustn't tell me that! My God, my Lady, can't you see the effect it has on me?

DONNA MATILDA [*she looks at him; then says in a very quiet voice, as if she is confiding in him*]: Do you still love her?

HENRY IV [*dismayed*]: Still? What do you mean . . . do I *still* love her? You know, then? But nobody knows! Nobody *must* know!

DONNA MATILDA: But *she* knows perhaps. Yes. And perhaps that is why she has pleaded so hard for you!

HENRY IV [*looks at her for a moment and then says*]: And you love your daughter? [*A short pause. He turns to the DOCTOR, a note of laughter in his voice.*] Ah, Monsignor, how true it is that I only realized I had a wife after I'd . . . Too late . . . Too late . . . And even now . . . Yes, I must have a wife. . . . There's no doubt, of course, that she *is* my wife. . . . But I swear to you . . . I hardly ever think of her. That's probably a sin. . . . But I don't feel anything for her at all. . . . In my heart I have no feeling for her at all. What's stranger still, however, is that her mother's heart is just as barren of feeling for her. Confess, my Lady, that she means very little to you! [*Turning to the DOCTOR, he says exasperatedly*] She talks to me about that other woman! [*And, getting more and more excited*] So persistently too! She keeps on talking about her! And I can't understand at all why she should want to!

LANDOLPH [*humbly*]: Perhaps, your Majesty, she does it so as to persuade you into giving up the unfavourable opinion which you've formed of the Marchioness of Tuscany. [*Then, dismayed at having permitted himself such an observation, he immediately adds*] I'm speaking, of course, of the way things are going at the moment. . . .

HENRY IV: Perhaps you, too, would maintain that she has been my friend?

LANDOLPH: Yes, at the moment, I should say she *is*, your Majesty!

DONNA MATILDA: Why yes, of course, she is! . . . And because of that . . .

HENRY IV: I understand. Which means, then, that you don't believe that I love her. I understand. I understand. No one has ever believed it. No one has ever suspected it. So much the better! That is just as it should be! It fits in well enough with my desires! [*He stops short and turns to the* DOCTOR, *his expression and his attitude completely altered.*] Have you realized, Monsignor, that the conditions which the Pope has laid down, the conditions with which I must comply before he will lift the ban of excommunication he has laid upon me, have nothing, *absolutely nothing*, to do with the reasons for which he excommunicated me? Tell Pope Gregory that we shall meet again at Bressanone. And you, my Lady, should you have the good fortune to meet your daughter down there in the courtyard of the castle of your friend the Marchioness, what message would you like me to give you for her? Ask her to come up here and visit me. We shall see whether I can succeed in keeping her close by my side. . . . My Empress and my wife! Oh, how many women have presented themselves here already, assuring me, assuring me that they were Bertha of Susa. . . . And I knew that Bertha was mine. . . . She belonged to me. . . . So several

times I . . . tried to take her . . . to have the woman who . .
There's nothing to be ashamed of in that. . . . After all, she is·
my wife! . . . But every one of them . . . Even while she was
telling me that she was Bertha . . . Bertha of Susa . . . began
. . . I don't know why . . . she began to laugh! [*Then, as if
in confidence*] Do you understand? In bed . . . I hadn't these
clothes on . . . and she . . . naked too . . . yes, my God! . . .
naked! . . . a man and a woman . . . It's all very natural! At
such times we're no longer concerned with what sort of
people we are! And our clothes . . . once we've taken them
off . . . they remain there, hanging on their pegs like so
many phantoms! [*Then in a changed tone, confidentially to
the* DOCTOR] I think, Monsignor, that phantoms in
general are, at bottom, nothing more or less than trifling
spiritual disorders. Images that we fail to keep within the
frontiers of sleep. They reveal themselves even when we're
awake . . . during the daytime. And they terrify us. I am
always afraid in the night, when I see them there before me.
. . . So many disordered images. . . . Down from their
horses now, laughing away. . . . And sometimes I'm even
afraid of my own blood pulsing through my arteries . . . like
the dull thudding of footsteps in the silence of the night
. . . treading their way through far-off rooms. . . . But, forgive me! I've kept you standing here far too long. Your
humble servant, my Lady! I kiss your hand, Monsignor!
[*He goes with them to the door and bids them farewell. As he
stands there on the threshold,* DONNA MATILDA *curtseys, the*
DOCTOR *bows, and out they go. He shuts the door behind them and
turns round immediately. He is a different person altogether now.*]
Fools! Fools! Fools! Pipes on which my fingers may play
what tune they please! The lightest of touches, and they
burst into the songs I bid them sing! And that fellow . . .
Peter Damiani! Ha! Ha! I caught him out beautifully! He's
too frightened to present himself before me again. [*Walks
up and down excitedly as he is saying this. There is a hectic gaiety
in his voice, a note of frenzy. Suddenly his darting glance falls on*

BERTHOLD *who is shrinking back, terrified out of his wits by* HENRY'S *sudden change. He stops in front of him and points him out to his three comrades, who are every bit as bewildered, dismayed, and terrified as he is.*] Oh, look at this idiot here! Look at him! Standing here gaping at me ... with his mouth wide open ... [*He shakes him by the shoulders.*] Don't you understand? Can't you see how I treat them? How I make them dress themselves up, just as my fancy takes me! How I force them to appear before me? Miserable, frightened clowns that they are! And what is it they're frightened of? This ... and this alone ... that I shall tear off their fool's mask and show up their disguise for what it is! As if it wasn't *I* myself who had forced them to assume that mask... so that my taste for playing the madman might be satisfied

| LANDOLPH HAROLD ORDULPH | [*dazedly looking at one another in utter bewilderment*] | What? What did he say? But, if that's how things are, what ...? |
|---|---|---|

HENRY IV [*immediately they start to speak he turns on them and cries imperiously*]: Silence! That will do! I've had enough! I'm fed-up with the whole affair! [*Then, immediately, as if the very thought of it brought him neither peace nor the ability fully to believe in the reality of what's happened.*] My God! What impudence! Coming here like that ... to see me ... now ... with her lover by her side ... pretending to dress themselves up out of compassion for me ... so as not to vex the mind of a poor devil who was already out of this world ... out of time ... out of life itself! Huh! Do you think that fellow would have put up with being pushed around like that, if it hadn't promised him so much amusement? Those people always demand that the rest of us should behave exactly as they wish. That every moment of every day should be lived out as they dictate. But of course there's nothing arrogant about that! Oh, no! No! Of course not! It's merely *their* way of thinking! *Their* way of seeing ... *their* way of feeling! Everybody's got his own way of ... You've got yours, too, haven't you? Of course, you have!

But what *is* your way? Your way is that of the common herd. You're a flock of sheep . . . wretched, uncertain, feeble . . . and *they* take advantage of it! They make you submit to their will. They make you accept their way of life. So that you feel and see as they do! At least, that's the illusion to which they blissfully cling. For, after all, what is it that they've succeeded in imposing upon you? Words! Words, that each one of us understands and gives out again in his own particular way. And that . . . that is how so-called public opinion is formed! And it's a poor lookout for the man who finds himself branded with one of these words which everybody goes about repeating . . . like *madman* or . . . oh, I don't know . . . *fool.* Tell me something . . . don't you think it's a bit much, expecting a man to keep quiet, when he knows that there's a fellow going about doing his damnedest to persuade other people that you're what he sees you as? When he's trying his utmost to fix in other people's minds *his* assessment of you . . . *his* judgement upon you! 'He's mad!' 'Quite out of his mind!' . . . Now I'm being serious. . . . I'm not talking any longer about the pleasure of making them act as I bid them. . . . Before I . . . before I fell from my horse and hurt my head . . . [*He breaks off short, noticing the dismay of the four young men. His speech has served only to increase their amazement and distress.*] Why are you looking at one another like that? [*He laughs mockingly at their stupefied expressions.*] Ha! Ha! Ha! What's the matter? Is it all a revelation to you? Am I mad, or aren't I mad? Go on! M'm? Yes, I'm mad all right! [*His manner becomes terrible.*] Well, then . . . down! My God! Down on your knees! Down on your knees! [*And one by one he forces them down on to their knees before him.*] I order you to go down on your knees before me . . . yes, like that! And touch the ground three times with your foreheads! Go on! Down with your heads! That's the way that everyone must present himself to a madman! [*At the sight of the four of them kneeling there he immediately feels his ferocious gaiety evaporat-*

*ing. He becomes contemptuous.*] Get up, you sheep! Go on, get up! . . . You obeyed me, didn't you? You might have put a strait-jacket on me! To crush a man like that . . . with the weight of a single word! But it's nothing really! What is it, in fact? A fly! And yet the whole of life is crushed out of you . . . like that . . . by the weight of words! The weight of the dead! . . . I stand here before you. Can you really believe that Henry IV is still alive? And yet . . . look! . . . you are living men, and I can speak to you and command you to do my will! And that is how I want you! Do you think this is a joke too, that the dead continue to live? Oh yes, it's a joke here all right! But suppose we leave here and go out into the world of the living. Dawn is breaking. All time is before us. Dawn . . . and the dawn of . . . and the day that lies before us. You say to yourselves . . . this day is ours to make of it what we will. And do you? *Do* you? To hell with tradition! To hell with the old conventions! Go on, talk away! You'll do nothing but repeat the same old words, over and over again, like countless generations before you! Do you really believe you're living? All that you're doing is chewing the cud of the life of the dead! [*Goes up to* BERTHOLD, *who has succumbed to a stupor of terror and amazement.*] You don't understand a word of all this, do you? . . . What's your name?

BERTHOLD: Me? . . . Oh! . . . Er . . . Berthold . . .

HENRY IV: Idiot! What do you mean, *Berthold*? Now tell me the truth, what's your *real* name?

BERTHOLD: Well, I . . . I . . . my real n-n-name's Fino . . .

HENRY IV [*turning quickly to quell a slight – Oh, very slight! – movement of warning and admonition on the part of the other three*]: Fino?

BERTHOLD: Yes, sir. . . . Fino Pagliuca.

HENRY IV [*turning again to the others*]: The number of times I've heard you calling one another by your real names, when you were by yourselves! [*To* LANDOLPH] Your name's Lolo, isn't it?

LANDOLPH: Yes, sir.... [*Then, bursting with joy*] Oh, God! Then...?

HENRY IV [*immediately, brusquely*]: What?

LANDOLPH [*immediately faltering*]: No.... I was only going to say...

HENRY IV: That I'm no longer mad? Of course I'm not! Can't you see? We're having a bit of fun at the expense of those who believe I am!

[*To* HAROLD] I know your name too.... It's Franco....
[*To* ORDULPH] And you... wait a moment...

ORDULPH: Momo!

HENRY IV: That's it, Momo! Wonderful, isn't it? *M'm?*

LANDOLPH [*joyfully*]: But, in that case...! Oh, my God!

HENRY IV [*brusquely*]: In that case what? In that case, *nothing!* Let's have a good long laugh together! [*And he laughs.*] Ha! Ha! Ha! Ha! Ha! Ha!

LANDOLPH ⎱ [*looking at one another in uncertainty and dismay. In*
HAROLD ⎰ *their faces joy and bewilderment conflict*]: Is he
ORDULPH ⎰ cured? Can it be true? But how on...?

HENRY IV: Silence! Silence! [*To* BERTHOLD] You're not laughing! Why not? Are you still offended? You mustn't be! I didn't just mean *you*, you know! Everybody, absolutely everybody, has to believe that certain people are mad, so as to have an excuse for keeping them locked up. Do you know why? Because otherwise you can't resist the temptation to listen to what they're saying. What shall I say about those people who've just left? Shall I tell you that one of them's a whore? Another a filthy libertine? And the third a charlatan? But it's not true! Nobody could ever possibly believe it! But they'd all stop and listen to me, terrified, every single one of them! Now, tell me why, if what I say isn't true? Oh, you mustn't believe what madmen say! Yet they stop and listen to them, with their eyes popping out of their heads with terror! Why? Tell me why! *You!* Tell me why! You see, I'm quite calm now.

BERTHOLD: Well, because... perhaps it's because they think that...

HENRY IV: No, my dear fellow, no! Look into my eyes . . .
deep down into them. . . . Don't be alarmed! I don't say
that it's true! Nothing is true! But look into my eyes!

BERTHOLD: Ye-es? And what am I . . .?

HENRY IV: You see? You see? You're afraid too! You too
have terror in your eyes! Because now I seem mad to you
too! There's the proof! There's the proof of what I was saying! [Laughs.]

LANDOLPH [is at the end of his tether. He plucks up courage and
steps forward, the spokesman of them all]: But . . . What proof?

HENRY IV: Why, your being so dismayed because now I seem
to you to be mad again! Oh, my God! Of course you know
what I mean! You believe it now. . . . And you believed it
before . . . believed that I was mad! Didn't you? Didn't you?
Right up till a moment or so ago! [They are terrified. He looks
at them for a moment.] You see? You feel that this dismay of
yours could so easily become terror, don't you? The terror
you'd know in the face of something that dashed away the
ground from under your feet, that snatched away the very
air you were breathing! And this, gentlemen, is what you
must feel. You can't help yourselves! Do you know what it's
like to find yourself face to face with a madman? To find
yourself face to face with someone who shakes the very
foundations of everything you've built up in yourselves?
Everything you've built up around you? Who challenges
the logic, the logic of all that you've constructed? H'm!
Well, what can one do about it? That's the way things are!
Lucky people, madmen! They construct without logic. . . .
Or, rather, with a logic all their own, that flies hither and
thither . . . light as a feather! Here one moment, gone the
next! Today things are like this . . . and tomorrow? Who
knows? You hold on tight to an idea and they . . . hold on
to nothing. Light as a feather, they float from idea to idea.
You say, 'But that's impossible!' But for them everything's
possible. 'But,' you reply, 'that's not true!' And why isn't it
true? Because it doesn't seem true to you . . . and you . . .

and you ... [*Pointing to the other three of them.*] And a hundred thousand other people! Ah, my dear fellows! And just look at the things that seem real to your hundred thousand other people! The ones who are not supposed to be mad! What a wonderful sight they afford, as they reach their solemn agreements on this or that! What flowers of logic they produce! I know that when I was a child, I thought the moon in the pond was real. Oh, how many things seemed real to me then! I believed everything that everyone told me, and I was happy, completely happy. Because it's a terrible thing if you don't hold on tight to what seems true to you today, to what will seem true to you tomorrow, even if it is the complete opposite of what seemed true to you yesterday! I would never wish you to think, as I have had to do, of that horrible thing which really drives you out of your mind. .... You're there, very close to someone, looking into his eyes, just as, one day, I looked into someone's eyes ... and you see yourself mirrored there. .... But it's not really yourself! No, you see yourself as a beggar, standing before a door through which you will never pass. The man who goes through that door will not be you ... you with that secret life, that world you have within you ... the familiar world of sight and touch ... It will be someone quite unknown to you who will pass in at that door. .... The man *he* sees you as ... The one he, in his own personal, impenetrable world, sees and touches. [*A long pause. Darkness gathers in the room, increasing the deep sense of dismay and consternation which fills the four young men. Four lesser masks, they are being removed even further away from the great Mask. He remains apart, absorbed in the contemplation of a terrifying world of wretchedness which is not the wretchedness of himself alone, but of all mankind. Then he shakes off his air of brooding and, as if feeling that he no longer has them with him, looks about him in search of the four young men.*] It's getting dark in here. ....

ORDULPH [*immediately stepping forward*]: Would you like me to go and fetch the lamp?

HENRY IV [*ironically*]: Oh, yes . . . the lamp! Do you really believe that I don't know that, once my back's turned and I've gone off to bed with my oil lamp, you switch on the electric light for your own benefit in here, and even in there, in the throne-room? I pretend not to notice. . . .

ORDULPH: Oh! Then would you like me to . . .?

HENRY IV: No, it would blind me! I want my lamp.

ORDULPH: I'll go and get it. It's probably ready by now . . . behind the door. [*He walks over to the principal exit, goes outside for a very brief moment and immediately returns with a lamp. It is an eleventh-century piece, one of those lamps you carry by a ring at the top.*]

HENRY IV [*taking the lamp and then pointing to the table on the small rostrum*]: Come over here. . . . Let's have a little light. Sit down there . . . round the table. But not like that! More at your ease . . . in more aesthetically pleasing positions . . . not so stiff . . . more relaxed. . . . [*To* HAROLD] That's it, like that! [*He places him in position. Then he says to* BERTHOLD] And you, like that. . . . [*Arranging him in position.*] That's it. . . . [*He sits down himself.*] And I'll sit here. . . . [*Turning his head towards one of the windows.*] One really ought to be able to command the moon to provide us with a fine decorative moonbeam. . . . The moon is very useful to us . . . very useful . . . most helpful! As for me . . . I feel a need for the moon, and quite often I get completely lost in wonderment as I gaze up at her from my window. Who would believe, to look at her, that she knows that eight hundred years have passed? And that I, who am seated at the window, looking up at the moon, like the poorest of poor devils, cannot really be Henry IV? But look . . . look what a magnificent night scene we make! The Emperor surrounded by his faithful counsellors. . . . Don't you find it rather pleasant?

LANDOLPH [*in a low voice to* HAROLD, *as if fearful of breaking the enchantment*]: Do you realize what? . . . To think that it wasn't true . . .!

HENRY IV: True? What wasn't true?

LANDOLPH [*timidly, apologetically*]: No ... I mean ... I was telling Berthold [*with a gesture in his direction*] only this morning ... You see, he was new to the job ... I said what a pity it was that ... with all these lovely costumes ... and all the others out there in the wardrobe ... and with a room like that ... [*A gesture in the direction of the throne-room.*]

HENRY IV: Well? Did you say it was a pity?

LANDOLPH: Yes ... I did ... I meant a pity we didn't know that ...

HENRY IV: That you were playing this thing out as a joke?

LANDOLPH: Because, you see ... we believed that ...

HAROLD [*coming to his assistance*]: Yes ... we believed that the whole thing was serious!

HENRY IV: And isn't it? Do you really think it's not serious?

LANDOLPH: Well, if you say that ...

HENRY IV: What I say is that you're a pack of fools! You ought to have known how to create the fantasy for yourselves! Not just known how to play your parts when you were with me ... or when people came to see me from time to time. ... They should have become second nature to you! You should have lived the part every minute of every day ... even when there was no one to see you. ... [*Then, to* BERTHOLD, *taking him by the arm*] So that this world of fiction which you had created for yourself. ... You'd eat in it ... sleep in it. ... You'd even scratch yourself in character when you felt your shoulder itching. [*He turns to the others*] And all the time you'd feel yourself to be living ... really to be living ... in the history of the eleventh century ... here at the Court of your Emperor, Henry IV! And to think that at a distance of eight centuries from this remote age of ours ... so colourful and yet so sepulchral ... to think that the men of the twentieth century are torturing themselves, in an absolute agony of anxiety, to know how things will work out. Painstakingly they rush around, frantic about fate and fortune, and about what they have in store for them. Whereas you are already in history with me! And sad as my lot is . . . hideous as are the events of my life . . . with all the bitterness and all the struggle . . . with all the sorrow and all the strife . . . nonetheless . . . it's all history. . . . Nothing can change! . . . Do you understand? . . . Nothing can possibly change! Everything is fixed for ever! And you can peacefully gaze on in admiration as effect follows obediently upon cause, with the most perfect logic . . . and as every event happens precisely and coherently, right down to the smallest detail. Yes, the pleasures of history . . . the pleasures of history . . . and they're so very great! All yours!

LANDOLPH: Beautiful . . . beautiful . . . oh!

HENRY IV: Beautiful . . . yes! But now it's all over. . . . Finished! Now that you know, I can no longer go on with it! [*Picks up the lamp to go to bed.*] Neither could you . . . if up till now you've not understood the reason why we've lived like this! Oh God, how sick I am of it now! [*Then almost to himself, his voice vibrant with restrained fury.*] By God I'll make her sorry she came here! Oh! Dressing herself up as my mother-in-law! And *he* . . . was a monk! A reverend father! . . . And they bring along a doctor with them, so that he can study me. . . . Who knows? Perhaps they hope they can cure me! . . . The stupid, stupid fools! There's one of them at least whose face I'd like to slap. . . . Yes, that fellow! They say he's an expert swordsman, don't they? He'll kill me. . . . Run me through just like . . . But we'll see . . . we'll see . . . [*A knock is heard at the door.*] Who is it?

JOHN'S VOICE: Deo Gratias!

HAROLD [*there is joy in his voice – perhaps he feels that there's still one joke left to play*]: Ah, it's John! It's John! He's come to do the old monk as usual! Every evening, regular as clockwork. . .!

ORDULPH [*rubbing his hands with glee*]: Yes, let's make him do it! Let's make him do it!

HENRY IV [*instantly, severely*]: You fool! Why? Don't you see what a fool you are? Making fun of a poor old man who plays his part out of love for me!

LANDOLPH [*to* ORDULPH]: Everything's got to be as if it were true! Didn't you understand that?

HENRY IV: Exactly! As if it were true! Because only when it's like that does the truth cease to be a joke! [*He goes and opens the door and lets in John, who is dressed as a humble friar and who is carrying a roll of parchment under his arm.*] Come in! Come in, Father! [*Then, assuming a tone of tragic gravity and of gloomy resentment.*] All the documents concerning my life and my reign which were favourable to me were destroyed, deliberately destroyed, by my enemies. Only one has escaped destruction . . . My life, written by a humble monk who is devoted to me . . . and you want to laugh at him! [*He turns affectionately to* JOHN *and invites him to sit down at the table, on the side nearest the audience.*] Sit down, Father! Sit down here. . . . Let me put the lamp near you. [*All through the preceding lines he has been holding the lamp. Now he puts it down on the table near* JOHN.] Write! Write!

JOHN [*unrolls the roll of parchment and gets ready to write at* HENRY'S *dictation*]: I am ready, your Majesty!

HENRY IV [*dictating*]: The decree of peace which was proclaimed at Mainz benefited the humble and the oppressed as much as it harmed the interests of the wicked and the powerful. [*The curtain begins to fall.*] It brought riches to the former . . . hunger and destitution to the latter . . .

# ACT THREE

*The scene is the throne-room. It is dark. The wall back can barely be distinguished in the darkness. The canvases of the two portraits have been removed and in their places, standing within the frames, which have been left there to give a framework to the emptiness of the niches, are* FRIDA *and* CHARLES DI NOLLI. *They are in exactly the same positions as the figures in the portraits.* FRIDA *is dressed as the 'Marchioness of Tuscany', as we saw her in Act Two, and* CHARLES DI NOLLI *is dressed as 'Henry IV'.*

[*For a moment or so after the curtain goes up the stage appears to be empty. The door left opens and* HENRY IV *enters, carrying his lamp by the ring at the top. He is looking back, talking to the four young men who, together with* JOHN, *are supposedly in the adjoining room, just as we left them at the end of Act Two.*]

HENRY IV: No! Stay where you are! Stay where you are! I can manage by myself. Good night! [*He closes the door behind him and moves, very sad and tired, across the room, in the direction of the second door on the right, which leads into his apartments.*]

FRIDA [*immediately she sees that he has gone a little way past the throne, she whispers from her niche. Her voice is that of a woman who feels herself fainting away through fear*]: Henry . . .

HENRY IV [*stopping at the sound of her voice, as if someone had treacherously stabbed him in the back. He turns a terror-stricken face towards the wall back, and instinctively half raises his arms, as if to ward off a blow*]: Who's calling me? [*It's not really a question. . . . It's more of an exclamation, an exclamation that vibrates with shuddering terror. It doesn't expect any reply from the darkness and the terrible silence of the throne-room, which quite suddenly have become filled for him with the suspicion that he really is mad.*]

FRIDA [*his gesture of terror has done nothing to mitigate her own terror at the part she is playing. Now she repeats a little more loudly*]: Henry ... [*And although she wishes still to maintain the part she has been given to play, she stretches her head a little way out of the frame and looks in the direction of the niche in which* DI NOLLI *is standing.*]

[HENRY IV *gives a dreadful cry and lets fall his lamp. Covering his head with his arms, he makes a movement as if to run away.* FRIDA *jumps out of the frame on to the ledge in front, and stands there screaming like a mad woman.*]

FRIDA: Henry! ... Henry! ... I'm afraid! ... I'm afraid!

[*Meanwhile* DI NOLLI *has also leapt out of his frame on to the ledge and thence to the floor. He rushes over to* FRIDA, *who is on the verge of fainting. She continues to scream, her face and voice convulsed with terror. The* DOCTOR, DONNA MATILDA (*also dressed as the 'Marchioness of Tuscany'*), TITO BEL-CREDI, LANDOLPH, HAROLD, ORDULPH, BERTHOLD, *and* JOHN *all burst in through the door left. One of them immediately turns on the light. It's a strange light, which comes from bulbs hidden in the ceiling, so that only the upper part of the set is well-lit.* HENRY IV *gazes on in utter astonishment at this unexpected inrush, coming as it does immediately after that moment of terror. He is still shuddering at the memory of it. The others ignore him and rush anxiously over to comfort and support* FRIDA. *She is lying trembling and sobbing in the arms of her fiancé. There is a babble of confused talk.*]

DI NOLLI: No! No! Frida! ... I'm here now! ... I'll look after you!

DOCTOR [*coming up with the others*]: Stop! Not another ... ! We mustn't go on with it. ... There's no need. ...

DONNA MATILDA: He's cured, Frida! Can't you see? He's cured! Can't you see?

DI NOLLI [*in utter amazement*]: Cured?

BELCREDI: It was all a joke. Now just be calm! Everything's all right!

FRIDA [*frenziedly*]: No! I'm afraid! I'm afraid!

DONNA MATILDA: But what are you afraid of? Look at him! He was never mad at all! He was never mad at all!

DI NOLLI [*still quite bewildered*]: He was never mad at all? What on earth are you talking about? He's cured?

DOCTOR: It certainly seems so! As far as I'm concerned, I should say . . .

BELCREDI: Of course he's cured! *They* told us so! [*He points to the four young men.*]

DONNA MATILDA: Yes, and has been for some time! He confided in them.

DI NOLLI [*now more indignant than bewildered*]: But what on earth . . .! What does it mean? If up until a short while ago . . .?

BELCREDI: Oh! He was acting! He wanted to have a good laugh at your expense! And at *our* expense too! And in all good faith we . . .

DI NOLLI: Is it really possible? Do you mean to say that he would even go so far as to deceive his own sister, right up until the day she died?

[HENRY IV *meanwhile has remained to one side, peering now at one, now at another, as the rain of mockery and accusations grows. To them quite obviously what is now revealed appears as a cruel jest. By the flashing of his eyes he shows that he is meditating revenge, though the violent anger which is raging like a tumult within him has so far prevented him from clearly defining to himself the nature of that revenge. At this point he is stung to the quick, and, with the clear intention of assuming as true the fiction they have so insidiously created for him, he now bursts out.*]

HENRY IV [*shouting at* DI NOLLI]: Go on! Go on!

DI NOLLI [*astounded, taken aback by the cry*]: Go on? What do you mean, go on?

HENRY IV: It's not only *your* sister that's dead!

DI NOLLI [*even more taken aback*]: My sister? I was talking about *your* sister . . . whom you compelled right up to the day she died to present herself here as your mother Agnes!

HENRY IV: Then she wasn't *your* mother?

DI NOLLI: Yes, she *was* my mother! *My* mother!

HENRY IV: But, for me ... and I am old and far away ... she is dead.... Your mother is dead! And you ... you have just tumbled down ... a brand new being ... from up there. [*He points to the niche from which* DI NOLLI *has leapt.*] And how do you know whether I've not wept for her ... wept a long time for her ... secretly ... even though I am dressed like this?

DONNA MATILDA [*in consternation, looking at the others*]: But what's he saying?

DOCTOR [*greatly affected, studying him*]: Quiet ... please! Please be quiet!

HENRY IV: What am I saying? I'm asking you all if Agnes was not the mother of Henry IV! [*He turns to* FRIDA, *as if indeed she really were the Marchioness of Tuscany.*] You, my dear Marchioness, ought to know! Or so it seems to me!

FRIDA [*still afraid, clinging more tightly to* DI NOLLI]: No! No! I don't know! I don't know anything at all about it!

DOCTOR: It's the madness returning.... Please be quiet, ladies and gentlemen!

BELCREDI [*angrily*]: Madness be damned, Doctor! He's picking up the play where he left off! He's acting again!

HENRY IV [*immediately*]: You accuse *me* of acting? It was you who emptied those niches there, and *he* stands before me as Henry IV ...

BELCREDI: Well anyway, let's have done with the joke now!

HENRY IV: Who said it was a joke?

DOCTOR [*loudly, to* BELCREDI]: Don't excite him, for the love of God!

BELCREDI [*not heeding him, even louder*]: Why, *they* said it was a joke! [*Again he points to the four young men.*] *They* said so! *They* said so!

HENRY IV [*turning to look at them*]: You? Did you say it was a joke?

LANDOLPH [*timidly, embarrassed*]: No ... to tell the truth ... we said that you were cured!

BELCREDI: Look here, I think we've all had about enough of

this! Let's have done! [*To* DONNA MATILDA] Don't you think, my dear Marchioness, that the sight of you and him [*pointing to* DI NOLLI] dressed up like that, is becoming more and more intolerable? It's all so childish!

DONNA MATILDA: Oh, be quiet! What does it matter how we're dressed, so long as he really is cured?

HENRY IV: Cured? Yes, I'm cured! [*To* BELCREDI] But I'm not going to let it all end like this . . . all at once . . . as *you* think I should. [*Attacking*] Do you know that for the last twenty years no one has ever dared to appear before me dressed like you and that gentleman? [*Pointing to the* DOCTOR.]

BELCREDI: Of course I know! As a matter of fact, this morning I appeared before you dressed . . .

HENRY IV: As a monk! Oh, yes!

BELCREDI: And you took me for Peter Damiani! And I didn't even laugh, because I believed . . .

HENRY IV: . . . That I was mad! And does it make you laugh, when you see her dressed up like that, now that I'm cured? And yet you might have remembered that in my eyes her appearance now . . . [*He interrupts himself suddenly with a gesture of contempt.*] Pah! [*And immediately he turns to the* DOCTOR.] You are a doctor?

DOCTOR: Yes, I . . .

HENRY IV: And it was you who dressed them *both* up as the Marchioness of Tuscany? Do you know, Doctor, that for one moment you ran the terrible risk of bringing black, empty night back into my brain? My God, to make those portraits speak! To make them come to life and leap out of their frames! [*He studies* FRIDA *and* DI NOLLI. *Then he looks at the* MARCHIONESS. *Finally he looks at the clothes he is wearing.*] A most beautiful pattern. . . . Two pairs. . . . Excellent, my dear Doctor. . . . Very good indeed. . . . And for a madman . . . [*A slight gesture with his hand in the direction of* BELCREDI.] He thinks it's a carnival out of season now, doesn't he? [*Turns and looks at him.*] Well then, I'll get rid of this fancy dress of mine, too! So that I can come away with you! Shall I?

BELCREDI: With me? With us?

HENRY IV: Where shall we go? To the Club? In tails and white tie? Or shall we go to the Marchioness's? Both of us together?

BELCREDI: Wherever you like! You surely wouldn't want to remain here alone, to perpetuate what was an unfortunate trick of fate that happened one carnival day! It's absolutely incredible . . . it really is incredible how you were able to go on as you have . . . once you'd shaken off the effects of the disaster that befell you!

HENRY IV: Yes, it is! You see how it was! The fact is that, falling from my horse and striking my head as I did, I was completely insane for . . . oh, I don't know how long . . .

DOCTOR: Ah, this is most important! Most important! Did this insanity last a *very* long time?

HENRY IV: [*to the* DOCTOR, *very rapidly*] Yes, Doctor, a very long time. . . . About twelve years. [*Then, immediately turning and speaking to* BELCREDI.] And so, my dear fellow, I saw nothing of what happened after that day of carnival. Of what happened for you, but not for me. I saw nothing of how things changed. Of how my friends betrayed me. For instance, I didn't see it when another man took my place in the heart of the woman I loved. . . . Perhaps it didn't happen! Who knows? But let's suppose that it did. I didn't know who'd died. Who'd disappeared from circulation. All this, you know, wasn't exactly a joke for me . . . as you seem to imagine!

BELCREDI: No! No! That wasn't what I meant at all! I was talking about afterwards!

HENRY IV: Oh, you were? Afterwards? One day . . . [*Stops and turns to the* DOCTOR.] A most interesting case, Doctor! Study me, study me carefully! [*As he speaks he is trembling all over.*] All by itself . . . one day . . . Heaven knows how or why! . . . the trouble here . . . [*He touches his forehead.*] righted itself. Little by little I opened my eyes again . . .

and at first I didn't know whether I was awake or dreaming! Yes, I was awake! I touched the things around me. I began to see clearly again! Ah!... and now, as he says [*alluding to* BELCREDI], off with this fancy dress! Off with this incubus! Let's fling open the windows, and breathe in life again! Let's get out of here! And away! Away! Let's rush out of here.... [*Suddenly pulling himself up.*] But, where? And to do what? To have myself slily pointed out as Henry IV? Even though I should no longer be as you see me now, but arm in arm with you and surrounded by all the dear friends of the life I used to lead?

BELCREDI: Oh, no! How can you suggest...? Why should they?

DONNA MATILDA: Who would dare? *Now!* Why it's not to be thought of! It was an accident!

HENRY IV: But they all said that I was mad before it happened. [*To* BELCREDI] And you know it! You were more ferocious than any of them in attacking anyone who tried to defend me!

BELCREDI: Oh, that was all a joke!

HENRY IV: Look at my hair! [*Shows him the hair on the nape of his neck.*]

BELCREDI: But my hair's grey too!

HENRY IV: Yes, but there's this difference.... Mine has gone grey here, you understand ... while I've been Henry IV ... and I never knew it! I became aware of it suddenly one day, just as I was opening my eyes! And it was terrifying, because all at once I realized that not only had my hair gone grey, but that I was all grey inside! That everything was finished. Crumbled into ruins. I should arrive hungry as a wolf at a banquet which had long since been cleared away.

BELCREDI: Yes, I know.... But the others...

HENRY IV [*immediately*]: I know, they couldn't even wait till I was cured! Not even those people who came up behind me and viciously stabbed my horse till it bled....

DI NOLLI [*startled, appalled by what this implies*]: What?... What did you say?

HENRY IV: Yes, treacherously . . . so as to make it rear and throw me.

DONNA MATILDA [*quickly, in horror*]: This is the first time I knew that that was what happened!

HENRY IV: That too was meant as a joke, probably!

DONNA MATILDA: But who did it? Who was riding behind us at that moment?

HENRY IV: It doesn't matter who it was! They all went on with the banquet, quite happy that I should arrive to find their leavings . . . their leavings, my dear Marchioness! A slobbered-out scraping of pity. . . . A dirty remnant or two of remorse left sticking to the filthy plate. Thank you, my dear friends! [*Suddenly turning to the* DOCTOR.] Now, Doctor, don't you think this case is absolutely unique in the annals of madness? I preferred to remain mad, because I found everything ready to my hand for this new and delightful experience. I preferred to live out this madness of mine, so that I might revenge myself on the brutality of a stone that had dinted my head! I would live it out with the most lucid consciousness of what I was doing. And solitude . . . *this* solitude . . . bleak and empty as it appeared when first I opened my eyes again . . . I immediately determined to make into something finer! I would trick it out in all the splendour, all the brilliant colours of that far-off day of carnival, when you . . . [*He looks at* DONNA MATILDA *and points out* FRIDA *to her.*] There you are, Marchioness, over there! . . . When you triumphed! And I would oblige all those who presented themselves before me to play out that famous pageant of the past, which had been . . . for you, but not for me . . . the jest of a day! And, my God, they'd play as I bid them now! I would turn that jest into a reality. . . . An everlasting reality . . . the reality of a true madness! Here . . . all in our costumes . . . the masks of the parts we were to play . . . with this throne-room . . . and these four counsellors of mine . . . Privy counsellors . . . Privy and, of course . . . traitors! [*He turns quickly towards them.*] I should like to know what you have gained by revealing the fact that I was cured! If I am cured, then there's no longer any need for you, and you'll be out of a job! To give anyone one's confidence . . . that is an act of real madness! Ah! And now I accuse you in my turn! Do you know what? They actually thought that we might carry on the joke . . . they and I . . . and have a lot of fun at your expense! [*He bursts out laughing. With the exception of* DONNA MATILDA, *the others also laugh . . . but they are clearly still thoroughly put out.*]

BELCREDI [*to* DI NOLLI]: Did you hear? That's not bad. . . .

DI NOLLI [*to the four young men*]: Did you?

HENRY IV: We must forgive them! This dress [*plucking at his robe*], which for me is the caricature . . . manifest and voluntary . . . of that other masquerade . . . that ceaseless, everlasting masquerade in which we are the involuntary actors . . . poor strolling players. . . . [*He points to* BELCREDI.] When . . . without knowing we're doing it . . . we mask ourselves with the semblance that we have for ourselves . . . And dress . . . their dress . . . well, we must forgive them! Since they do not yet see it as one and the same thing with themselves. [*Turning again to* BELCREDI.] You know, it's quite easy to get accustomed to it. You walk about like this, playing the part of a tragic character . . . just as if it were nothing . . . [*Walks about in a tragic manner.*] . . . in a room like this! Listen, Doctor! I remember one sunny day in November seeing a priest . . . an Irishman, by the look of him . . . a handsome fellow . . . asleep on a bench in a public garden . . . with his arm resting on the back of it. He was lost in the golden delight of the warm sunny air, which must have seemed almost like a breath of summer to him. We can be quite sure that, at that moment, he was completely oblivious of the fact that he was a priest, completely oblivious even of where he was. He was dreaming! And who knows what he was dreaming! A little urchin came past with a flower in his hand. He'd torn it up somewhere, roots and all. As he went by, he tickled the priest with it, here on the throat. I saw him open his smiling eyes, and his whole mouth laughed with the beauty and the blessedness of the laughter of his dream. The world did not exist for him at that moment! Then all at once he stiffened back into his priest's cassock, and there came back into his eyes that same seriousness which you have seen in mine. Because Irish priests defend the seriousness of their catholic faith with the same zeal with which I defend the sacred rights of hereditary monarchy. Ladies and gentlemen, I am cured! Because I know perfectly well that I'm playing the madman here! And I do so very quietly. You are the ones who are to be pitied, for you live out *your* madness in a state of constant agitation . . . without seeing it . . . without knowing it.

BELCREDI: So that's what it all boils down to, is it? *We're* the ones who are mad!

HENRY IV [*with an effort he restrains the violence of his emotions*]: But if you weren't mad, would you have come to see me . . . together? . . . the two of you together! [*A gesture in the direction of the* MARCHIONESS.]

BELCREDI: Well, to tell you the honest truth, *I* came here believing that you were the one who was mad.

HENRY IV [*immediately, in a loud voice, pointing to the* MARCHIONESS]: And she?

BELCREDI: Ah! . . . she . . . as for her . . . I don't know . . . I see, however, that what you've been saying has . . . how shall I put it? . . . enchanted her. . . . She's spell-bound by your words. . . . Fascinated by this *conscious* madness of yours! [*He turns to her*] Dressed as you are, my dear Marchioness, you might even remain here and live out that madness with him. . . .

DONNA MATILDA: You are insolent!

HENRY IV [*immediately, placating her*]: Don't bother about him! Don't bother about him! Let him go on tormenting me . . . although the Doctor has told him not to. [*Turning to* BELCREDI] But do you really think I'm going to trouble myself any more about what happened between us. . .? About the part you played in my misfortune . . . the misfortune that lost me . . . her! [*Pointing to the* MARCHIONESS. *Then he turns to her and points to* BELCREDI.] Or about the part he now plays in your life! *This* is my life! Quite a different sort of life from the one you lead! Your life . . . the life in which you have grown old . . . I have not lived that life! . . . [*To* DONNA MATILDA] Was that what you wanted to tell me? Was that what you wanted to show me with this sacrifice of yours? Dressing yourself up like this . . . so that the Doctor could play his little scene. . . . Oh, it was very well done, my dear Doctor! As I said . . . 'As we were then, eh? And as we are now.' But I'm not a madman in your sense of the word, Doctor! I know quite well that [*pointing to* DI NOLLI] that man cannot possibly be me . . . because *I* am Henry IV . . . and have been these last twenty years . . . here . . . fixed in this eternal mask! She has lived through these twenty years. . . . [*Pointing to the* MARCHIONESS] She has enjoyed them . . . and she has become . . . look at her . . . a woman I can no longer recognize . . . because it is like that that I know her! [*Pointing to* FRIDA, *and then going over to her.*] For me she is always *this* woman! You seem just like a lot of children to me. . . . Children that I can frighten so easily! [*To* FRIDA] And you're frightened, too, little girl, aren't you, by the joke they persuaded you to play on me? And they didn't understand that for me it couldn't possibly be the joke they meant it to be. No, it became this terrible prodigy . . . a dream that came alive in you . . . more alive than ever before! You were there . . . a picture . . . and they've turned you into a living being! You're mine! You're mine! Mine! Mine in my own right! [*He clasps her in his arms, laughing like a madman, while all the others cry out in terror. But when they rush over to tear* FRIDA *from his arms, he becomes furious, terrible, and cries out to the four young men.*]

HENRY IV: Hold them! Hold them! I order you to hold them! [*So astounded are the four young men that, as if mesmerized,*

*they try automatically to prevent* DI NOLLI, *the* DOCTOR, *and*
BELCREDI *from reaching* HENRY IV.]

BELCREDI [*freeing himself without difficulty and hurling himself at*
HENRY IV]: Let her go! Let her go! You're not mad!

HENRY IV [*in a flash he turns to* LANDOLPH, *who is standing near
him, and draws his sword*]: So I'm not mad, eh? Take that,
you . . .! [*And he drives* LANDOLPH'S *sword into* BELCREDI'S
*belly. A cry of horror goes up. Everyone rushes to help* BELCREDI.
*General uproar, during which the following exclamations are
uttered*]:

DI NOLLI: Are you badly hurt?

BERTHOLD: Yes! He's wounded him pretty badly! It's pretty
serious!

DOCTOR: I told you so!

FRIDA: Oh, God!

DI NOLLI: Frida, come here!

DONNA MATILDA: He's mad! Mad!

DI NOLLI: Hold him!

BELCREDI [*as they carry him through the door left, he protests
fiercely*]: No! No! You're not mad! He's not mad! *He's
not mad!*

    [*They go out through the door left and the confused noise of
their cries can be heard from off-stage. Suddenly a sharper,
piercing cry from* DONNA MATILDA *is heard above the
general din. And then . . . silence.*]

HENRY IV [*has remained on-stage, surrounded by* LANDOLPH,
ORDULPH, *and* HAROLD. *His eyes are staring. He is terrified by
the life of the fiction which he himself has created, and which in one
fleeting moment has driven him to commit a crime*]: And now . . .
yes . . . inevitably . . . [*He calls them around him, as if to protect himself.*] Here . . . we must remain here . . . together . . .
together . . . for ever!

*A further selection from Pirandello,
and some other volumes in the
Penguin Plays series,
are described on the
next few pages*

# LUIGI PIRANDELLO

PL34

The first volume of Pirandello's plays to be published by Penguin Books contains three plays and is introduced and edited by E. Martin Browne.

## The Rules of the Game

TRANSLATED BY ROBERT RIETTY

## The Life I Gave You

TRANSLATED BY FREDERICK MAY

## Lazarus

TRANSLATED BY FREDERICK MAY

# SOME PLAYS IN PENGUIN CLASSICS

### EDITED BY E. V. RIEU

## Chehov · *Plays*

*The Cherry Orchard · Three Sisters · Ivanov*
*The Seagull · Uncle Vania · The Bear*
*The Proposal · A Jubilee*

### TRANSLATED BY ELISAVETA FEN

## Ibsen · *Hedda Gabler & Other Plays*

*The Pillars of the Community*
*The Wild Duck · Hedda Gabler*

## *The Master Builder & Other Plays*

*Rosmersholm · The Master Builder*
*Little Eyolf · John Gabriel Borkman*

### TRANSLATED BY UNA ELLIS-FERMOR

## Strindberg · *Three Plays*

*The Father · Miss Julia · Easter*

### TRANSLATED BY PETER WATTS

# FOUR MODERN VERSE PLAYS

PL 37

T. S. Eliot · *The Family Reunion*

Christopher Fry · *A Phoenix Too Frequent*

Charles Williams · *Thomas Cranmer of Canterbury*

Donagh MacDonagh · *Happy as Larry*

NOT FOR SALE IN THE U.S.A. OR CANADA

# FOUR ENGLISH COMEDIES

EDITED BY J. M. MORRELL

PL 33

Jonson · *Volpone*

Congreve · *The Way of the World*

Goldsmith · *She Stoops to Conquer*

Sheridan · *The School for Scandal*

# NEW ENGLISH DRAMATISTS

# THREE EUROPEAN PLAYS

### Ring Round the Moon · *Jean Anouilh*

At the Globe Theatre the play was a resounding success. 'On this occasion,' said *The Times*, 'Mr Christopher Fry is writing in prose and his pen (for the first time) is yoked to well-constructed fantasy. ... Subdued to its new medium, the poet's pen turns the French dialogue into coloured but not too highly figured English speech. The result is an enchanting little fairy tale of laughing, Musset-like grace, its sentiment masked by cool, brittle, elegant mockery.'

### The Queen and the Rebels · *Ugo Betti*

Henry Reed writes: 'Long before his death Betti had become accepted as the leading dramatist in Italy in the generation that followed Pirandello.' More and more, during the last few years, Ugo Betti has been coming to be recognized as one of the really great dramatists of modern times.

### In Camera · *Jean-Paul Sartre*

'*In Camera* proves that Sartre is an artist of a high order, with many of the traditional French dramatist's virtues intact' – *Tribune*

'*In Camera* is a masterly piece of imaginary conversation in Hell. This book will delight anyone with a taste for slick intellectual drama' – *Scotsman*

# TWO OTHER VOLUMES IN THE PENGUIN PLAYS SERIES

*Three Irish Plays*

PL 35

THE MOON IN THE YELLOW RIVER · *Denis Johnston*

THE IRON HARP · *Joseph O'Conor*

STEP-IN-THE-HOLLOW · *Donagh MacDonagh*

*Gallows Glorious*

PL 31

GALLOWS GLORIOUS · *Ronald Gow*

LADY PRECIOUS STREAM · *S. I. Hsiung*

RICHARD OF BORDEAUX · *Gordon Daviot*

20      1